FILM AS ARGUMENT

FILM AS ARGUMENT

THE SECRET TO FEATURE FILM STORYTELLING

DARREN PAUL FISHER

RUTGERS UNIVERSITY PRESS
New Brunswick, Camden, and Newark, New Jersey
London and Oxford

Rutgers University Press is a department of Rutgers, The State University of New Jersey, one of the leading public research universities in the nation. By publishing worldwide, it furthers the University's mission of dedication to excellence in teaching, scholarship, research, and clinical care.

Library of Congress Cataloging-in-Publication Data

Names: Fisher, Darren Paul author
Title: Film as argument : the secret to feature film storytelling / Darren Paul Fisher.
Description: New Brunswick : Rutgers University Press, 2025. | Includes bibliographical references and index.
Identifiers: LCCN 2024058489 (print) | LCCN 2024058490 (ebook) | ISBN 9781978841130 paperback | ISBN 9781978841147 hardback | ISBN 9781978841154 epub
Subjects: LCSH: Motion pictures—Production and direction | Motion pictures—Philosophy
Classification: LCC PN1995.9.P7 F495 2025 (print) | LCC PN1995.9.P7 (ebook) | DDC 791.4302/32—dc23/eng/20250401
LC record available at https://lccn.loc.gov/2024058489
LC ebook record available at https://lccn.loc.gov/2024058490

A British Cataloging-in-Publication record for this book is available from the British Library.

∞ The paper used in this publication meets the requirements of the American National Standard for Information Sciences—Permanence of Paper for Printed Library Materials, ANSI Z39.48-1992.

rutgersuniversitypress.org

For Lucy, Scarlett, and Miles

CONTENTS

NOTE ON SCREEN REFERENCES

MOST FILM EXAMPLES are of current or popular feature films that should be widely available and easy to access for most readers. Whenever a film is referenced, convention dictates that the director be credited as the author of the work in the main text, with the producers, screenwriters, and production companies fully credited in the filmography. With respect to television shows, due to the number of producers, screenwriters, and directors who work on a show during its lifetime, for purely practical reasons only the creator(s) of the show are credited.

All film budgets and gross profits are quoted in U.S. dollars (noted as US$), with figures supplied by Box Office Mojo, a subsidiary of the Internet Movie Database (IMDb), both owned by Amazon.com, Inc.

FILM AS ARGUMENT

PART I

THE ELEPHANT IN THE SCREENING ROOM

CHAPTER 1

What's the Big Secret?

IF YOU'VE PICKED up this book, it's most likely that you have an interest in movies over and above the typical audience member. You may be a film aficionado or a creative practice researcher, but most likely you are a screenwriter, producer, or director looking to improve your work, on a constant search for any and all insights that will result in great cinematic storytelling.

If that's the case, then the good news is that this is the book for you.

More accurately this is one of the books for you, as there are many excellent titles that will deepen your understanding of the filmmaking process. However, what is unique about this book is that as much as it will be used (and rightfully so) as a "how-to" book, at its heart it is really a "why we" book.

It has become very fashionable in business circles to ask the why of a company, then build out the how and then finally the what (product) that is actually sold to the customer.[1] However, despite some books taking this approach to story more generally,[2] this has never been done before specifically for feature films. Yet how can we really gain insight into our practice and improve it if we haven't really explored or understood why we make films in the first place?

As you've already read the title of this book and picked it up (and are either scanning the introduction to try before you buy or carefully reading it after purchasing), there's no spoilers if we jump to the conclusion and work our way back from there.

Why Do We Make Feature Films?

To move the audience to a worthwhile conclusion in a worthwhile way.

A bold idea, to be sure. So to directly answer the title of the chapter, the big secret is that the single defining characteristic of the practice of making feature films is for filmmakers to make meaningful arguments with integrity. This is what it means to excel at the practice. If a film fails to do this, then the filmmaker has failed to a greater or lesser degree, even if critical acclaim or gross profits suggest otherwise.

If we take this to be true, it inspires a second, equally controversial statement: most filmmakers are unaware of the true nature of their practice.

If you were being uncharitable, you may feel that this explains a lot, but as our central film-as-worthwhile-argument idea does not represent current dominant industry thinking, it is an inevitable result. Yet, as with most things, it's not quite as simple as that. As we'll see, conventional cinematic storytelling wisdom has talked around film as argument (in a general sense) for decades, almost but not quite committing to the concept, creating an elephant in the screening room, if you will.

But we're not talking about film as argument in a general sense. The current practice of feature filmmaking is to move us to a very specific kind of conclusion in a very specific way.

Is it possible to be this simplistic? How can it be that all mainstream feature films can fit neatly into one sweeping statement? They're both fair questions. This book lays out the case for film-as-worthwhile-argument, a deep dive into how filmmakers are trained and taught to think about their practice, and what traditions they are following. We'll look at a substantial number of films and some major case studies to explore how and what films argue, and why knowing this can both unlock both a greater appreciation of the form and improve the impact your films make.

I'd like to say that this understanding of feature filmmaking practice was not simply pulled from thin air, yet there certainly was an epiphany moment—even if it was inspiration borne from a lifetime working, studying, and teaching in the industry. However, the conceptualization has since been interrogated and refined through substantial research drawn from various bodies of knowledge: film philosophy, industry best practice, core notions of morality and virtue, and inevitably the great Aristotle himself (more than just the usual *Poetics*, but we'll return to that later).

Industry responses to film-as-worthwhile-argument fell into three main camps: most were excited by the idea, some believed it so self-evident to the point of banality, others were horrified and believed it blasphemy. What is clear is that no other book is talking about films in this way, which, to reference the business world again, gives you first-mover advantage.

Most practical filmmaking manuals necessarily tend to concentrate on technique and their nuances, so as controversial as film-as-worthwhile-argument might be, this book should complement those others on your shelf: it's designed to play very well with others.

A Few Key Terms and Concepts

The approach of this book is primarily based on the work of Alasdair MacIntyre. If you're screen-industry centric in your reading, he will likely be unknown to you, but he is a giant in the field of social practice theory. MacIntyre, a pioneer in his field, was one of the first to attempt to define practices in terms of their ends—to ask, "Why do we do these things, and how do we excel at them?" His seminal work *After Virtue* set out concepts that have been debated and developed by critics since but remain fundamentally intact.[3]

FILMMAKING PRACTICE

What do we really mean by filmmaking practice? Creative practice to be sure, but it fits under a wider concept of social practice. Examples given of social practices are often games or sports such as football or chess, as they are defined as a complex form of socially established activity that require people to cooperate.[4] Kicking a ball with incredible skill is simply not enough. They are also activities where intrinsic benefits are realized when attempting to excel in that activity. These benefits are referred to as "internal goods" (see below) and define that activity, inviting reflection that should increase understanding and ability to achieve in that field.[5]

So, in our case, feature filmmaking qualifies as a social practice: an established and highly social creative activity composed of many intricate stages, with constant reflection of what it means to succeed an embedded part of the process.

This is also what Aristotle referred to as a *tekhnê*: an art, craft, or skill informed by its own innate rationale. The first activities were about achieving the necessities for existence, next came the recreational arts that enhanced the quality of life, then those based around satisfying the desire to know, until finally philosophy. For Aristotle, this does not mean that the artists are necessarily aware of the rules of their own practice: instinct and unreflective experience can produce the same result as tekhnê.[6]

INTERNAL GOODS

As internal goods define both a practice and what it means to be truly exceptional, identifying them is critical to developing a deep knowledge of any field. MacIntyre believes that they must be specific to the practice and can be recognized only by the practitioners themselves; insight can come only from within. For us, this means that only mainstream feature filmmakers can correctly judge the internal goods of mainstream feature filmmaking.[7]

Is the internal good of chess simply to win by any means necessary? If so, cheating is very much on the table, and those who follow the game would idolize those players who bend the rules to their will. Or is the internal good not just to win within the rules of the game but win with an elegance that evolves the gameplay for the wider chess community?

To use MacIntyre's terminology, the central idea of this book is that the internal good of mainstream feature filmmaking is to move the audience to a worthwhile conclusion in a worthwhile way.

EXTERNAL GOODS

External goods are defined as someone's property and possession, with no benefit to the wider community. Take the cheating chess player, who may achieve glory, status, money, and power, but the game is not improved.[8]

External goods are also not practice-specific: they can be the result of many different kinds of endeavors. There is often conflict between practitioners and their institutions, and this can be thought of as a battle between internal and external goods. There is a dramatic irony here; the institution enables the practice but is its most significant enemy. This is the cliché of the studio versus the filmmaker, the eternal battle of art versus commerce.

It's worth noting that MacIntyre is not saying that external goods are necessarily negative, simply delineating the difference between internal and external. A practitioner who is fixated on external goods is likely to—but will not necessarily—fall foul of the internal goods of the practice. For instance, a filmmaker may be wholly fixated on fame and money, but if they believe the best way to achieve that is through film-as-worthwhile-argument, it's possible to fulfil both simultaneously.

GENERAL VIRTUES

MacIntyre is aware that any human quality that motivates behavior could be regarded as a virtue, depending on the social conventions of their particular culture. He examines three prominent thinkers on the topic: Aristotle, Homer, and Franklin.

Aristotle holds, rightly or wrongly, that humans must have an overall objective or final end and articulates this in his *Nicomachean Ethics* as achieving "eudaimonia"—a good life.[9] This good life is achieved through the exercise of virtues. MacIntyre notes that all three thinkers consider virtue to be a secondary concept, capable of being expressed only within social and moral life.[10]

It does feel a little counterintuitive: virtues are defined in terms of social practices, not the other way around. Social practices are not defined in terms of the exercise of virtues. Virtues are traits that are necessary for practitioners to excel—they are not definitional of what it is to excel. This is where the concept of the internal good becomes critical—it is how practitioners understand success specific to their field, which in our case is to move the audience to a worthwhile conclusion in a worthwhile way.

MacIntyre believes that internal goods are based on three universal human virtues, which will also serve to protect the practice from corruption by their institutions: justice, courage, and honesty.[11]

In mainstream feature filmmaking they represent both a creative and moral compass. As this book is not an exploration of the nuances of human morality, we will accept this logic as virtues are typically uncontroversial. Who doesn't want to aspire to justice, courage, and honesty? Their agreeable nature is also due to their subjectivity. What is "just" varies from culture to culture, courage can be misguided, and honesty is very much about personal perspective.

FILM-SPECIFIC VIRTUES

In addition to the universal human virtues, I suggest three further film-specific virtues: those of curiosity, compassion, and generosity.[12] This makes the full set of filmmaker virtues as follows (defined in creative terms):

COURAGE:	Courage to tell the story (at the risk of physical or emotional harm)
HONESTY:	Telling the story honestly
JUSTICE:	To be fair in the telling of the story
CURIOSITY:	The constant inspiration to explore and understand
COMPASSION:	Empathy for all characters
GENEROSITY:	Desire to share your story to enrich others

It's important to remember that a screenwriter or director who embodies these virtues may still make a cinematic failure by any definition (artistic, commercial, failure of argumentation) due to a lack of advanced craft skill-sets, such as the ability to get performances from actors or write convincing dialogue. However, if they have no sense of honesty, courage, justice, compassion, generosity, or curiosity for the world, any filmmaker is unlikely to recognize or achieve either internal or external goods.

As with all things human, these virtues are not static. A filmmaker such as Terrence Malick is a good example, as arguably his skills as a filmmaker are undiminished, but the way he has chosen to express his virtues has affected his impact. Despite an initial miniscule output, he was widely considered to be one of the finest screenwriters and directors of his generation. In recent times, his output has increased but his reputation has almost universally declined.[13]

His debut, *Badlands* (1973), attempts to tell a difficult truth rather than a comforting lie: that sometimes there is no satisfactory explanation for extreme amoral human behavior and, furthermore, that it may inspire not just notoriety but popularity. It was highly provocative, set up to challenge conventional understanding of human motivation and evil, but Malick demonstrates a voracious curiosity in human behavior and bravely tells his story in an honest, just, compassionate, and accessible way.

Compare this to *Knight of Cups* (2015). Although technically and creatively polished, the film failed critically, financially, and as film-as-worthwhile-argument due to a failure to express creative generosity. He may have expressed his creative curiosity and honesty, but the film was almost completely inaccessible to an audience, appearing to be a work made not just for a niche audience but purely for Malick himself; he did not allow anyone else to share in his journey.

SUCCESS

This book often talks of success in critical and financial terms, those useful external goods, as they are key concerns of any filmmaker and undeniable markers of a film's impact. However, for our purposes, a film is considered successful only if it truly fulfills the internal goods of the practice: to move an audience to a worthwhile conclusion in a worthwhile way. Yet obviously, all three versions of success are connected, and it is very much the expectation that a film that argues well will lead to higher ratings and grosses.

MAINSTREAM NARRATIVE FEATURE FILM

When we say "film" or "feature film" in this book, we typically mean a mainstream fictional narrative feature film. The definition is the broadest possible. A mainstream fictional narrative feature film is

- a fictional story that runs between 65 and 300 minutes, where
- a series of events unfold
- usually with obvious causal connections, and
- typically with the same group of characters
- intended to be seen in one sitting
- requiring continuous attention from the audience, and
- deemed releasable to the general public by current established multiplex or art house feature film distribution companies (this includes streamers)

This definition is not platform specific; it is fully independent of the type of screen on which the film should be viewed. It is also necessarily linked to the practices of current film distribution companies. Because the mainstream evolves as the medium evolves, the definition must have the capacity to develop also.

What counts as a mainstream narrative feature film varies over time and in different cultural contexts: mainstream narrative feature films in the United States in 1927 were silent films, making the first ever "talkie" (even if it was merely five minutes of sound at the end of a silent movie) *The Jazz Singer* (Crosland 1927) the risky avant-garde outlier; a current mainstream Bollywood feature film is considered to be a predominantly Indian cast in a musical/action epic spectacular in the Hindi language, such as the romantic-comedy-adventure *Chennai Express* (Shetty 2013).

It is also key that the narrative (and therefore the argument) is completed in some way, even if the films are released in two halves (see *Spider-Man: Across the Spider-Verse* and *Spider-Man: Beyond the Spider-Verse*; Dos Santos, Thompson, and Powers 2023 and 2027) or three thirds (*The Lord of the Rings* trilogy; Jackson 2001–2003).[14] Any ongoing series or serial is designed to be open-ended, which fundamentally alters the capabilities of the form and therefore the practice.[15]

Narrative completion is why the practice of making episodic television did not develop as argument. It is not that the form is incapable of making an argument but that the realities of production did not allow for that form of expression to manifest. Fiction television in all its guises is very similar to mainstream feature films in that all forms usually contain both characters and events that are causally linked. However, three forms—serial, series, and soap operas—are open-ended, in that even if they ultimately are axed as a show, as they inevitably must be (even *Coronation Street* [Warren 1960–] and *Eastenders* [Smith and Holland 1985–] will eventually cease broadcasting), the makers of those shows will often not know which will be the last series and would be unable to write a cohesive conclusion even if they wished to do so. The current trend is for season finales to leave more questions than answers to convince the audience and networks that the show must be renewed. On very rare occasions, such as *Breaking Bad* (Gilligan 2008–2013), the makers of the show have the power to end the narrative on their own terms.[16] This is rare as the networks will want a series to continue as long as there is money to be made from its exploitation, but in this case film-as-worthwhile-argument could function in this format, even if it is not a tradition of the practice of making serialized television.

Traditionally, if a series, serial, or soap opera is open-ended, it cannot function as a coherent argument as there is no conclusion. That is not to say these formats do not have a creative voice, as they can still contain a consistent sensibility. For example, *The West Wing* (Sorkin 1999–2006) clearly has a left-leaning liberal progressive bias, but there is little more structure that can be developed within it. Another factor restricting the development of television-as-worthwhile-argument is that the longer a show continues, the more likely the key creative personnel will change, and with it a change of sensibility, however subtle or extreme. Writers are replaced throughout the duration of a single series, and the showrunners may have longer tenures but often will be replaced.[17]

This means that the fixed episode miniseries, now also referred to as "limited" or "event" series, could certainly function as film-as-worthwhile-argument, whether or not it is a tradition of the practice.[18] That is not the focus of this book, but clearly the principles discussed here can technically apply to those formats, even if they are not fully definitive of that practice.

In recent years the worlds of television and narrative feature films have been converging ever closer together in terms of both visuals and artists involved, and the argument could be made (although I won't make it here) that modern serials, miniseries, and event series such as *Stranger Things* (Duffer and Duffer 2016–) and *True Detective* (Pizzolatto 2014–) are being thought of as more cinematic not because of high production value, camera, and sound techniques or the presence of Hollywood stars but due to definite ends and the ability to binge watch.[19] This allows for them to be seen in one (very long) sitting, which enables the writers, directors, and showrunners to create something much like an eight- to thirteen-hour mainstream narrative feature film. Anthology series such as *True Detective,* with each returning season based around a whole new cast and scenario, are essentially series of separate long, standalone feature films.

ARGUMENT

To be as inclusive as possible, we're working with a minimalist conception of what constitutes an argument. This can be stated as follows: *An argument is an assertion supported by reasons to believe such assertion.*

Typically film arguments will be inductive, as they inevitably present a specific set of circumstances to prove a general point or worldview that could be contradicted by further evidence. They may wish or even attempt to function as deductive arguments that once we agree the general premises the specific conclusion is incontestable, but this is problematic and something we'll explore in further chapters.

We also must define what we consider logical argument, sound argument, and rhetoric. Here, rhetoric is considered a bad form of argument, persuading others through the appearance of truth. A logical but unsound argument (sometimes called a valid argument) is one that has a clear internal logic but starts from a false premise, such as arguments made arising from racist or sexist assumptions. A sound argument is what we aspire to, a logically credible argument that starts from true premises.

FILMMAKERS

This is a deceptively fluid term. Every cast and crew member could be considered a filmmaker, as they make a creative and technical contribution to the film. However, for our purposes, we typically use the term as a shorthand to mean screenwriters, directors, and creative producers. Our basic means test is that to qualify as a filmmaker, the role in the production is defined by a primary responsibility to develop and deliver the overall story.

Some Quick Notes on Directing

As we are talking about the practice of filmmaking, rather than solely screenwriting, we need to place the director within the context of film-as-worthwhile-argument. They can essentially be thought to embody filmmaking practice, even if only symbolically. The film director is in a unique position as chief creative, the only role given direct hands-on responsibility to mold the work from development to release.

Focusing specifically on story (as opposed to other areas of directing, such as management of cast and crew), it would in no way be intellectually or professionally contentious to regard their creative responsibility as fundamentally a process of interpretation and adaptation: directors interpret the script and then adapt the writing to the visual and audio form.[20] Legendary American playwright and filmmaker David Mamet was particularly vocal in viewing the director as merely the extension of the screenwriter.[21]

John Mateer provides a useful summary of the director's role: that of "transportation." Originally designed to analyze written stories, transportation is a measure of how much or little an individual is absorbed into a story world by the melding of attention, imagery, and feelings.[22]

The consensus is that the director's role is actually a three-stage process: interpretation, adaptation, and transportation.[23] Mateer provides a useful summary of how this three-stage process is broken down. The director analyzes the script to

- formulate their interpretation of the story
- define the overall theme and message

- define how information will be revealed
- define the overall objectives of core characters and the dynamics between them
- extract story elements to inform realization and creative production choices

This idea of director as transporter in no way diminishes their creative influence, even though ultimate creative responsibility typically lies with the producer or studio. The development process is usually circular, with ideas from the director feeding back to the writer for rewrites, and the writer/director is a common role.[24]

Although the director ultimately is concerned with the intangible (story, theme, tone, audience response), they must manipulate a varied range of tangible elements including production design, lighting, lens choice, camera movement, sound, blocking, and performance. These all have an influence on meaning and are not directly referenced in a conventional screenplay. If the film has a different writer than director, it is integral that they both agree that the movie is making the same argument. If not, the film essentially has two conflicting authors, a common industry problem. This can also be compounded if the producer has yet a third take on the material. In these cases, the argument breaks down in the physical telling of the story: adaptation and transportation may have been successful, but the process of interpretation has failed. Ultimately the screenplay is not the film.

What This Book Won't Do

The book certainly makes some provocative, sweeping claims about filmmaking practice but is not a conventional "how-to" book of film technique. It does not explore film spectatorship. It is not attempting to be a general theory of story or narrative, nor any unified conception of cinema or art. It is not looking to define what mainstream narrative feature films are, nor speculate on what films could or should be doing.

No book is without its biases and limitations. A diverse range of films and filmmakers are used when discussing individual examples and more in-depth case studies, however there is a strong, almost exclusively English-speaking film bias. This is not to say that film-as-worthwhile-argument does not apply to global mainstream cinema in non-English-speaking territories, but this has not been investigated to a degree that would provide sufficient or compelling evidence to support such a claim.

You may decide that some of the ideas we explore here may be relevant to other traditional or emerging screen forms, but that's up to you—this book is focused purely on mainstream feature film. All other mass-media fiction such as novels, short stories, radio plays, television series, and serials are well beyond our brief.

This book is a snapshot in time. It lays out, without judgment, how mainstream feature filmmaking practice defines itself at this point in history. Hopefully, this knowledge will deepen your understanding and enjoyment of the medium and/or help you make films that truly connect with an audience.

Now let's dig in. Literally.

CHAPTER 2

The Other Half of the Story

A Brief History of Film as Argument

THERE IS A central visual metaphor for this book, and it's the medallion from *Raiders of the Lost Ark* (Spielberg 1981). The medallion is actually the headpiece of the Staff of Ra, which when positioned in the right place at the right time will reveal the buried location of the Ark of the Covenant. The headpiece itself details how high the staff should be—but to avoid a casual, undeserving observer stealing its secrets, both of its sides need to be read. One side gives what appears to be the correct height, but the other reveals what length then must be deducted to achieve the true measure.[1] Only then will we know where to dig.

The first side of the headpiece is Aristotle's *Poetics.* Most books on drama and storytelling will at some point reference what is indisputably considered the mother text of Western drama, relevant to any and all forms and platforms, even if the precise meaning of much of the terminology continues to be hotly debated. In many cases, especially when it comes to the screenplay, it is often imperfectly quoted, understood, and applied.[2] But that is not our concern here. Even if what is available to read today is incomplete, it still offers great insight and rightly informs inquiries into the fundamentals of storytelling. It is not that this work is overutilized or misused but that when it comes to feature film there is another of Aristotle's works equally relevant that when used together with *Poetics* offers far deeper understanding of the process.

If you're familiar with Aristotle's writings, you'll have guessed that the other work is *Rhetoric,* his exploration of persuasion that lays out the fundamentals of effective argument. Our second side of the headpiece. It's this combination of *Poetics* and *Rhetoric* that gives us full insight into mainstream feature filmmaking. To complete the metaphor, to use only one or the other would mean we're digging in the wrong place.

Specificity is key. It's very seductive to attempt to make general points about all stories—to solve everything, everywhere, all at once. But unfortunately for those of us who like things neat and tidy, the reality is that there are medium-specific fundamentals that don't fit neatly into overall conceptions of art. This is why we are not suggesting that all art—or even all screen stories—is worthwhile argument, just that the tradition of mainstream feature filmmaking appears to be so, and one that uses more of Aristotle than just his direct teachings on drama.

I have previously noted that this book is potentially controversial, but it really shouldn't be; ultimately it is an observation of a join-the-dots variety. To use a film-centric idiom, it is a "you had the red shoes on all the time, Dorothy" epiphany.[3] It builds, very much inside the box, on current dominant thinking in the field from various branches of industry and academia. Before jumping wholeheartedly into how (and what) films argue, let us take a deep dive into that orthodox thinking here and speculate why, despite the apparent consensus, there will counterproductively be resistance to the idea of film-as-worthwhile-argument.

There are two broad groups whose thoughts support the idea of feature film as a general type of argument, albeit in very different ways. We can think of them as the film philosophers and the film gurus.

The Film Philosophers

Plenty of thinking has already been done when it comes to film as argument by the film philosophers.[4] Film philosophy is an area that concentrates precisely on how the areas of film and philosophy intersect. It is also where academic debate on film's ability to argue primarily takes place.

This debate focuses on philosophical argument, a far higher bar than our broad definition of reasons to believe an assertion, and includes film of all kinds (mainstream, feature, or otherwise). There are four main theories when it comes to the ability (or not) for film to argue: the Bold Thesis, Null Thesis, Modest Thesis, and Moderate Thesis.[5]

The Bold Thesis claims that film can be considered as doing genuine philosophical work only if the argument cannot be replaced or reduced to any other form of communication. The Null Thesis suggests a film can never be anything more than inspiration or source material to support philosophical argument. The Modest Thesis puts film on an even footing with other forms of argument, citing that it does not need to be untranslatable into other media, and the Moderate Thesis adds further weight to the idea of film being able to argue as it takes into account that film has ways of arguing that are particularly powerful—especially when it comes to emotionally engaging and entertaining an audience.[6]

Our definition of argument falls firmly within the Moderate Thesis camp. Many influential film philosophers whom we'll briefly look at here make the case that films state assertions and hypotheses for audiences and explore the nuances of the human experience far more effectively than written texts. This doesn't necessarily mean, however, that this is the intention of the artist.

What is of particular relevance is precisely how film argues, that it can weave the emotional and intellectual to focus attention on elements of an argument that may otherwise be dismissed. Film philosophers Cox and Levine make the case that "belief is more often than not a function of desire and emotion as well as reasons and evidence."[7] As anyone who has ever attempted to change anyone's mind will realize, logic is simply not enough, and this is something that Aristotle explored in his *Rhetoric*. The ability to effectively stimulate emotion is a significant power of mainstream narrative feature film. It is film's ability to argue well that has allowed the social practice of film-as-worthwhile-argument to evolve.

A strong supporter of the film-as-philosophy concept is Stephen Mulhall. In his book *On Film*, Mulhall classifies the *Alien* series of films (1979–) as anything but disposable popular culture, instead "thinking seriously and systematically about them [philosophical arguments] in just the way that philosophers do. . . . They [the films] are philosophical exercises, philosophy in action—film as philosophizing."[8]

However, Mulhall does not make the claim that argument is essential to the practice, just that certain films are able to argue philosophically. This is a view shared by most prominent film philosophers, including Noël Carroll and Thomas Wartenberg.[9]

Wartenberg claims not only that some films can argue philosophically but that the very idea of films illustrating certain philosophical positions is in itself a form of argument. He uses a scene from *Modern Times* (Chaplin 1936), where Chaplin's production line worker continues to act as if he is on the line in other social situations, to demonstrate the film's ability to make philosophical points about the "*mechanization of the human under capitalism*."[10]

Wartenberg makes a strong case for film as philosophical argument.[11] He invokes a point made by Carl Plantinga that a key distinguishing feature separating documentary films from fiction films is that audiences not just accept but assume that documentary films make assertions.[12] This must prove, at least to some degree, the ability of the film form to argue using narratives.

Wartenberg directly addresses Carroll, who believes that films can be very persuasive but make arguments by example, which typically makes them invalid arguments, this due to what is termed inductive inference: a fallacy to use just one case to create a general rule. Take *Moonlight* (Jenkins 2016), a film that—to heavily simplify for our purposes—makes a case through the experiences of the main character Chiron that conventional ideals of masculinity can be problematic. For Carroll, this is obviously not a compelling argument, as just one example should not imply that conventional ideas of masculinity are always a problem. This returns us to films' natural inclination to be inductive arguments (always disprovable by further evidence) and therefore potentially fatally flawed (as philosophical arguments).

Wartenberg refutes this in two ways. First, there is at least one instance where a sample size of one creates a valid inference: the thought experiment. A thought experiment is often used to test a universal philosophical claim or definition (the definition of a "good action," for instance). Films can function very well when they become a counterexample to an idea—by showing one single instance that contradicts the claim, so making a compelling case against. This is functional inductive argumentation.

Wartenberg's second approach is particularly relevant for film-as-worthwhile-argument: some films are enthymemes. The concept is again something we have to thank Aristotle for, articulated in his *Rhetoric*. An enthymeme is a deductive argument where one or more of the premises (or the conclusion) is missing, working on the assumption that the audience will be able to provide it. What is missing or implicit is typically something considered common knowledge, or a universal truth, by the culture to whom the enthymeme is targeted.

So, for instance, a film such as *Parasite* (Joon-ho 2019) expects the audience to complete the argument of the film by bringing with it the assumption that class inequalities are intrinsically bad for society. This will happen irrespective of the intention of the filmmakers and perhaps even of the viewers; the highly influential film theorist David Bordwell called enthymeme making a "hypothesis-forming activity."[13] It is this combination of film and audience that makes enthymematic argument so effective. Aristotle believed so strongly in the power of enthymematic argument, that he called it "the flesh and blood of proof."[14]

In this way, Wartenberg makes the case that film argumentation functions both inductively and deductively. There are two parts: the counterexample (as provided by the film, presenting inductive reason(s) to believe), followed by the reasoning process (a deductive exercise by the audience, using their own previously held assumptions). The result should be coherent philosophical argument.[15]

Carroll ultimately allows that films can argue philosophically, but that it is phenomenally rare. He considers that only one film he has encountered, *Serene Velocity* (Gehr 1970), can be genuinely proved to do so. Yet by citing just one example, he also could be taking the moderate line that some films in some circumstances can argue philosophy better than written texts.

What is especially interesting is Carroll's invention of a fictional "skeptic." This skeptic is looking not at film as argument but at film as evidence; and they have concerns about its validity. It's worth quoting Carroll directly here: "[The film] is still evidentially challenged, since the 'evidence' has been constructed precisely to cast to best effect the general hypothesis the film is advocating. Or, to put it less charitably, the evidence has been cooked. Moreover, when one recalls that many of the films that may be said to do philosophy are fictional—with made-up stories expressly designed to fit their general theme—one may feel compelled to agree with the skeptic that much of the evidence in fiction films is not only statistically insufficient, but arguably tainted (or skewed) to boot."[16] This idea of film-as-evidence, Aristotle's "flesh and blood of proof," is central to feature film's power of persuasion, and we will return to it many times throughout the book. It may well be "cooked," but is no less powerful for it.

Carroll's fictional skeptic also worries that films might evoke a belief by encouraging the viewer to think about the theme, guiding their meditation but not formally arguing. In other words, as with Wartenberg, films can be thought experiments, but not arguments. Carroll disagrees with his fictional counterpart and invokes Wittgenstein to make the claim that this is simply the case of arguments being more or less user-friendly.[17]

Robert Sinnerbrink has developed some highly detailed theories of cinematic ethics, especially in how films express ethical ideas and the kinds of ethical experience cinema is able to evoke.[18] Sinnerbrink believes that "there are four dimensions to the cinema-ethics relationship, including an aesthetic dimension."[19] His ideas regarding how narrative frames thematic ideas and the moral code to which practitioners hold themselves during production relate directly to MacIntyre's ideas of internal goods and virtues. Sinnerbrink strongly promotes the theory that cinema is a meaningful vessel to present ethical ideas and meaning and through emotional engagement have an impact on the viewer's beliefs.

The Real Skeptics

As with any field, the general consensus is never unanimous. Two notable naysayers to film as philosophy are Murray Smith and Paisley Livingston. Smith is particularly significant as he wrote the paper that inspired this entire book. In "Film Art, Argument and Ambiguity," Smith doubts the ability of narrative feature film to argue, and not just philosophically.

It is a terrific paper, and I disagreed with almost every word.

Smith makes the claim that a narrative is not an argument, despite a well-established assumption that it can imply or attempt to realize one. He notes that some critics such as André Bazin have spelled this out more literally, but that "the precise relationship between narrative and argument remains impressionistic and undertheorized." He calls for a more comprehensive analysis of how narrative can deliver the basic elements of argument, which must include premises, a pattern of inference, and a conclusion.[20]

Smith's main point is that there is a fundamental conflict of purpose: narrative feature films serve primarily artistic rather than argumentative purposes, so can never truly argue—even if it takes the form of a thought experiment. Smith uses the Steve Martin / Lily Tomlin comedy *All of Me* (Reiner 1984) as an example, claiming that the demands of comedy outweigh any other priority.[21]

What Smith suggests seems highly plausible—and will often be the case—but in fact does not contradict film-as-worthwhile-argument, or even current industry best practice. It is an industry truism that for a narrative feature film to function correctly, all must be unified—theme, plot, character—as this is what will make (in this example) the comedy work; we'll laugh harder if we're fully convinced by the piece. For a filmmaker to sacrifice conceptual logic for a gag merely represents a poor creative choice.

Smith also believes that a film has too many elements with which to conduct a coherent argument. He worries about all the detail required but seems to be a case of claiming something is unlikely because it is highly complex.[22] Smith does however allow that genre is key, citing documentary as a form of narrative film that might prioritize the artistic and the intellectual equally.

In contrast to Smith, Livingston's rejection of film's ability to argue philosophy is by strict adherence to the high demands of the Bold Thesis. He requires that for films to be able to make significant philosophical contributions they will have to use techniques exclusive to film, be historically innovative, and not require paraphrase to be understood.

Livingston's use of the word "paraphrase" is not the same as used in everyday language. Livingston's paraphrase of a film contains the complete argument inspired by events on-screen: the film does not argue, the argument is created from interpreting the content of the film. This in itself does not necessarily mean the film did not have an argument of its own.

He does give some concessions, however, based around ideas of artist intentionality. For Livingston, this is key. He allows that films can do philosophy—can argue—if it can be proved using public commentaries surrounding the film that the director intended to philosophize seriously and significantly, in what he calls "partial intentionalism."[23]

The Film Gurus

The other main group that gives weight to film-as-worthwhile-argument are the stars of film industry education. These are the thought leaders whose books most screenwriters and directors (emerging or established) will have on their shelves. They are primarily outlining theories of screenwriting rather than directing, as the screenplay is the foundation of any film story.[24]

Unlike the film philosophers, these feature film gurus do not explicitly discuss film as argument, but this does not make their case any less valid. As we will see, they will often use quite convoluted verbal gymnastics *not* to mention it, creating that perfect elephant-in-the-screening-room shape: film-as-worthwhile-argument.

In selecting what works to reference, I've necessarily been quite brutal. Selection is based purely on evidence of influence and impact on filmmakers: the metrics include a combination of book sales, use in industry-facing film schools, academic discourses, and specialist discussions in various professional, public, and industry circles.

Due to the high odds against any given screenplay reaching production, the screenwriting profession is predominantly a freelance one and as such has created a strong market for "how-to" self-help manuals. Despite each taking a slightly different approach in vision or suggested methodology, these books are very efficient in articulating the received wisdom of screenwriting. Between 2007 and 2012 there were more than a hundred new books on screenwriting accessioned into the U.S. Library of Congress alone.[25]

As part of a research project into screenwriting as practice, teaching, and labor, academic Bridget Conor builds a list of popular and classic screenwriting manuals.[26] There are two tiers of guru: first tier for individuals who have written canonical texts; second tier for significant but less widespread influencers.

The top five books written by first-tier gurus, listed by sales figures, are the following:

1. *Story* (1997) by Robert McKee
2. *The Writer's Journey* (1998) by Christopher Vogler
3. *Making a Good Script Great* (1994) by Linda Seger
4. *Screenwriting Updated* (2000) by Linda Aronson
5. *Screenplay* (1979) by Syd Field

These five books continue to form the foundation that informs, educates, and inducts members into the feature film profession. They establish what are considered the current traditions of the screenwriting element of the practice as well as giving strong indications of the likely internal goods of the practice overall.[27]

This is not to claim that other works in this area are not of equal value or insight, just that they are less widely read and have yet to make a significant impact on industry or dominant thinking in the field.

Screenplay: The Foundations of Screenwriting, Syd Field

It is worth moving in chronological order to get a sense of how reflection on screenwriting practice has evolved and been finessed by a succession of story analysts.

With its first edition published in 1979, *Screenplay* was one of the first books to formalize practical screenwriting theory for a general audience. To put this into context, although the Moscow Film School was founded in 1919, it was very much a technical school based on cinematography (between 1934 and 1991 it was named the All-Union Institute of Cinematography), and the idea of a degree in film took root in the West only in the 1960s. Columbia University School of the Arts and the New York University Tisch School of the Arts were both founded in 1965. This means there had been only ten graduating film school classes by the time Field's book was first published.

Like many books dedicated to professional practice, especially at the time, it is primarily concerned with improving the how rather than focusing on the why. Field goes into detail on all key areas of screenplay storytelling, with chapters on the creation of subject, character, structure, plotting, scenes, sequences, form, adaptation, and collaboration. The three most relevant concepts for film-as-worthwhile-argument are the "idea," "subject," and "dramatic premise." Field's basic conception of story is that "you have to set up your characters, introduce the dramatic premise (what the story is about) and the dramatic situation (the circumstances surrounding the action), create obstacles for your characters to confront and overcome, then resolve the story."[28]

Field does not mention any deeper underlying element to the story, such as theme. Like MacIntyre, he uses chess as a metaphor for the relationships between the various storytelling elements. He isolates four parts—the pieces, players, board, and rules—and believes it is the relationship between them that defines the game. Field's component parts of story comprise action, characters, conflicts, scenes, sequences, dialogue, action, the various acts, incidents, episodes, events, music, and locations. What is fascinating is that despite the attempt to be exhaustive, Field makes no mention of theme or any other unifying concept. However, he approaches what could be considered thematic concepts with his thoughts on the idea for a screenplay, which he notes as a vague notion but does not elaborate.

Field's definition of the subject of a screenplay is quite straightforward: an action (what the story is about) and a character (whom the story is about).

Nonetheless, Field's discussion of *The Last Samurai* (Zwick 2003) does indicate more subtextual elements but offers no further development. He notes that the film is really about how the lead character learns to embody the virtues of honor and loyalty, which on the surface feels like a point about theme but remains confined to the character's learning of those virtues rather than a wider thematic point of view. Often they are closely connected, but a main character may learn to value honor and loyalty in a film that makes the case that they are misguided principles.

Field's idea of a dramatic premise does seem at first glance to be a discussion of theme, yet the conception is inconsistent and remains confined to the level of an individual character going on a journey. At various points, dramatic premise is described as (1) what the screenplay is about (that provides dramatic thrust), (2) synonymous with theme (but defined as internal character motivation to action), or (3) the surface-level plot setup hook of the film. This inconsistency when discussing wider storytelling concepts is problematic. *Screenplay* laid the foundations of best industry practice in so many areas, but for the purposes of film-as-worthwhile-argument is the least relevant of the screenwriting manuals we'll look at here.

Making a Good Script Great, Linda Seger

Seger develops the conventional wisdom of feature film storytelling but, as with Field, defines terms inconsistently throughout the book. Seger's core definition of "idea" also differs markedly from Field's. It's worth noting that this is an ongoing issue across the literature; an analysis of twelve prominent manuals identified 17 common terms in over half the texts examined but disparity between 397 other terms.[29]

Seger initially uses idea to mean both theme (as in abstract concept, such as love) and the entire viewpoint of the film. To use her terminology, the idea of *Fatal Attraction* (Lyne 1987) is that "if you're reckless in sex, you can jeopardize your family." Yet Seger does take for granted that there is "an underlying message that the writer wants to communicate through a story rather than through an essay." However, this point is not further developed.[30]

When Seger talks about theme explicitly, she uses it to refer to the central abstract concept on which the film will hold a point of view (corruption, greed) but also to concept and point of view combined (triumph of the human spirit). Seger then focuses on how best to communicate theme by taking a "show, don't tell" approach without indicating what precise screenplay elements entail a thematic point of view. Like Field, Seger is justifiably focused on guiding the reader on how to maximize drama rather than understand the practice itself.

Yet it's with Seger where the shape of film as argument begins, even if not deliberately stated. When talking of theme, she asks aspiring writers to ask themselves a series of questions and makes a point that having a character "give a message" to the audience is objectively bad. This is not about Seger making a case for or against film as argument; rather, the comment is based on the unspoken assumption that all feature films have messages—not just art films or prestige pictures but mainstream feature films that appeal to wide audiences. It recalls (by immediately contradicting) the famous Samuel Goldwyn maxim about the film business, that "pictures are for entertainment, messages are for Western Union."[31] Seger believes all films are in the message business.

Story: Substance, Structure, Style, and the Principles of Screenwriting, Robert McKee

Robert McKee is undoubtedly the most well-known and still the most influential of the gurus. His 1997 book *Story: Substance, Structure, Style, and the Principles of Screenwriting* is much maligned, but despite the public criticism is still considered by the industry as the mother text of all screenwriting books.[32] It is here that film as argument is described in detail—in all but name.

In keeping with the inconsistency and fluidity of key terms, McKee defines story as "not only what you say but how you say it." The book is split into four unequal parts: "The Writer and the Art of Story," "The Elements of Story," "The Principles of Story Design," and "The Writer at Work." McKee invokes Aristotle early, initially citing not his *Poetics* or *Rhetoric* but his *Ethics*. It mirrors MacIntyre in that he claims we all ask how we should best live our lives and seek answers in the four wisdoms: philosophy, science, religion, and art.[33]

McKee also makes some interesting points about entertainment, a concept we'll examine in detail later in the book. He sees entertainment as reliant on experiencing the story's meaning and insight, and that "all coherent tales express an idea veiled inside an emotional spell." Could this coherence be the result of a convincing argument? A worthwhile one at that?

McKee focuses on what he refers to as "aesthetic emotion." It's the idea that unlike in life where meaning is separated from emotion, story unites them to create epiphanies in the audience. Even if McKee does not deliberately develop this concept in terms of argument, aesthetic emotion indicates that feelings can supply reasons for thought—to reveal to us (emotional) reasons to believe ideas.

Yet as McKee explains further, we see the first indication of his resistance to any idea of film as argument. He sees story as completely nonintellectual, citing that films do "not express ideas in the dry, intellectual arguments of an essay." McKee sees these ideas as expressed "directly through the senses and perceptions, intuition and emotion," with no mediator, claiming "a well-told story neither expresses the clockwork reasonings of a thesis nor vents raging inchoate emotions. It triumphs in the marriage of the rational with the irrational."

Note the terminology, the vilification of argument and thesis as dry and clockwork: never terms to describe great art. Even if you don't agree, this makes perfect sense as a point of view that prioritizes a need to balance reason with emotion, even if McKee seems to dismiss the idea that one can serve the other or that emotions can be rational.

Yet as with the other film gurus, McKee is not consistent here, continuing to conceptualize film story using very argument-like logic. He writes about story structure as a strategic sequence to arouse specific emotions to express a specific view of life. When discussing point of view, he claims that if "a writer's final statement about life appears dogmatic and opinionated, so be it," that "we want unfettered souls with the courage to take a point of view, artists whose insights startle and excite."

Depending on the precise unpacking of what it means to use a strategic sequence to express a view of life, these ideas could be regarded as remarkably similar to a broad definition of argument. A potential work-around is that the filmmaker is just expressing a view, rather than trying to convince anyone that it is a right or valid view. However, McKee soon goes all in, and we enter the land of euphemism: "An artist must have not only ideas to express, but ideas to prove. Expressing an idea, in the sense of exposing it, is never enough. The audience must not just understand; it must believe. You want the world to leave your story convinced that yours is a truthful metaphor for life. And the means by which you bring the audience to your point of view resides in the very design you give your telling. As you create your story you create your proof; idea and structure intertwine in a rhetorical relationship."[34] McKee is describing argument here. If I were to design a structure to prove an idea, not just to make you understand it but to believe it, to convince you that it is at least subjectively truthful, what other word better describes it?

The verbal gymnastics continue. McKee uses the term "controlling idea" (which actually has its origins in essay writing) as it encompasses idea and function, but as he continues his description it sounds increasingly like film as argument. He makes the point that although stories have an "irreducible meaning" they cannot be reduced to rubrics, that they are too rich with subtleties and subtexts so can be described only by another euphemistic term: story as "living philosophy." This term is far more exciting than argument, but the description of our elephant in the screening room is now complete: if a feature film is a living philosophy led by a controlling idea that expresses a story's irreducible meaning, then we've arrived at a general conception of film as argument.

When McKee talks specifically of the craft of delivering this living philosophy, the term "argument" and its technical language inevitably begin to appear. He talks of constructing a film sequence by sequence where "the positive Idea and its negative Counter Idea argue, so to speak, back and forth, creating a dramatized dialectical debate."

The way McKee writes (or doesn't write) about argument is reminiscent of the introduction to Mark Twain's *The Adventures of Huckleberry Finn*, in which the narrator tells readers, "Persons attempting to find a motive in this narrative will be prosecuted; persons attempting to find a moral in it will be banished; persons attempting to find a plot in it will be shot." The protestation is in equal proportion to the true nature of the form.

But why is McKee resistant to the idea of film as argument? Potentially it is the fear of explanation over dramatization. He believes master storytellers never explain, that audiences are not interested or convinced by a discussion of ideas, only by consequences of human choice and action. Yet this is a concern of execution, not conception. Fear of poor application should not result in a false conceptualization of the practice.

However, McKee's greatest fear appears to be that of didacticism: the act of obviously teaching the audience or appearing to tell them what to think.

Below is one of the few occasions McKee talks explicitly about cinematic argument:

> A note of caution: In creating the dimensions of your story's "argument," take great care to build the power of both sides . . . in other words, do not slant your "argument" . . . the danger is this: when your Premise is an idea you feel you must prove to the world, and you design your story as an undeniable certification of that idea, you set yourself on the road to didacticism. In your zeal to persuade, you will stifle the voice of the other side. Misusing and abusing art to preach, your screenplay will become a thesis film, a thinly disguised sermon as you strive in a single stroke to convert the whole world. Didacticism results from the naïve enthusiasm that fiction can be used like a scalpel to cut out the cancers of society.[35]

Note the use of the scare quotes for "argument," as if the term must be quarantined: not the way to conceptualize story. No other concept receives the same treatment. Again, it appears that McKee is primarily concerned with execution, with the slanting of the argument, rather than a fundamental issue with film as argument itself. His definition of thesis film is also his own, implying a thesis will not examine different views or evidence in an attempt to prove its validity.

In McKee's defense, as a writer with the goal to improve screenwriting technique, his concern with application is understandable. He makes clear that he fears a plethora of badly written didactic films: "When talented people write badly it's generally for one of two reasons: Either they're blinded by an idea they feel compelled to prove or they're driven by an emotion they must express."

Yet there is perhaps a further fear: revealing the true influence, reach, and impact of mainstream narrative feature films. McKee concedes that writers deal with ideas, not in the rational way of philosophers, but concealed within the "seductive emotions of art," and that "the persuasive power of a story is so great that we may believe its meaning even if we find it morally repellent."

This persuasive power is beginning to be quantified through academic analysis. The work of Green and Brock investigates narrative feature film's power not only to convince the audience of things that they know to be factually untrue (even if only for a short period of time) but also to influence the identity and self-perception of the viewer themselves.[36]

This conception of film, not film-as-worthwhile-argument but simply film-as-highly-efficient-persuasive-argument, could be viewed as the industry's dirty and dangerous secret. Later in the book we'll take a deeper dive into why it is politically expedient for the screen trade that mainstream films and television are generally viewed as harmless entertainment, but suffice to say here that if they were widely accepted as structured persuasion it could endanger the industry itself. The worry is that quality would tumble not simply due to a plethora of bad didactic writing but from threats from external regulators and government.[37]

To combat potential didacticism from his readers, McKee invokes Aristotle again, to contrast the clumsy didactic writer with the virtuous writer. McKee's writers' virtues require a writer to possess a love of story, the dramatic, truth, humanity, sensation, dreaming, humor, language, duality, perfection, uniqueness, beauty, and self. His use of Aristotle is perhaps a symbolic summary of conventional industry wisdom: conscious attention to his *Poetics* and *Ethics*, but not his *Rhetoric*. If there's a through line to our book, it's that there's just not enough Aristotle.

The Writer's Journey: Mythic Structure for Writers, Christopher Vogler

Vogler's book came in the wake of *Story* and is a shorter, much less dense work that mirrors its origins as an internal Hollywood memo. As with the other literature, *The Writer's Journey* is primarily concerned with craft, but unlike McKee, Vogler spends much less time discussing precisely what story is and why humanity needs it.

Vogler's work is built on the studies of Joseph Campbell in comparative mythology.[38] The book essentially outlines Campbell's theories and applies them specifically to feature film (although there is the occasional reference to readers having used his work in television also). Vogler believes that the hero's journey, the monomyth that Campbell explores, can be used to structure, pace, and characterize not just story but also the life of the writer.[39]

Vogler claims myths are "not an untruth but a way of reaching profound truth" and that "these ancient tolls of the storyteller's craft still have tremendous power to heal our people and make the world a better place."

This assumption that stories make the world a better place does align Vogler with the central importance of the practice of telling worthwhile stories, although these ideas are not developed as his priority is to show how story manifests itself through character archetype and mythic structure. Vogler lays out seven archetypes: hero, mentor, threshold guardian, herald, shapeshifter, shadow, and trickster (although these forms owe as much to Russian formalist Vladimir Propp as to Campbell).[40] Vogler also outlines twelve stages of the hero's journey: ordinary world; call to adventure; refusal of the call; meeting the mentor; crossing the first threshold; test, allies, enemies; approach to the innermost cave; supreme ordeal; reward; the road back; resurrection; and return with the elixir.

For Vogler, these elements represent the epitome of effective storytelling across all media: "They deal with the child-like universal questions: Who am I? Where did I come from? Where will I go when I die? What is good and what is evil? What must I do about it? What will tomorrow be like? Where did yesterday go? Is there anybody else out there?"

These are all obviously questions of theme, and unsurprisingly for a book highlighting structure, Vogler leads with where it should be stated. He defines theme as "an underlying statement or assumption about an aspect of life," and adds, "Knowing the theme is essential to making the final choices in dialogue, action and set dressing that turn a story into a coherent design. In a good story, everything is related somehow to the theme, and the Ordinary World is the place to make the first statement of the main idea."

Vogler gives the examples of "love conquers all" and "money is the root of all evil," among others. As with Seger and McKee, Vogler refers inconsistently to theme as both plural and singular, sometimes talking about the theme or themes of the film without clarifying whether he considers all stories to have one central theme supported by subthemes or whether stories can support multiple main themes simultaneously.

As with McKee, Vogler has his own set of euphemisms that can be used instead of a film as argument vocabulary. His conceptualization of story is that of metaphor, "a model of some aspect of human behaviour. It is a thought machine, by which we test out our ideas and feelings about some human quality and try to learn more about it." This aligns well with downplaying the influence of film as persuasion: quite harmless if all films do is learn, as oppose to convince.

Further euphemisms include attitude (argument), mood (argument), chain of thought (argument), comparisons (evidence), feelings about life (conclusion), dramatic point of view (conclusion), and declarative statement (conclusion). These terms taken together quite comprehensively describe the elements and shape of film as argument with the benefit of not having to publicly commit to the concept.[41]

Screenwriting Updated: New (and Conventional) Ways of Writing for the Screen, Linda Aronson

Aronson's work most closely echoes the traditional self-help book style. There are charts and diagrams, and wherever possible Aronson delves into the specifics of how to apply the various theories, including exercises for the would-be screenwriter.

Aronson conceptualizes screen narratives as fables, seeing them as useful models due to their strongly defined characters, their compelling character-driven plots, and their nature to demonstrate the flaws of the main players.[42] Interestingly, she doesn't draw out the thematic implications of this, instead almost exclusively focusing on character.

Where Aronson branches into new territory not covered by the other gurus is her work on the expectation of the audience when it comes to the meaning of the stories they are seeing. She makes the point that they actively seek a moral—surprising, immoral, or depressing—and will complain if they don't get it. Although Aronson accepts this necessary presence of a moral as a current truism, the narrowness of the mainstream feature film form is not something that she appears to be happy about. She floats the idea that audiences would need to be reeducated not to need a moral, so they could be happy just to journey with the film.[43]

This truism lends significant weight to the idea of film as argument, even if Aronson does not define it by name. If the received wisdom is that film audiences expect a moral from the form, it is an integral part of the social contract between the viewer and film. Whether market forces have conditioned the films or the films have conditioned the audience is moot: the expectation gives us insight into the practice.

Like McKee, Aronson is fearful of how theme-led stories will be executed. She creates the concept of "strongly felt themes" and believes that they often inspire particularly passionate—but flawed—writing: clumsy structure, prone to cliché, stereotypes, and didactic preachiness.[44] Usefully, Aronson creates a unique practical approach to solving these issues, citing that as themes are intellectual in nature, they are ruled by what she refers to as vertical thinking.

Aronson divides human thinking into two categories: vertical and lateral. Vertical thinking is good at "keeping it real," and she lists nineteen separate things it is good at, including logic, structural instinct, learned knowledge, technique, a socially conditioned worldview, objectivity, sound judgment, caution, concentration, and cliché. Alternatively, lateral thinking is good at intuition, inspiration, originality, energy, receptiveness to new ideas, writing emotion, associational tasks, subjectivity, and melodrama.[45]

The exercises in the book push the theme-concerned writer toward lateral thinking, which can also be viewed as developing cinematic technique to argue effectively. This includes ways to disguise the argument, something we will explore in more detail when we look at our case studies in the second half of the book, most notably in the discussions of *Brave* (Andrews and Chapman 2012), *Frozen* (Buck and Lee 2013), and *Barbie* (Gerwig 2023).[46]

Honorable Mentions

There are many brilliant books on feature film screenwriting and cinematic technique that add to the conversation even if their sales and impact are not as widespread as those of the first-tier gurus. Although they do not talk of film as argument explicitly, Steven Maras's *Screenwriting: History, Theory and Practice* and Ken Dancyger and Jeff Rush's *Alternative Screenwriting* are worthy of note.

Maras provides a great overview of the evolution of professional screenwriting practice, especially of the early screenwriting manuals.[47] Dancyger and Rush put forward the idea that overt concentration on theme takes the writer away from the "concrete texture of experience" that they see as fundamental to alternative styles. Most critically, their definition of what is alternative also defines conventional screen storytelling. For Dancyger and Rush, randomness is key to alternative screenwriting, as opposed to the standard method where every storytelling element is used to illustrate meaning. Talking of both feature film and television series, they suggest that focus on theme is likely counterproductive for the alternative feature film screenwriter but useful for the conventional television series writer where randomness is almost unavoidable in material of that length. For the television writer, close attention to theme is the only way to keep the overall story coherent.[48]

However, the most significant honorable mention is for *Dramatica* (1993), the only widespread industry-facing book on story and screenwriting craft that to date explicitly discusses the idea of film as argument.

Dramatica: A New Theory of Story, Melanie Anne Phillips and Chris Huntley

Dramatica originated as a piece of software whose associated glossary of terms grew into a book. It is officially relevant to all story forms but does have a clear focus on the feature film screenwriter. Phillips and Huntley take a descriptive approach, outlining the various story options a writer has at their disposal. Two of these are different versions of argument. The first variation is classed as "the progression of logistic and emotional meanings that combine to prove a story's message." Phillips and Huntley define emotional as passionate and logistic as dispassionate, with meaning created by the interactions of character, plot, theme, and genre.

Their definition of dispassionate argument is quite specific: where the story makes a case that a singular approach is best for a given issue in a given context. Passionate argument attempts to prove that "one world view is better than another in terms of leading to personal fulfillment." A story's argument can be conveyed directly, indirectly by inference, and by using an exaggerated argument to make the opposite case. Critically, a single story can comprise multiple arguments: both passionate and dispassionate can run simultaneously.[49]

Phillips and Huntley contrast this with the particularly complex form they title Grand Argument Story (GAS). This variation takes the approach of a story with a single argument. Essentially both the passionate and dispassionate arguments form a whole where different perspectives are explored and the only possible conclusion reached. A Grand Argument is flawless and cannot be disproved on its own terms, only disputed based on the givens of the initial circumstances. Using our terminology, these Grand Arguments are logical rather than sound arguments, as they don't necessarily have to be based on true premises.[50]

Phillips and Huntley offer a third principal conceptualization of story. It is that of "following the muse," which they describe as authors writing without intent: simply concerned with recording their journey through a topic or just wanting to wander. This often results in work that is highly ambiguous yet still may elicit strong emotions and conclusions by the audience.[51] Films such as Chloé Zhao's *Nomadland* (2020) or Wong Kar-wai's *Chungking Express* (1994) could be considered mainstream examples of this form of storytelling.

The first two theories represent a view of story as sometimes being a general form of argument, be it one that can carry many separate arguments at once or a single grand argument. Even though clearly aimed at screenwriters, *Dramatica* does not suggest that argument is the fundamental nature of the practice, just that it is the basis of two possible forms to follow: story-as-sometimes-argument, rather than our film-as-worthwhile-argument.

Cognizant Filmmaking

Whether or not the first-tier gurus are oblivious to film as argument in a general sense is perhaps the wrong question to ask. They may believe film as argument as a dirty secret or be utterly unaware of its presence, but ultimately the fact that none of them partially or fully acknowledge it is decisive. These books, whether we rage against it or not, represent how the mainstream film industry understands and thinks about feature film stories. If we agree that film-as-worthwhile-argument is the practice, this lack of acknowledgment means it is rarely practiced consciously, and this can create all manner of problems.

If filmmakers follow the conventional thinking that these books articulate, be it euphemistically thinking of feature film stories as living philosophies or chains of thought, their conscious practice could be very close to film as argument in a general sense. Film-as-worthwhile-argument could happen, but as Aristotle suspected with the poets, it would be by accident rather than by design. As is the danger with most slight—but key—misconceptions, all is fine until things go wrong. Then there aren't the right tools to locate the problem. If you think you're driving a car but you're actually piloting a boat, you will coast along happily until you hit land, then won't understand why you can't move forward.

CHAPTER 3

What and How Films Argue

THE WHAT AND how of film argument is really a deconstruction of the term "worthwhile." Our central idea uses it twice: to move the audience to a worthwhile conclusion in a worthwhile way. It's a very useful adjective, but one that is highly subjective—explaining and obscuring in equal measure.

Cinematic Arguments

As we defined earlier in the book, a cinematic argument is simply an assertion supported by reasons to believe it. It does not matter if it works inductively or deductively. Successful cinematic argument need not even be intentional and likely represents the majority of cases—yet coincidental success is still bona fide success.

As the film philosophers have shown us, fully formed fictional worlds do excel in making certain types of argument. For their purposes, a film can work as a perfect thought experiment to provide a counterexample to a universally accepted truth. Obviously, their standards of argument are set far higher than ours, but what they have shown us is two key ways in which cinema can argue effectively, over and above a simple appeal to emotion.

First is enthymematic argument, working in partnership with an audience to lead them to a conclusion that is not explicitly stated. It is a particularly formidable and well-used (if unconsciously) film technique that we'll look at more closely in the full case studies in the second half of the book.[1]

The second aspect, not openly discussed in the professional literature, is film's capacity to function as both the argument and the evidence for that argument simultaneously. This is an extraordinarily critical strength. Film philosopher Carroll may be concerned that this evidence is tainted but is no less powerful for it.[2]

What Films Argue

This is not about defining what films argue in terms of their actual subject matter or specific arguments. To attempt to find material trends across the myriad story worlds and subjective points of view would be a book in itself, if not a fruitless exercise: any categorization would likely have to be so nuanced to have little practical value.[3] Yet it is possible to define what films argue in a general sense. All argue for their conclusions, to persuade us that their perspective is, if not universally true, at least valid. This we define as a "worthwhile conclusion."

On face value this seems so straightforward as to be simple common sense. But what is worthwhile to one person is trivial to another, and this subjectivity limits the usefulness of our understanding. But we can dig a little deeper, as what filmmaking practice appears to define as worthwhile is not completely open.

So what is a worthwhile conclusion? This relates back to the virtues of the filmmaker, from Aristotle by way of MacIntyre: to live a good life, to exercise justice, courage, and honesty.[4] Yet it needs to be stressed that worthwhile is not necessarily the same as worthy; this is not about films pursuing wokeness or even insight, although some form of audience enrichment, of a story worth telling, is certainly part of the goal. Sinnerbrink holds that films are vessels for aesthetic ethical experience, able to meaningfully challenge and potentially even change beliefs and opinions in the mind of the audience[5]—therefore it might justifiably be expected that knowledge or at least truth is a worthwhile target. However, perhaps counterintuitively, neither is a necessary bar. Film-as-worthwhile-argument does not require feature filmmaking to contribute to global knowledge or articulate an objective truth, just that the conclusion has some intrinsic value.

Feature film conclusions need merely to be edifying, so rather than knowledge and truth, plausibility and significance are the requirements. Implausible conclusions usually require deceptive argumentation; trivial conclusions are simply not worthwhile.

There are plenty of worthwhile conclusions that ultimately are proved wrong. Until the third century BCE almost every civilization believed the Earth was flat.[6] This conclusion was clearly edifying (both plausible and significant), and the arguments put forward were usually well-reasoned—albeit just all of them completely wrong. A conclusion that would not be considered edifying, although plausible, significant, and well-argued, would be "it's important that kids should eat their greens so they grow up big and strong." It is an assertion that—if not self-evident from tacit knowledge—children (and parents) are likely to have already been consistently told, certainly in Western culture. It may well be true, but there is little value in its social or cultural reinforcement.

How Films Argue

Before we fully invoke Aristotle's theories of persuasion from his *Rhetoric,* we need to more fully define our version of worthwhile argument. Again, it is based on the virtues of the filmmaker and is essentially making any argument with integrity, in a sincere, nonmanipulative way using reason as opposed to misleading claims or appeals to emotion—even if the ultimate conclusion is edifying, plausible, and significant.

This disqualifies such techniques as rhetorical argument, which attempts to persuade others through the appearance of truth and may employ false reasoning. However, it does not rule out unsound arguments, which are internally systematic and logically valid but start from false premises.

Cinematic arguments presented in a worthwhile way are not as straightforward as they seem, as cinematic technique itself is fundamentally audience manipulation that appeals to emotion. The question of how a film argues well really becomes a question of how a film sincerely convinces us of a plausible, significant conclusion. To do this, a film must convince us in all areas of story: that the world, characters, motivations, situations, and resolution (or nonresolution) are authentic. If it fails in any of these factors, the argument is lost.

When engaging with any piece of art, audiences are expected to suspend disbelief to the form-relevant degree—this means that genres such as comedy require a higher suspension of disbelief than domestic drama. A conventional moviegoer will accept plot contrivances such as coincidence far more readily in the French farce *Le Dîner de Cons* (Veber 1998) than in the war drama *The Hurt Locker* (Bigelow 2008), as well as the impossible over the improbable. As long as the logic of the story world is consistent, audiences are much more likely to suspend their disbelief that an alien can fly (Superman) than the reputed top investigative reporter in Metropolis (Lois Lane) cannot recognize him when he wears spectacles.

Aristotelian Modes of Persuasion

In *Poetics,* Aristotle did nominally consider how persuasion would function in drama, making reference to his *Rhetoric,* but his approach and application were very different to ours. Depending on which translation is used (we're using both Butcher's 1907 and Heath's 1996 translations), Aristotle refers to "thought" or "reasoning" being present in drama.[7]

Rather than applying thought/reasoning to the drama overall, Aristotle is concerned only with how this element plays out within character. He initially discusses how a character reasons within their circumstances based on their morals: Should I steal? Will I get caught? The character will often vocalize this and make a declaration about their situation: I'm in a place of opportunity. This is ultimately expanded to include how one character will use dialogue to influence another. It is here that he invokes *Rhetoric* as a guide.[8]

Rhetoric is split into three books, with the first advancing the view that persuasion is achieved by the combination of three main elements:[9]

Ethos: the source of the argument being credible
Logos: the argument is internally logical, sometimes with appeal to facts and statistics
Pathos: the argument invokes the emotions and senses

Ethos is from the Greek word for "character" and means a set of core, guiding beliefs that inform a community or ideology. The idea of the source of the argument being credible can be interpreted in two equally valid ways. It can be taken to mean that the author of the work is credible, be it the filmmakers or the institutions responsible for the film. Taking the example of Paul Thomas Anderson's drama *Phantom Thread* (2017), the ethos could come from Anderson's reputation, from that of production company Annapurna Pictures, or from distributor Focus Features, a subsidiary of NBC

Universal. The alternate interpretation is that the world of the film itself is credible, convincing in terms of the aforementioned genre-consistent suspension of disbelief.

Logos, the internal logic of the argument, refers to all the complex storytelling elements combining to make a cohesive case for the conclusion: essentially the bulk building blocks of what we would understand as filmic persuasion. Yet as noted in chapter 2, it is pathos that is key, that gives written drama more impact than simple intellectual debate, performed drama further impact over written drama, with film (and its ability to combine performance with other purely emotive elements such as music) perhaps providing the most impact of all.[10]

In a film that argues in a worthwhile fashion, the logos should be supported and augmented by ethos and pathos. They are not to be distractions from either the conclusion or the argumentation. However, with so many elements to balance, this is a difficult process that requires a mastery of the craft. As we'll explore in later chapters, a film can argue in an insincere way simply by emphasis, by too much reliance on desire or sentimentality to cover a flaw in logic or even to disguise false premises.

Film Streams

The overarching view from many film philosophers is the false notion that somehow theme and argument are separate from action on-screen—as if one exists before the other is somehow inserted or one stops when the other begins.[11] Yet in mainstream narrative cinema, every moment, every image, every sound contributes: action is very much the argument. Seger uses the example of a character mugged as they were in the wrong place at the wrong time to communicate that life is haphazard.[12]

The film gurus tend to isolate the key thematic element in a film by observing what idea is being consistently tested, usually on a scene-by-scene basis.[13] The screenplay can be thought of as being split into two distinct streams that must be unified for the film to function correctly; we'll call them the Dramatic Stream and the Thematic Stream.

Most screenwriting "how-to" books typically concentrate on the Dramatic Stream, the fundamentals of main character / goal / conflict / resolution straightforward to explain, comprehend, and refine. The Thematic Stream is a little more nebulous, as it governs the Dramatic Stream and the way they relate to each other is particularly fluid. It is relatively simple to ensure your main character has an internal and/or external goal, less so to decide how your complex ideas on sexual identity are communicated without relying on clunky exposition.

The Thematic Stream contains the assertion, composed of a central singular abstract concept, a standpoint to that concept, and the reasons why that standpoint is valid. In a film that functions well, it is wholly constructed around demonstrating that assertion (even if the filmmaker is not explicitly aware they are doing this or conceptualizes it in a different way, using different terminology) with every creative element unified in this goal. The scriptwriting process can begin with the assertion, but this is rare as it is more likely to lead to those problematic didactic films. Usually there is another inspiration (scenario, character, music, sequence, genre) with development and fine-tuning of the assertion coming at a later time in the development process.[14]

The traditional tools of the screenwriter are time, place, characters, and events. Propp suggested that all stories in any medium can be made up of a combination of seven character types and thirty-one story functions.[15] The primary reader of the screenplay is an industry professional who is looking to draw out relevant material for their particular department: an actor looking for indications of character and dialogue, a production designer looking for clues as to physical setting, and so on. However, it is the craft of the director that constitutes how the film is ultimately delivered to the audience.

The director must create a myriad of distinctly cinematic moments, each of which must make precisely the right impact if the argument is to succeed. These moments may be intellectual, emotional, sensual, or sexual.[16] Using the case study of Michael Haneke's bleak drama *Amour* (2012), Sinnerbrink demonstrates that impact by emotional engagement can counterintuitively include both emotional estrangement (invoking ambivalence, clashing emotional and evaluative responses that resist reconciliation or unification) and moral-cognitive dissonance (as opposed to unified emotional and intellectual understanding).[17]

The director's tools overlap but fundamentally differ from those of the screenwriter—the screenwriter can describe or indicate a shot, but it is a wholly different experience to read a description of a picture than to actually see the picture. Directors always have to show, not tell; a screenplay can indicate an emotion, but the film must make us experience it. In a purely practical sense, the screenplay can be considered as a blueprint of gaps that the director fills using their understanding of the medium. If the script was an exhaustive and objectively prescriptive list of instructions, the director would be superfluous; but—for now—the raw material requires humans to creatively shepherd it to the screen.[18]

In contrast to the screenwriter, who has only words on a page in which to communicate, the director has a profusion of medium-specific techniques at their disposal that has built on or simply uses many of the other arts, be it photography, theater, or music.[19] In isolation all are phenomenally powerful argumentative devices and, even if nonverbal, are capable of influencing the audience's opinion of a moment or scene and therefore entire argument. In combination they can be virtually irresistible.

Butch Cassidy and the Sundance Kid

As we're looking at the practice of film-as-worthwhile-argument rather than screenplay-as-worthwhile-argument, the best way to demonstrate the mechanics of the process is to examine completed films. The nuances of a shot, look, or gesture can communicate compelling information that was never on the page. Here, we use the western *Butch Cassidy and the Sundance Kid* (Hill 1969) as a quick initial illustration of the key concepts.

The Dramatic Stream of main character / goal / conflict can be stated as follows: *two bandits want to maintain their lifestyle but are prevented by the "Wild West" rapidly becoming developed by the industrial age*. The Thematic Stream could be stated as this: *people need to evolve both who they are and how they fit into their community if they are to survive, even if they will not thrive.* As we've seen, the Thematic Stream is referred to in many different ways in the industry and professional literature, but most commonly as creative voice. Yet however it is referenced, it functions as the conclusion to an argument to which all creative elements combine to prove. This is creative unity.

To apply Aristotle's elements of persuasion, the ethos is provided by the filmmakers and studio: written by William Goldman, directed by George Roy Hill, and released by 20th Century Fox. Goldman had not yet achieved worldwide fame as the epitome of a critically and commercially successful screenwriter but had already had modest success with studio film *Masquerade* (Dearden 1965), and Hill had previously directed Julie Andrews in the well-received *Thoroughly Modern Millie* (1967). Both were highly credible, as was the studio. The film world presented is also strongly plausible; artistic license is taken in terms of its Hollywoodization (overly handsome leads, for instance), but it is in line with genre conventions.

The story lays out logical reasons why Butch and Sundance have to change (mostly by showing the inevitability of social and societal evolution) using various techniques, from the visual metaphor of the railroad bringing civilization to the Wild West to the dialogue with which Butch, Sundance, and their mutual friend Etta discuss their futures. The central values of the film are completely consistent; all characters who embrace change are rewarded, and all who reject it are punished, most critically the titular characters themselves. At one point in the narrative Butch and Sundance attempt to go straight but find they neither have the authentic desire to do so nor are their best selves when trying to play by the rules.

Pathos is provided by the presentation of the cinematic elements, invoking not just emotion but also the senses and desires in the audience. This begins with the casting: Paul Newman, Robert Redford, and Katherine Ross. All are hugely attractive and charismatic individuals whose natural essence, played up for the screen, is to invite desire and empathy. This is further intensified by the use of camera and light, both highlighting their attractiveness and giving the audience insight into the nuances of their feelings, especially through the use of close-ups. If we truly care about these characters and become emotionally invested in their journey, what happens to them will have an impact on our beliefs. An individual glance or subtle intonation can carry great power to make us like, hate, or doubt a character—and each moment builds toward the conclusion that unless these men can change, they will metaphorically or physically die.

The conclusion is more nuanced, and the film demonstrates this through a significant moment when Sundance realizes he needs the adrenaline in order to remain the fastest shot in the West. It builds to the realization in both characters—and the audience—that perhaps death is their best option; they might survive if they succeed in changing—but they will not thrive. A substantial level of detail is required in order for us to fully understand and empathize with these men. The conclusion is essentially about immobility of innate nature, told through personal tragedy. When Butch and Sundance realize they can't change at the end of the second act, the scene is played as a death scene, even though their literal deaths don't take place until (just after) the final frame of the film.

On a well-constructed film, be it film-as-worthwhile-argument or just film as argument, the key elements are always clear: what theme is consistently being tested (necessity for change), what happens in the end and why (death through lack of change). It would likely be a mistake to attempt to make the entire argument within each scene (such as in an Eisensteinian intellectual montage),[20] but each is an important building block required to convince the audience of the validity of the conclusion. This is why the ending is decisive and precludes ongoing story forms to function efficiently as arguments.

So is *Butch Cassidy and the Sundance Kid* a successful film, in the sense that it achieved the internal goods of feature filmmaking practice? Is it film-as-worthwhile-argument? To answer that we have to assess if (1) the conclusion is edifying (plausible and significant) and (2) the argument relies on reason with appeals to emotion, desire, and the senses without reliance on misleading facts or inferences, sentimentality or sensation.

This is of course subjective and relies heavily on context, but a film that reminds us of the difficult necessities of personal development is both plausible and significant. As it makes its case in a way that is internally consistent and not reliant on exploitative techniques (such as manufactured melodrama or gratuitous sex, nudity, or violence), the answer is a very unsurprising yes, *Butch Cassidy and the Sundance Kid* is a strong example of film-as-worthwhile-argument. As it was also both a critical and commercial triumph, it is a film that can be considered a success in all senses of the term.

CHAPTER 4

Alternate Conceptions

The internal and external goods of feature filmmaking are regularly referenced by mainstream filmmakers and commentators, although almost never conceptualized as such. Whenever an attempt is made to universalize what filmmakers are trying to do—or what films are—the discussion is typically based on an assumption of what it means to make a creatively successful film, often tempered with whether or not this was reflected in the box office.

There are three particularly prevalent assumptions that, for shorthand, we'll refer to as Just Entertainment, Just Telling Stories, and Emotional Manipulation. Like film-as-worthwhile- argument, these assumptions have not been pulled from thin air but are based on a combination of observation and considered reflection. This is not an attempt to undermine any of these ways of understanding, as each makes a genuinely compelling case. It's just that all are incomplete, none offering a full account of the practice.

Just Entertainment

This is perhaps the most popular way of thinking about mainstream feature films, relating directly back to that infamous Sam Goldwyn quote: "Pictures are for entertainment, messages are for Western Union."[1]

It's a quite neat and direct denial of film-as-worthwhile-argument. Translated into our terms, the view claims that the internal good of the practice is to just entertain; the simple provision of amusement and enjoyment. This is all that filmmakers should attempt to do, and when it is achieved, they may deem themselves successful. No matter if the subject matter is dishonest, divisive, and destructive, as long as the audience is diverted in a pleasurable way, the internal good of the practice has been satisfied.

If we're going to fully interrogate this, it is critical to clarify precisely what is meant by "entertainment." Most filmmakers are likely to have in mind the conventional dictionary definition of the word, where a piece of entertainment is something designed to provoke delight or amusement. Richard Dyer, in *Only Entertainment*, defines entertainment more precisely as a performance that has the sole conscious aim of providing pleasure.[2]

What both definitions lack is the impact of timing. Perhaps a more accurate definition of entertainment is one that takes into account the immediacy of the reaction it inspires. In this way, entertainment is a type of performance or artwork that triggers amusement or joy that the audience is aware of at the time. Where an audience is entirely unaware of their enjoyment, they have not been entertained—even if, on reflection, they realize the work had merit or benefit. They may have been interested, engaged, and absorbed (or alternatively resistant, bored, and distressed) at the time of viewing only to come to a different conclusion once other internal processes have taken place—but ultimately it was not an entertaining experience.

Both Dyer's definition and Goldwyn's maxim contain an implicit idea of entertainment-as-merely-pleasure-giving that attempts to diminish both its significance and its influence.

The popularity of the idea of film as just entertainment can in part be attributed to the fact that it serves the purposes of both the promoters and the detractors of the filmic arts. For the promoters—primarily filmmakers and film institutions—it is a useful articulation of the practice as it absolves the industry of any social or cultural responsibility. This is most explicitly spelled out when the industry comes under attack by politicians and various media and cultural commentators for its potential influence on real-world violence. In the early 1980s this occurred with the rise of "video-nasty" VHS rentals and then a decade later with *Child's Play 3* (Bender 1991), with the film being quoted in court by the child defendants in a child murder case in the United Kingdom.[3]

In these cases, the defense of film as just entertainment had real-world stakes and consequences. In many countries the film industry is self-regulating. This means the industry bodies responsible for classifying films are funded by the industry itself, with little or no government involvement or oversight. If more weight were given to the influence of film, more regulation would likely follow.

The detractors of mainstream narrative feature film consist of individuals and institutions that believe film is an inferior art form compared to other modes of creative expression. Again, this belief does not exist purely as theory and has significant real-world implications. Almost all film industries globally are heavily supported by public arts funding, as are most other conventional performing arts. It is unlikely that any meaningful arts organizations would survive without such government support, yet funding is finite and industries compete for their respective share. This creates an inevitable political situation where each art form must justify its relevance and significance to the culture at the direct fiscal expense of the other forms. By definition, mainstream feature film is undeniably for the masses, so the Just Entertainment view suits other art forms that can position themselves, despite their smaller audiences, as providers of a more significant cultural experience. These tend to be battles between what has been traditionally regarded as high and low culture, and since both supporters and rivals of mainstream narrative film tend to push the same low-cultural conception of the practice, it has widespread currency.

This is not to deny the significance of entertainment in mainstream filmmaking practice. It would be false to state that films have nothing to do with entertainment, in the same way it would be false to state that chess playing has nothing to do with entertainment. Entertainment is a key element in the practice of mainstream narrative filmmaking—but it is not foundational, and therefore cannot be the internal good of the practice.

Yet surely that can't be right? If you're feeling resistance to this idea, you won't be alone. The idea of film as entertainment is so embedded in the way film is talked about, so encouraged as a general understanding of the medium, it's absence as an intrinsic element to the practice is likely to receive a hostile reception. And does it have to be so? To argue in a worthwhile way invokes the virtues of honesty, courage, justice, creative generosity, and compassion, with filmmakers not manipulating audiences dishonestly, even if they bring them to a conclusion that they believe to be just. But could not entertainment be included in this definition of a worthwhile way to deliver film stories?

Robert McKee certainly believes so: "All fine films, novels and plays, through all the shades of the comic and tragic, entertain when they give the audience a fresh model of life empowered with an affective meaning."[4] The idea also has support from a less likely source—Joel Silver, producer of action blockbusters such as *Lethal Weapon* (Donner 1987) and *Die Hard* (McTiernan 1988). He claims that films are perceived to be lesser if they don't have a message, but to him the message is entertainment.[5]

Yet these comments, although welcome and giving huge weight to the idea of film-as-worthwhile-argument, stretch the definition of entertainment to its breaking point. There is a substantial difference between entertainment and engagement. One is the bringing of joy, the other emotional involvement or commitment. This is not an exercise in unnecessary semantics; the distinction is critical as the word "entertainment" has useful connotations of disposability that "engagement" does not. You will never hear the phrase "We're just in the engagement industry," not simply because it lacks a certain excitement, but because it implies a more significant connection with the audience. It is certainly possible to view entertainment as a worthwhile endeavor—even a desired part of filmic storytelling—but it is ultimately not a necessary part.

This is demonstrated regularly by various well-known films that have been embraced by academics, critics, and audiences—often with strong cultural impact—but cannot be considered entertaining. One of the biggest successes of 1993 was *Schindler's List* (Spielberg), the story of an industrialist and war profiteer, Oskar Schindler, who had a change of heart and used his profits to rescue Jews destined for the death camps. It is an undeniably confronting and brutal film. Its aim is not to generate pleasure in an audience but to move and edify them. It is an absorbing and interesting film certainly, but not one that seeks to delight its audience. It can be appreciated, revered, and understood to have had a positive impact on the viewer, but not one that is designed to bring joy at the time of viewing. *Fruitvale Station* (Coogler 2013) is another such film, a brutal drama about institutional racism and state-sanctioned violence.[6]

On the other end of the filmmaking spectrum, to illustrate a second reason the Just Entertainment narrative is disingenuous, we need to bring in two outlier genres of feature film. One sits on the fringes of the mainstream, the other well beyond it: exploitation and pornographic films.

A good working definition of exploitation films is those that are "tawdry exercises in catering to audiences' primal urges."[7] Famous examples of the genre, which had its heyday in the 1970s pre-VHS era, were films such as the women-in-prison escape movie *Big Bird Cage* (Hill 1972) and violent revenge thriller *I Spit on Your Grave* (Zarchi 1978). These films clearly prioritize sensationalist and extreme renditions of sex, violence, and often sexual violence over other artistic considerations.[8]

An official, global definition of pornographic feature films does not exist, and what is considered pornographic in any media is delegated to the judicial systems under obscenity laws. However, like exploitation films, pornographic narrative feature films can be defined as prioritizing scenes of sexual intercourse (often real sexual intercourse) over the needs of the storytelling.

Exploitation and pornographic films are relevant as they are both genres of narrative feature film that undeniably place entertainment of the audience front and center of the cinematic experience. Both genres aim to bring joy to the viewer, be it fetishistic or more conventionally sexual. Yet the labels pornographer and exploitation filmmaker are pejorative terms. It would be highly unlikely (although not impossible) that anyone inspired by the magic of cinema would aspire to be a pornographer.

If the internal good of mainstream narrative feature films was just to entertain, then pornographers and exploitation filmmakers would not be seen as separate from mainstream film culture. This indicates that the tradition is more than simply bringing delight to an audience.

This leads to a third challenge to the Just Entertainment idea: put simply, there are far easier ways to entertain than making often hugely expensive and complex narrative feature films. If an individual wishes to entertain an audience, they can tell a joke. They can be a magician, an illusionist, an equestrian in a circus. They can write a short story, a novella, or a novel that simply requires themselves and an editor. In the world of moving pictures, they don't even have to go so far as exploitation or pornography, instead making cat videos or any bite-size content in their homes that routinely gets millions of hits on social media sites. These are all more straightforward ways to entertain. So if the attraction, the desire, the vocation is to be a mainstream narrative feature film storyteller, then there is something else at work.

Finally, even film industry lobbyists undermine the Just Entertainment theory as a matter of policy. National screen bodies such as the British Film Institute and Screen Australia give the global film industry something of a split personality. When it comes to the social impact of violence on-screen, the influence of narrative feature film is argued to be negligible by all stakeholders. When public funding is in question, the cultural impact of the form is claimed to be substantial.[9]

Just Telling Stories

This popular conception seems to be another attempt to minimize the (perception of) cultural impact of feature filmmaking, this time by reducing its complexity. This can be called the We Just Tell Stories approach.[10]

Taken at face value, the claim that "storytellers just tell stories" is so reductive it does not even appear to qualify as an alternative understanding of the practice. Yet even the most minimal scratching of the surface reveals it is based on some conventional assumptions on how and why we tell stories across all forms.

Obviously, these terms need qualifying: what do they mean by stories and storytelling? Story is a particularly fluid term. As with much terminology used in the creative industries, the industrial, academic, and everyday usages diverge significantly. The *Oxford English Dictionary* defines story as "an account of imaginary or real people and events told for entertainment" and as "a plot or storyline." So to the common observer, the terms "story," "plot," and "storyline" are all synonymous.

The academic discipline of narratology offers much more precise definitions, even if inevitably they are not completely consistent. Also somewhat predictably, the origins of narratology can be traced back to *Poetics*. The Russian formalists created the discipline in the early twentieth century, but it must be noted that they never came to a consensus other than over the fact that poetic and practical language were distinct entities worthy of theorization.[11]

Narratology is founded on the distinctions between "story" and "storytelling." In fact, *Narrative*, the official journal of the International Society for the Study of Narrative, is specifically interested in the powers and limits of the story-discourse distinction. Two key concepts in narratology are those of the *fabula* and the *syuzhet*. These terms are also somewhat fluid, so for clarity we'll use Bordwell's definitions. The fabula is the chronological-causal string of events; the syuzhet is their presentation, the configuration of the events in the narrative.[12]

So to go down a semantic rabbit hole, for narratologists story is fabula and storytelling is syuzhet. Another synonym narratologists use for storytelling is narrative, although in everyday language this also means story, storytelling, and plot. It is yet a different definition of the word "narrative" than we used to define mainstream narrative feature films in terms of film-as-worthwhile-argument at the start of the book.

In the most fundamental sense, a story is something that can never be reached. Once there is an attempt to specify it, it is not story but storytelling. Story is an abstract object in logical space; only a representation of the story can be given, not the story itself, communicated via the encoding process of the storytelling. However, as Bordwell rightly points out, the construction of the story in the head of the audience member during and after the telling is highly imperfect.[13]

To return to the idea of Just Telling Stories—it is now possible to distinguish two versions, dependent on who is making the claim. A filmmaker with no formal knowledge of narrative theory will still be able to claim the general "we're storytellers, we just tell stories," whereas the narratologist would claim the more specific "we are fabula-tellers, we just present syuzhet."

Yet having its origins in linguistic study, narratology is only one approach to investigate story. Another branch of analysis is that of comparative mythology, exemplified by Joseph Campbell in his major work *Hero of a Thousand Faces*. This will be familiar to screenwriters everywhere, even if, as we noted in the previous chapter, it is solely via their reading of Christopher Vogler's *The Writer's Journey*. Campbell compares myths from various cultures and historical periods in order to assess similarities and points of difference. Unlike the more limited scope of narratology, comparative mythology allows for an attempt to understand why human beings tell stories.

In *Into the Woods: A Five-Act Journey into Story*, John Yorke takes both a narratological and comparative approach to storytelling across most popular forms, although, being the former Head of Channel Four Drama and Controller of BBC Drama Production in the United Kingdom, he defaults mainly to film and television. Yorke posits seven distinct reasons why human beings tell stories:[14]

1. Societal: The story as a blueprint for human survival. A view that believes societies survive by adaptation, rejecting the conventional and embracing change—and stories are a codification of this process, a guide to show us how to break free of repression.
2. Rehearsal: Stories as safe places to understand and navigate the complexities of real life.

3. Healing: Similar to rehearsal, but here the story is a model specifically for overcoming and resolving faults—a structure to enable healing.
4. Information retrieval: Story as knowledge database, the narrative allowing for efficient and outsourced mental storage.
5. Panacea: Stories to provide hope by making order out of chaos. They make reality palatable and give it meaning.
6. Procreation: Based on the sheer prevalence of stories that conclude with sex or marriage. They indicate a necessary or pleasurable template for healthy propagation of the human race.
7. Psychological: Based more specifically on Jungian psychology, this reason is yet another user manual for the human condition. This states that humans have to be psychologically balanced in order to achieve fulfilment. Mental health depends on resolving contradictory elements represented by elements of character: how the protagonist integrates wisdom from a mentor or learns from the flaws of the antagonist.

Yorke takes a similar approach to this book in asking the "why" before moving to the "how" and "what," yet his primary focus is to defend a thesis that five-act structure is the true structure of storytelling, rather than the dominant three-act shape. He uses the caveat that anyone certain of a single reason for storytelling faces public condemnation, but eventually settles (if not with complete certainty) on one overarching motive: we tell stories to impose order on the world.

In this way, all storytelling (filmic or otherwise) is an exercise of existential control. The horror of meaningless survival is too difficult to bear, so we use stories to find patterns, order, and meaning in our lives. For Yorke, ordering is an act of perception that gives us narrative, the "dramatization of the process of knowledge assimilation."[15] He goes further and begins to touch upon a drama-as-argument concept, claiming drama mimics the way the brain assimilates knowledge, which is why it's "identical to both legal argument and the basic essay structure we're taught at school." Yorke believes this is "why theme is essential and why it arises unbidden from any work. Consciously or unconsciously, all drama is an argument with reality in which a conclusion is drawn and reality tamed."[16] Yorke uses a slightly different idea of argument than we have been using. Argument with reality implies that the truths, subjective or otherwise, within the story are at odds with reality as experienced, rather than a simple assertion and reasons to believe that assertion.

So to bring us back full circle and align Yorke's terminology within the "storytellers just tell stories" maxim, he would state that "we're knowledge dramatizers: we just dramatize knowledge assimilation."

This makes Yorke's point of view closely aligned with film-as-worthwhile-argument, although he does not make this claim; it is a side observation used to justify his championing of the five-act structure. Nevertheless, could "knowledge-assimilation dramatization" be a viable—or superior—alternative internal good of feature filmmaking?

It is certainly feasible, but we are concerned not with what is possible—or even preferable—but with what constitutes the current tradition of the practice. There is an issue with knowledge as the fundamental target of filmmaking practice, as the goal is simply not realistic within the confines of mainstream narrative feature filmmaking: any tradition is highly unlikely to evolve around such an aim. Film argument is concerned with reasoned opinion of ideas plausible and significant, something the definition of knowledge does not accommodate. It is not outside the realms of probability that some of the plausible and significant assertions may at some point qualify as knowledge, but that is not under the control of the filmmakers. To be fair, Yorke does not clarify precisely what he means by knowledge. But an argument to convince others of an opinion (which may not be held as certainly true, even by the author) need not be aimed at knowledge, given any reasonable conception of knowledge. So even when using Yorke to provide a more complex and complete interpretation of Just Telling Stories, it does not become a viable overall conception of the practice.

Another flaw with Just Telling Stories is the assumption that all stories in all formats can be reduced to universal general principles. This reductivism negates the idea that different forms have critical nuances with different traditions and internal goods that may not be compatible with any central unifying claim. Film-as-worthwhile-argument is a declaration not about all drama but about a very specific form of narrative. This particularity is crucial as there are many ways of telling stories that are not suited to mainstream narrative feature film. Think of *The Odyssey* by Homer. Noted as a definitive work of epic poetry, it should be highly surprising that there have been no significant film adaptations of the complete story in the history of mainstream narrative feature filmmaking. The most substantial attempt was a 1930s-set reinterpretation by the Coen Brothers entitled *O Brother, Where Art Thou?* (Coen 2000), but it was the structure that was subsumed, with other elements only very loosely inspired by the original text. We are also not making the claim that the internal good of the television soap opera is worthwhile argument in a worthwhile way. This form, due to its endless nature and the inevitable and constant turnover of practitioners during the life of the production, means that the idea of these shows being formed as any kind of argument is nonsensical, in precisely the same way that an endless argument that never reaches a conclusion is nonsensical: as we noted above, it is neither practical nor rational to form a tradition around a self-defeating principle.

Emotional Manipulation

The third most plausible alternate understanding of mainstream filmmaking is to simplify our original idea and lean further into pathos. What if the practice was not to move an audience to a worthwhile conclusion in a worthwhile way but simply to use creative expression to move an audience?

"It's a punch. It's a total punch." This is screenwriter and director Darren Aronofsky defending his film *mother!* (2017), which had become only one of eleven films in the history of Western cinema to receive an "F" rating by Cinemascore, a review aggregator in existence since 1978 that polls cinemagoers on the first night of release.[17] Aronofsky called it a punk movie that would come at the audience, that he was sad and wanted to howl, and that the film was his howl, and that it's okay if some people don't want to listen to it.[18]

The idea of a movie that just punches you was front and center in the reviews of the film. Owen Gleiberman, chief film critic for *Variety*, commented that the film could be considered a masterpiece if the only thing you needed from a horror film was to get a series of visceral reactions.[19] Gleiberman believes that horror films need to be more than this, but concedes that for a section of the audience this may be enough. Is he right? And does this not reveal an underlying truth? If audiences are happy to be punched or hear a howl, could simply telling emotionally charged and moving stories be a more justifiable internal good of the practice? It is both plausible and highly achievable, as it doesn't have the demands of entertainment, knowledge production, or structured argument of any kind.

EMOTIONAL CHARGE

An academic who works in this area is French film theorist Martine Beugnet. In *Cinema and Sensation: French Film and the Art of Transgression,* Beugnet coined the term "cinema of sensation" when looking at the release of a successive series of French mainstream narrative feature films that clearly prioritize the form's capability to impact the emotions and the senses, the most high-profile being (English title in parentheses) *Baise Moi* (Rape Me) (Despentes and Trinh Thi 2000), *Demonlover* (Assayas 2002), *Lady Chatterley* (Ferran 2006), *Romance* (Breillat 1999), and *Venredi Soir* (Friday Night) (Denis 2002). Beugnet prioritized the visceral element of the films, but the investigation still examined the works as intersections between the intellectual and the biological. (In fact, she considers film as embodied thought, clearly a concept compatible with film-as-worthwhile-argument.) Obviously Beugnet is making claims about the nature of the films themselves rather than filmmaking, but her work still opens the way to an academic defense of emotionally charged sensation-led cinema.[20]

Some objections to this version of the internal good are identical to those challenging the idea of cinema as purely entertainment. If simple emotional manipulation is the goal, there are many easier ways to perform the same function—all of which are less time-consuming, expensive, and difficult to control as the creation of a feature film. This returns us in no particular order to exploitation film, pornography, and cat videos.

Another indication that untethered emotional impact is not the tradition of the practice is that Aronofsky is having to strenuously defend the point of his film to critics and audiences alike. Yet this is not to say that there is no merit to the idea. Emotional engagement is a key strength of cinematic storytelling, so could a modified version function as the internal good?

DESIRE SATISFACTION

It is received wisdom that most individual scenes within a film set up a desire or desires to be satisfied, be they significant or trivial.[21] This relates back to common concepts of all film scenes requiring if not conflict, then constant tension.[22] Films are often referred to as fantasy, so can wish fulfilment be the ultimate point of mainstream cinematic storytelling?

This view takes a cue from Yorke, who takes a fractal approach to storytelling by arguing that scene structure mirrors overall film structure.[23] There is a critical difference between being moved and having a desire satisfied, but is this distinction decisive? Could the internal good of mainstream narrative feature films be the straightforward practice of setting up and then satisfying desire?

This conception carries weight and brings with it all the work of psychoanalytic film theory. Many of Freud's concepts were used in its construction, among them the id, ego, superego, Oedipal complex, narcissism, the unconscious, hysteria, and castration.[24] For our purposes, it is not relevant whether the audience desire is perceived as conscious or unconscious, merely that the definitive tradition of filmmaking practice is to satisfy it. There are many variations in such a wide field of study, but most film psychoanalytic theories are based around the idea of the incomplete audience becoming symbolically complete through the experience of watching the film, be it through a process of identification or by positioning all viewers as male and creating the female as the object of desire.[25] Laura Mulvey brought the Freudian term "scopophilia" (pleasure from looking) into the academic mainstream and with it the very specific sexual connotations of erotic pleasure from looking at the cinematic image.[26] In this way, on an intrinsic level the film does not even have to set up desire in order to satisfy it—if there is an instinctive desire to look, it is a preexisting want that film satisfies simply by the act of display.

These conscious/unconscious desires can be frivolous or significant and can function as simple wish fulfilment or psychological need. An audience member will pick a given film for its palette of desires: to live life as a pilot, to get him/her/they, to have power over anyone—the list is quite literally endless. Genre can be viewed in this way, the social and financial contract that certain desires will be fulfilled by the close of the narrative. In a romantic comedy, the couple will be formed, in a conventional action thriller good will overcome evil.[27]

Discarding those moment-to-moment sensory or sexual satisfactions, desire satisfaction is a primary function of plot, character, and theme. If the internal good was primarily through surface-level plot and character satisfactions, then feature filmmaking would have evolved into essentially an anti-art practice—the training not so much about a filmmaker finding their voice as about finding ways to pander to their audiences. This is clearly not the case. Discussions surrounding screenwriter and director Jordan Peele and his horror film *Get Out* (2017) demonstrate quite clearly that he became one of the hottest properties in Hollywood because his film did not simply deliver genre expectations but also elegantly spoke a difficult truth regarding race relations in America.[28]

But let us say that the feature filmmaker wishes to pander to a viewer of enlightened self-interest, one that will feel symbolically whole by satisfying their primary desire to understand the world, even if told a difficult truth. Or, as is often the case, a viewer simply concerned with self-interest who wishes to see a story that reinforces their view of the world, even if a comforting lie.

This circumstance is highly plausible. As we previously noted, film guru Linda Aronson believes that audiences consciously want a moral to their stories and express their irritation when it is not present. This is thematic desire satisfaction and brings us full circle to film-as-worthwhile-argument. It is simply a shifting of viewpoint from the filmmaker perspective to the audience perspective: "what is the internal good of feature filmmaking?" becomes "what is the fundamental human desire to be satisfied by feature filmmaking?" The answer is the same: to be moved to a worthwhile conclusion in a worthwhile way. Untethered exploration of an abstract concept is not enough; a thematic question has to be set up and paid off in a convincing way to satisfy.

A genre that illustrates this, perhaps the purest genre as relates to plot-based desire satisfaction, is the whodunnit. The crime (usually a murder) is set up at the start, creating with it a desire to know who committed it. This desire must sustain the complete running time of the film, when the identity of the criminal or criminals is finally revealed and their motivations laid bare. Few, if any, whodunnits in cinematic history fail to reveal the perpetrators at the close. That is not to say that all loose ends are tied up, *The Big Sleep* (Hawks 1946) a famous example of this, but the solving of the puzzle is the key joy of the experience.

The whodunnit is the most successful literary genre. Agatha Christie (1890–1976) worked almost exclusively in this field and is the best-selling author of all time with an estimated two billion books sold, a figure potentially matched or surpassed only by Shakespeare and the Bible.[29]

To use some simple calculus, if (1) the internal good of feature filmmaking is desire satisfaction, (2) the whodunnit creates a strong single desire to sustain a feature-length running time, (3) literary whodunnits are the best-selling genre of all time, and (4) Agatha Christie is the best-selling whodunnit author of all time, then this introduces the question as to why most filmmakers are not attempting to make whodunnits. Further, why are whodunnit filmmakers not canonized by critics and the public, and, by extension, why are not most financially successful films whodunnits?

As of writing, the most successful film whodunnit, *Murder on the Orient Express* (Branagh 2017), has made just under US$352 million at the international box office, from a US$55 million budget. The current highest grossing film ever is *Avatar* (Cameron 2009) with over US$2.9 billion.[30] At this moment, there is not a whodunnit in the top fifty grossing films. A reasonable objection to this would be that whodunnits simply satisfy the wrong desire, that mainstream narrative feature films set up various specific desires and finding out "who did it" is not one with widespread appeal. This might explain the lack of grosses but does not fully account for their status. Whodunnits are not seen as prestige pictures; they do not win significant awards for direction or screenwriting, have never won a best picture Academy Award, and are viewed at the low end of the genre hierarchy.

There seems to be a public admission of the problem of adapting Agatha Christie to the screen in how the films are cast. *Murder on the Orient Express* is arguably the most famous work by the best-selling author of all time. With underlying intellectual property of this strength, any resulting film should not be cast dependent (the film should work with any set of talented actors). The heavy marketing weight is being lifted by the author and the genre. Yet in both Hollywood feature film adaptations of the book (the other being directed by Sidney Lumet in 1974) the cast has been packed full of stars: Albert Finney, Richard Widmark, Sean Connery, Lauren Bacall, Anthony Perkins, John Gielgud, Michael York, Vanessa Redgrave, and Ingrid Bergman in the former and Johnny Depp, Penelope Cruz, Daisy Ridley, Dame Judi Dench, Sir Derek Jacobi, and Willem Dafoe in the latter. This inevitably betrays a lack of confidence in the source material. Stars are expensive and used only when required. Even Agatha Christie pastiches by writer and director Rian Johnson, *Knives Out* (2019) and its sequel *Glass Onion: A Knives Out Mystery* (2022), are cast similarly, with Daniel Craig, Chris Evans, Jamie Lee Curtis, Toni Collette, Christopher Plummer, Edward Norton, and Kate Hudson taking key roles across the two films.

How the genre decisively demonstrates that desire satisfaction cannot be the internal good of feature filmmaking is through the following thought experiment: imagine that, as a viewer, once the setup of the crime and the suspects have been laid out in front of you, you skip directly to the reveal at the end of the film. Your desire would be sated without having to watch the middle of the film. Most Sherlock Holmes short stories are structured like this: the mystery is told to Holmes in the first half, then Holmes tells Watson how he solved it in the second half.[31] It is highly unlikely that the internal good would be based around a concept that allows for removal of most of the narrative yet still remain a generally satisfying experience.[32] In terms of argumentation, most whodunnits are not particularly edifying or nuanced, rarely about anything other than crime doesn't pay; a point of view encoded into the DNA of the genre, requiring little reflection or awareness on the part of the filmmakers.

However, the ability to function with large sections of narrative missing or a lack of edifying argument may be why the whodunnit is a phenomenally successful episodic television genre, typified by American shows such as *CSI: Crime Scene Investigation* (Zuiker 2000–2015), *NCIS: Naval Criminal Investigation Service* (Bellisario and McGill 2003–), and *Law & Order* (Wolf 1990–) and their various spin-offs.[33] Episodic television is a different form, with a different set of traditions and audience expectations. A format that is viewed at home where distractions are often unavoidable may benefit from being able to function without every scene being the sole focus of concentration (watching television at home is now regarded as a multiscreen experience with viewers often on other devices at the same time).[34] A weekly television show, in this case a crime procedural, is also an endless format not well suited to develop a tradition of edifying argument, and as such the television audience is less likely to require a moral in the same way they would from a feature film.

Like emotional punch, desire satisfaction should not be mistaken for the internal good. Yet is it possible to combine both? Could feature filmmaking primarily be the practice of providing emotionally charged desire satisfaction?

Films that exemplify emotionally charged desire are those that are able to provoke an audience to really care about something (usually the fate of a character), then continually build the desire through obstacles before finding an emotional punch to satisfy that desire. Successful examples of this are pure revenge films such as both volumes of *Kill Bill* (Tarantino 2003 and

2004) and *Mad Max* (Miller 1979). The ending of *Mad Max* provided such an impactful body blow that it inspired the entire *Saw* franchise.[35] However, there is a reason revenge films are also a staple subgenre of exploitation films, as although they might satisfy an emotionally charged desire they are thematically shallow, instead prioritizing the mechanics of the reprisal.

A film such as the aforementioned *Schindler's List* also conforms to the emotionally charged desire-satisfaction model and is far removed from any hint of exploitation. Yet although the film creates a powerful emotional desire—for Schindler's workers to be protected and rescued—that is duly satisfied, the value of the film is not purely in the rescue. An alternate scenario where the workers were buried in a mudslide and Schindler successfully supervised their extraction would likely result in a lesser film.

However, there are many films that undermine the idea of emotionally charged desire satisfaction as a viable internal good: those lauded cases of mainstream narrative feature films that provide neither significant emotional charge nor desire satisfaction. These films are less common but high-profile and include Martin Scorsese's *Taxi Driver* (1976), *Raging Bull* (1980), and *The Irishman* (2019). These films operate as Sinnerbrink outlined, by invoking ambivalence and moral cognitive dissonance.[36] They may incite brief strong emotional responses to certain moments (such as sudden violence) but resist building traditional characters the audience are invited to root for, instead choosing to focus on difficult to relate to antiheroes in compelling situations, minimizing any desires as to individual fates. Yet the films are certainly mainstream, embraced by audiences and critics alike, and are capable of making coherent arguments. *Bad Lieutenant* (Ferrara 1992) is another such example.

Why?

All of the alternative conceptions we've looked at here are susceptible to the question of why. Why tell emotionally charged and moving stories? Why set up desires to be satisfied? Whether it is to entertain or help dramatize knowledge assimilation, they do not categorize the practice as a whole—a film that attempts either would be by definition an empty experience. To return to Darren Aronofsky, his film "howl" may have satisfied his own desire, but the story did not impact in any significant or meaningful sense. The audience might have been provoked emotionally but not in the service of anything larger than the sensation itself. This demonstrates that it is not enough to simply move the audience; it is necessary to move them somewhere worthwhile. Emotional manipulation in all its forms is also susceptible to the general objection that it is an internal good far simpler achieved using the myriad of other storytelling forms or other arts. Essentially there are far more efficient ways to punch.

PART II

THE CASE STUDIES

General Notes on the Case Studies

FILM-AS-WORTHWHILE-ARGUMENT IS ABOUT the intention of the practice, not—perhaps counterintuitively—the actual result. Therefore, it is fair to question if in-depth case studies of completed films are going to lend any significant weight to our understanding of the process.

The answer is twofold: yes, it is possible to think of these case studies as superfluous, that most of the heavy lifting has already been done by examining the history and evolution of feature filmmaking practice—how we are taught to think about and experience films as both creators and consumers. However, as film philosopher Sinnerbrink believes, detailed analysis and critical interpretation are the best ways to convince that a theory is sound.[1] If key examples can be carefully selected where the worthwhile argument is either well executed or illuminatingly flawed, then the film in question can provide compelling insight.

So how to choose from all of mainstream film? Ideally it would be films where the director had final cut.[2] This way we can best guarantee, as much as is reasonably possible, that we're seeing the result of the filmmaker's work, rather than a film heavily influenced by non-filmmakers. This narrows the pool significantly, as the final cut privilege is afforded to precious few filmmakers, even those working independent of the studio system. The decision as to which films have a well-executed argument is slightly more problematic. The case studies will inevitably rely on justifying precise interpretations of the films as definitive, so what of Barthes's still prevalent contention that the author is dead? How can film-as-worthwhile-argument function if various, often conflicting interpretations are equally valid?[3]

The response is again perhaps counterintuitive. Notwithstanding any valid theoretical objections to Barthes,[4] all interpretations of the films here are offered not as speculation on what any actual viewer may comprehend but rather (using the film in conjunction with the conventions of the practice) as informed judgments on what the filmmakers were intending to communicate, essentially to reverse engineer the argument of the film. The approach has strong precedence, especially in the study of screenwriting, where the priority is with what screenwriters thought would be effective rather than any ultimate effect.[5]

In this way, the viewer is an entity that exists only in the mind of the filmmaker, a theoretical construct that they use all their talents and training to move to a worthwhile conclusion in a worthwhile way. The filmmakers may completely misjudge their ultimate real-life audience, but nevertheless their speculation guides their process.

Exhaustive synopses are provided for all case studies; however, the analysis is written on the assumption that the reader will have previously viewed a release copy of the original film.

CHAPTER 5

The Exemplar

Toy Story 3

So WHY *TOY STORY 3* as the key exemplar? It is not only animation (which the majority of mainstream narrative feature films are not) but also a second sequel, rarely an indication of quality. Nonetheless, the film is a particularly accessible example of successful cinematic argument in modern mainstream narrative cinema and one that we can have a high degree of confidence was completed free from any undue outside influences that would impact the storytelling.

The fact that the film was made by Pixar is particularly relevant, as their track record at the time of almost flawless critical and commercial success ensured that their filmmakers had critical autonomy.[1] Here we can say it is highly probable that *Toy Story 3* is the film story contributor/director Lee Unkrich, screenwriter Michael Arndt, and story contributors John Lasseter (also studio head at the time) and Andrew Stanton wanted it to be.

However, as we've already noted, although these filmmakers have developed and delivered a successful cinematic argument, it does not necessarily follow that they think of their practice in this way. In fact, it is highly probable that they do not. Pixar is well-known for crediting their success to prioritizing story over animation tricks or technologies and is remarkably transparent about their project development process. Quite dogmatic in their approach, Pixar holds that conventional cinematic storytelling evolved naturally as it was the form that best served the audience of the time in terms of accessibility and emotional connection, and to work against that paradigm is to merely narrow your audience. They conceive the conventional storytelling/viewer relationship as a two-dimensional pyramid: the ultimate conventional storyteller works at the bottom, providing access to the largest possible audience, whereas the epitome of the avant-garde storyteller works at the top, essentially an artist making work only for other artists or themselves.[2]

Synopsis

The film begins with a toy adventure all set in young boy (and toy owner) ANDY's head. WOODY (Cowboy), BUZZ (Astronaut), JESSIE (Cowgirl), BULLSEYE (Horse), and SLINK (a slinky dog) are the goodies, MR. & MRS. POTATO HEAD, THE THREE ALIENS, and REX (Dinosaur) are the baddies, with HAM (Piggy Bank) as the master villain. Until the climax, the audience is in the world of the adventure (in the real Wild West), but as the goodies save the day, we cut to what is really happening—Andy playing with toys in his room. The sequence continues with a montage to show Andy growing up until about twelve years old.

The main story of the film opens with the toys in a trunk, about to execute an important plan. They have two telephones—a landline handset and a cellphone. Rex dials from the landline and the cellphone rings. We hear Andy searching for it. Then the lid of the trunk opens and we see Andy is now seventeen.

He takes his phone from Rex (who won't let go), but the dinosaur doesn't break the cardinal rule of toys staying inanimate when a human can see them. Andy wrenches the device from Rex, thinks for a brief moment about his toys, then throws Rex back in the trunk and blames his sister for taking his phone.

Once Andy has left, the toys get out. It was all a ruse to get Andy to play with them again. Leader Woody makes an announcement and tells the group that that was their last, best chance, and now they should "close up shop" and prepare for life in the attic. It is not a thrilling prospect for any of them, despite other toys being up there. There is a debate about loyalty to Andy: a toy's duty is "to be there" for their owner whenever they want to play with them. But what to do when their owner grows up and doesn't want to play with them anymore? How long should their loyalty last? They all love Andy, but now their future is unclear. Woody is adamant—as long as they are owned by Andy, they should always be there, even if in the attic.

Mr. Potato Head, always the voice of dissention, disagrees—but there is no consensus reached before they are interrupted.

Andy is leaving for college in a few days, and his mother wants him to clear out his room: things need to be taken to college, put in the attic, or thrown away. She mentions that Andy should think about donating his old toys to SUNNYSIDE DAYCARE, as they are always looking for new toys for the kids. Hassled and irritated, Andy tells her that they're all junk and no one would want them. He looks at his toys, plastic bin liner in hand, and puts all in except Woody, whom he is going to take to college with him.

Andy intends to put the bag in the attic but is distracted by his sister. His mother sees the bag, thinks it is trash, and throws it out by mistake. Woody sees this, but the toys in the bag do not. They escape and climb into Andy's mother's car—into the donation box for Sunnyside. The toys are hurt by what they feel was a betrayal by Andy and think they would be better off going somewhere where they might be played with. Woody gets into the car to convince them otherwise, and again there is the debate about their duty to their owner—especially as this was just a mistake. But suddenly the door shuts and all are taken to the daycare center.

Andy's toys are welcomed by the Sunnyside toys, led by big pink bear LOTSO, an affable old patriarch, and handsome figurine KEN. Ken makes an instant and inevitable connection with BARBIE (thrown out by Andy's sister). All but Woody are excited that Sunnyside never runs out of children to play with, a veritable paradise for a toy. But Woody sees this as a betrayal of Andy—and after a mean-spirited argument with best friend Buzz, Woody leaves them and makes his way out.

Things do not go to plan, and instead of getting back to Andy, Woody is picked up by sweet, young four-year-old BONNIE, whose mother works at the daycare center. She brings him home and plays with him and her other toys, and—despite himself—Woody enjoys it. Then he learns a dark truth from a miserable clown toy called CHUCKLES. Chuckles explains that he, Lotso, and BIG BABY (a large battered baby doll) had a lovely owner called DAISY who adored Lotso the most. She lost them on a family outing, but when they managed to finally struggle home Lotso had already been replaced. Lotso snapped—he told Big Baby that Daisy had replaced all of them and they all ran away, finding Sunnyside. The newly bitter Lotso took control, turning the center into a toy prison run by his rules. Chuckles escaped only when Bonnie took him home.

Back at Sunnyside, Andy's toys are thrilled for their first real playtime in years but are put in the toddlers' room and brutalized by the young children who play roughly. Buzz asks Lotso to move them to one of the more appropriate older children's rooms, but the true nature of Sunnyside is revealed. Lotso is using the new toys as cannon fodder—they need a constant supply of toys for the toddlers' room, as most don't last long. Before Buzz can escape and tell the others, Lotso and his cronies return Buzz to his original factory setting, both erasing his memory and returning his personality to that of a by-the-book obedient soldier.

At around the same time Mrs. Potato Head, through an eye she lost in Andy's room, sees Andy searching for them. They realize Woody was telling the truth and try to leave Sunnyside to get back to him. Unfortunately, they find themselves literally imprisoned in the room with Buzz as their guard.

Woody returns to Sunnyside to save his friends. He learns from a world-weary CHATTER TELEPHONE that the only way out is through the trash chute. He quickly finds everyone, and all are overjoyed to see him. Woody rescues them from Buzz, but in doing so Buzz is accidentally reset to Spanish Mode instead of his original persona.

Spanish Buzz instantly falls in love with Jessie and (incorrectly) sees Woody as a romantic rival. In a complex prison-break sequence, the toys make it all the way to the trash chute and are about to escape to freedom when they are ambushed by Lotso and his gang. Ken, still in love with Barbie, changes sides and joins Woody. As a garbage truck approaches, Woody reveals Lotso's deception to Big Baby, who in an act of revenge throws Lotso into a dumpster about to be collected. Woody and the gang jump over it to escape, but Lotso grabs Woody's leg and drags him down with him. The rest of the toys also fall in trying to rescue him (except Barbie, Ken, and Big Baby), and the garbage truck picks them all up.

A television falls on Buzz, and his original memory and personality return. The truck drops them at a landfill site, and the Aliens are swept away by a digger. The rest of the toys find themselves on a conveyor belt that recycles metal—and chops up the rest. They all hold onto something magnetic that will lift them over the spinning blades—but Lotso is stuck. Despite his misdeeds, Woody and Buzz risk their lives to help him. All avoid the chopper but then realize the conveyor belt now leads to an incinerator. Woody and Buzz help Lotso reach an EMERGENCY STOP button, only for Lotso to betray them again—abandoning everyone to escape. The toys fall into the incinerator and after some initial, frantic struggle, realize finally that this is their end. They stop trying to escape and hold hands as the heat is about to melt them. But at the final moment a GIANT MECHANICAL CLAW, operated by the Aliens, reaches down and pulls them clear.

Outside, Lotso is found by a GARBAGE TRUCK DRIVER, who, remembering the bear as a beloved old toy, ties him to his truck's radiator grille and drives away. Woody and the other toys board another truck back to Andy's house.

Now safe at home, Woody helps everyone into a box for the attic before saying his goodbyes and getting in a different box bound for college. The room now empty, Andy's mom walks in—only to have an emotional moment, declaring to Andy that she wishes she could always be with him. He hugs her and tells her she always will be. This strikes a chord with Woody, and he has a change of heart. As they leave the room, he jumps out of his box, grabs a sticky note and pen, and writes a hasty note that he sticks to the top of the box full of his friends, before jumping in himself.

Andy reads the note and, thinking the note is from his mother, donates the toys to Bonnie. It is not easy for Andy, especially when—to his surprise—he finds Woody at the bottom of the box. He's even more surprised when Bonnie recognizes Woody. Initially he takes his cowboy back, but then—realizing they have some special connection—passes Woody on to Bonnie, and they play together all afternoon. Woody and the other toys watch Andy go and say their silent goodbyes as they begin their new lives with Bonnie.

Over the credits, we see life in the new version of Sunnyside. Barbie and Ken have taken over, and it is now a lovely place to be with a fair tag-team system of being played with by the younger ones.

The Argument

Our earlier look at industry literature noted that the concept of argument is given various different names—the two most common being "the vision" and "the controlling idea."[3] Essentially, both can be reduced to the idea of a narrative feature film having a singular theme and singular (but not necessarily simple) standpoint to that theme. Current dominant thinking allows for subthemes and unlimited narrative complexity, but just one strongly articulated idea guides all creative choices. This is not to say that the argument has to be obvious or redundant, but it does need to be expressed in a way accessible to the intended audience.

Toy Story 3 is an effective exemplar to demonstrate how film-as-worthwhile-argument functions, as the argument the film makes is signposted with great clarity. The worthwhile conclusion the film wants to move the audience to in a worthwhile way could be expressed thus: *friendships and relationships should not be thought of as requiring eternal loyalty under any and all circumstances, so in order to live a fulfilled life—manifested by the ability to form new meaningful friendships and relationships—it is necessary, however emotionally painful, to sever or transform an existing friendship or relationship that has lost its intrinsic value.*

In the scenario specific to *Toy Story 3*, in order to thrive, Woody must move on from original friend and owner Andy (not necessarily end the friendship, but certainly move it from a primary relationship to a secondary one) as the relationship has lost its intrinsic value. Through no fault of his own, Andy is older now and has grown out of his toys (who will never change). This means he never plays with them anymore—and the intrinsic value of this particular friendship is that Andy thrives as he plays with the toys and the toys thrive because he plays with them. When Andy no longer fulfils his side of the relationship contract, it loses value for all concerned. If the toys attempt to hold on to the friendship with Andy, flagged in the film as a sense of loyalty and duty to always be there for him, it will mean they will fail to thrive as they will, at best, spend decades sitting in the attic, not played with.

So, how can we be confident that (1) this is the correct conclusion or (2) this conclusion is worthwhile? To convincingly demonstrate film-as-worthwhile-argument we also have to show (3) how precisely the film constructs a compelling argument using cinematic storytelling technique and (4) how the film does this in a worthwhile way that does not rely on unreasonable manipulation. It's worth noting that the correct conclusion does not necessarily have to be the conclusion intended by the filmmaker(s), even if this is often the case.

To first address (2), that the above conclusion is worthwhile, this is not a question of technique, just whether the assertion has any essential value. An edifying conclusion is one that we have previously defined as plausible and significant. If the conclusion is wholly implausible, the argument constructed in support of it will, in all likelihood, be superficial. Alternatively, if the conclusion is trivial, it is not worthwhile. We must remember that the question of whether or not the conclusion is somehow objectively true is not a strict requirement. *Toy Story 3* gives a conclusion around ideas of loyalty and friendship that, while accessible and plausible, is certainly complex and perhaps even unexpected to a child still learning how to make and maintain friendships. The idea that personal loyalty does not necessarily mean blindly committing to the romantic ideal of, to use tween parlance, a BFF (best friend forever) is something that requires a strongly developed sense of emotional stability, confidence, and maturity. In this way, we can judge the film to be drawing an edifying conclusion.

How to Read a Cinematic Argument

To prove (1), that the above is the correct conclusion, it is also necessary to simultaneously explore (3), how precisely the film constructs a compelling argument. Previously, we have defined filmic arguments as ones that aim to convince us of a stated assertion, providing us reasons to believe within a dramatic context. To isolate the key thematic element of an argument is a process of observing what idea is being consistently tested, almost on a scene-by-scene basis, by the film.

To initially use a McKee-based analysis, it would be to find the story's ultimate meaning by seeing what exactly is expressed through the action and aesthetic emotion of the last act's climax. McKee's equivalent to general cinematic argumentation is his controlling idea, defined as value plus cause, where value is the central thematic concept that includes a positive or negative judgment. Scene-by-scene "positive idea and counter idea argue back-and-forth until at climax one voice wins" and is revealed as the controlling idea.[4]

So what is the action and aesthetic emotion of the film's last act's climax? For McKee, aesthetic emotion is meaningful emotional experience. The last climax of *Toy Story 3* is Woody telling Andy (via a note that he knows that Andy will mistake to be from Andy's mom) to pass on the toys to Bonnie—and Andy doing it, with a little resistance when he realizes that Woody is in the box along with the rest of his old toys. The emotions are strong—the physical and emotional separation of two lifelong friends—but the meaning in context is clear—both parties are better for it. And there is yet another beneficiary—Bonnie.

So for McKee, the value must be friendship, as expressed through ideas of loyalty. The positive idea is that friendship is defined by unrelenting loyalty, the negative counteridea that loyalty has limits. The relationship is not that of the toys to each other, but of the toys to their owner Andy. This play between idea and counteridea is present in almost every scene in the film. It is first (and necessarily) flagged as a central concept at the start of the film, as conventional narrative feature filmmaking dictates, when Woody and the other toys try (and fail) for one last play time with Andy. What follows is a robust discussion between the toys about their future, and the ideological battle lines are drawn with the key thematic question articulated in the dialogue, paraphrased here as "despite our positive history/love, what loyalty do we have to a relationship when the other party has emotionally moved on?" Essentially it represents two choices: cling on to the past with ever diminishing returns (as demonstrated by an articulation of what failure looks like—the toys being consigned to the attic, safe but never being fulfilled again other than the long shot that Andy will someday have kids who might want to play with them) or move on to the scary unknown.

This unknown becomes more formed with the option of Sunnyside, but it is still a newness that contains its own inherent terrors. Even when the toys discover the daycare center is essentially a corrupt prison and want to escape, it still presents the dramatic question of "what now?" The attic might be a refuge, but hardly a long-term solution. To return home cowed, however grateful to be alive, is not presented in the film as a positive option, as the previous realities of life in the attic are not questioned or modified. It would represent a possible, if unsatisfying end to the story and would form an assertion along the lines of *you should retain loyalty out of fear of your life—there is worse out there.* This argumentative move would not work as life is not the theme; it would instead create two themes—loyalty and survival—and they will begin to conflict.

Yet this is not to deny that there are subthemes. As long as there is one overarching assertion regarding a single theme, there can be any number of subthemes that don't necessarily have to correspond to fully formed assertions or arguments, as long as they augment, not undermine, the central point of the film. A good example of this in *Toy Story 3* is furnished by looking at the film's narrative from Andy's perspective. Another way of isolating the main theme and argument is simply to ask what the main character learns (or what the main character does not learn to their detriment). This is not always as simple as it seems, as it is not always clear precisely who the main character is—either to the filmmaker or to the audience. Consider another highly successful animated film, *Frozen* (Buck and Lee 2013), which forms one of our later case studies. Is the main character Anna or Elsa? Both have the same journey. Or is this a case of the rare dual protagonist story?[5] A similar argument could be made for Andy being the main character, or at least an equal dual protagonist with Woody, as he has a similar journey and performs the final dramatic action in the film (giving Woody away to Bonnie). However, categorizing Andy as the main character would be incorrect, as his epiphany is instead a good example of a subthematic argument. Andy comes to understand the need to move on in relationships that have lost their intrinsic value, but it is through the prism of coming of age; what Andy learns is the need to fully let go of your childhood in order to become an adult. This is demonstrated by Andy finally passing over Woody, his final and most beloved toy. If he were to keep Woody and take him to college, it would be a metaphor for not fully letting go.

Further subthematic arguments worthy of mention, especially in the light of *Toy Story 4* (Cooley 2019), are those concerning religion, community, and parenthood. The religious argument implicit in this series views children as godlike beings who give a toy's life meaning and value through their imagination during play, less a conventional friendship than a deity-acolyte relationship. To be played with is to live a meaningful life. As Andy gets older, he is no longer the source of meaning, and neither are the younger children who damage the toys through inappropriate play. The community argument relates to Woody's connection to the rest of the gang. If he goes to college, the gang will be broken up, and the recognition of the need of community is one that is tacitly made by Woody at the close of the film. Woody could also be used to represent not Andy's friend or acolyte but father figure—scared of his son outgrowing him and learning to deal with that loss.

These arguments are subthematic as they are worthwhile, valid, and complementary to the main argument—but less fully developed, providing fewer reasons to believe their assertions. The religious metaphor is not developed in the story, the conception of play left vague and the viewer invited to interpret the Woody-Andy relationship as conventional friendship (no awe of hierarchy present). The community aspect is not highlighted or raised as a thematic concern, and the parenthood aspect is inconsistent (it is potentially an awkward stretching of the metaphor if Woody being passed on to Bonnie is supposed to represent the grandparent-grandchild relationship). It is interesting to note that *Toy Story 4* has developed the parent/grandparent metaphor further, although it is primarily making a case for personal evolution late in life, knowing when it is time not just for post-child/owner life but for new community life.

However, to decisively illustrate how *Toy Story 3* sets out its argument with such success, we need to return to Aristotle's *Rhetoric*. The film conforms quite clearly to Aristotle's three modes of persuasion. First is ethos: that the film comes from a credible source. Source can be defined two ways—as a consistent and convincing screen world or those presenting the film possessing great authority. Here both are credible, whether you consider the presenter of the argument to be the individual filmmakers, the franchise (*Toy Story*), the production company (Pixar), or the studio (Disney).[6]

Second is logos: that the argument is internally logical. The central idea of the film is one that should be tested scene by scene, and *Toy Story 3* does this in a highly efficient manner. The core thematic question of how to remain loyal when the other party in the friendship has moved on is raised at the start of the film and then is revisited and developed at regular intervals:

- when the toys escape from the trash
- at Sunnyside when Woody leaves for the first time
- at Bonnie's when Woody enjoys himself
- when Chuckles tells his story about Lotso
- during the confrontation at the garbage chute
- when Lotso betrays the toys on the conveyor belt
- when the toys settle for the attic
- when Andy's mom enters Andy's empty room
- when Andy donates the toys to Bonnie, including Woody

Some of these thematic moments are more explicit than others and exist on three levels of presentation—which we refer to here as direct thematic dialogue, indirect thematic dialogue, and thematic action. The latter two directly relate to the concept of enthymematic arguments we touched upon earlier in the book. As these arguments work by deliberately leaving key premises or even the conclusion unstated (typically as these are considered common sense) the fact that the viewers supply the missing element(s) themselves should make the argument more impactful. The idea of "unstated" in cinematic terms does not necessarily have to mean not in the dialogue, even if this is often the case. It may feel very true to Aristotle, who was working in a time before film and focused primarily on the spoken word when it came to persuasion, but films can also state their positions in a purely visual and aural sense.

Examples of direct thematic dialogue are when the toys escape from the trash and when Woody leaves Sunnyside for the first time—the thematic ideas stated plainly in the dialogue with the characters literally debating the core theme (with Woody arguing for loyalty). Indirect thematic dialogue is a less obvious form of presentation, such as moments when Andy's mom enters his room or the toys settle for the attic—there is dialogue around the core theme, but it is either oblique or subtextual. Finally, thematic action is demonstrated in the moment when Woody enjoys himself with Bonnie, in a very effective nondialogue thematic beat played out purely through action. As film guru Linda Seger notes, theme is the least interesting when it's communicated through talky dialogue and far better expressed by concentrating on other more cinematic choices.[7]

In constructing the logic of its argument, *Toy Story 3* demonstrates a common cinematic approach where the precise thematic question is laid out in the dialogue, but the answer (and hence the conclusion to the argument) is formed in thematic action. Why this is common is revealed by how these cinematic choices exploit Aristotle's third category of pathos.

For Aristotle, in order to win an argument, the senses and emotions have to be invoked. This can certainly be done with emotive text, but as we've previously explored, the engagement of the emotions and senses is where cinema excels, especially over the written word. It is one thing to be told that someone is attractive, quite another to experience that attractiveness for yourself.[8]

We've also noted that conversion from script to screen is a process of interpretation, adaptation, and transportation, the director using a myriad of tools specific and often unique to the visual and audio arts. Yet so far this case study has discussed only techniques that are wholly text-based without exploring how these moments are delivered with sound and vision (all analysis could have been identical by referring only to the screenplay). Therefore, we need to move on to a second stage of (3) how precisely the film constructs a compelling argument using cinematic storytelling technique.

One particular scene is highly illustrative. Near the end of the film the toys end up fighting for their lives at the dump, and at one point all appears lost. Below is how the moment was written in the original screenplay:

Woody grabs Rex's hand, slides further toward the inferno. They are all being pulled inescapably downward. There's no way out. Jessie looks at Buzz.

JESSIE

Buzz . . . ! What do we do?

Buzz looks at her. He reaches out, takes her hand. Jessie grabs Bullseye's hoof. Slinky takes Hamm's hand. Hamm reaches out to Rex. The Potato Heads hold each other. Mr. Potato Head grabs Rex. Buzz reaches out to Woody . . .

Woody takes Buzz's hand, and the circle is complete.

As they approach the vortex, heat waves blast their faces. The Toys close their eyes, turn away. Woody stares at the fire, shuts his eyes.

This is the end.

A LIGHT from above shines in Woody's face. He opens his eyes. A giant mechanical Claw lowers towards them.

The Claw plunges into the trash around them, closing them in its grip, then raises them up. They soar into the air, away from the ROARING incinerator. Woody looks around in disbelief. The Claw spins, passing in front of the crane booth.

The sequence is quite moving on the page, but on-screen the emotion is further intensified and manipulated by cinematic technique.

The most dominant of these not referenced at any time in the script is the music, scored by Randy Newman. It gives the sequence a gravitas, seriousness, and sense of scale that is not present in any other part of the film. As an audience we are mostly confident that no harm will befall the toys at this point, but are never completely sure—especially as this is near the end of a second sequel. Music is emotional information that tells the audience how to read a scene. Here, the music pushes the significance of the moment.

Perhaps the best demonstration of this is to imagine music that is comedic and comforting. It would indicate that everyone is going to be safe and undermine the drama of the situation (this is not a film franchise that uses music as counterpoint).

Another technique not referenced on the page is juxtaposition. It is unworkable to constantly remind the reader of the look of each character, but critically the script does not highlight the visual juxtaposition of harmless, childlike toys in a horrific physical situation. This juxtaposition is aided by various cinematic and visual tricks, primarily character design (most of the toys have large eyes that invite audience empathy, Jessie's hand is made to look much more human as Buzz takes it) and set design—the environment is utterly hellish with the palette completely made up from reds, yellows, and oranges that communicate extreme heat.

Further, more exclusively cinematic techniques maximize the dramatic tension and emotional reaction from the audience. A major moment of the scene is the toys accepting their own deaths. Buzz is first to do this in the exchange with Jessie, and it is notable in a film that is dialogue heavy that this moment becomes completely nonverbal. The question of "What should we do?" is answered simply by an offer of a hand. As Woody is the central protagonist with the main character trait of never giving up, the pivotal moment is when he finally stops struggling and takes Buzz's hand. It is here that the film uses the standard technique of giving Woody a bigger close-up than anyone else—communicating the significance of both his character and the moment and allowing that moment to be read in all its subtlety and complexity.

Editing is another unique film technique that maximizes emotional impact. The timing of the sequence is one that can be only approximated in written form and is critical to the viewing experience. The toys struggle for a long time, and the seeing of this struggle is necessary yet difficult to watch—a delicate balance. Too much struggle and viewers feel bored or emotionally exploited, not enough and they are not experiencing the moment fully. The sense of character desperation is one that is most impactful on the screen rather than the page. The director here made the toys struggle for thirty seconds before Buzz takes Jessie's hand. The time taken between Woody accepting his own death and the rescue is a further twenty-seven seconds. This is much longer than indicated in the script, which reads at approximately ten seconds. This timing is critical for the audience to wrestle with the potential for the toys' demise, even if they resist it. *Toy Story 3* stretches this duration to breaking point—pushing (especially the adult section of) the audience to consider the death of the toys, before giving them the release of a happy end to the sequence.

As Aristotle tells us, this emotional engagement is key to the film arguing effectively. The sequence is a culmination of a path that should not have been taken, Woody being punished for clinging to Andy, the others for severing rather than evolving their relationship with their owner.

Now we come to (4): How does *Toy Story 3* construct a compelling argument in a worthwhile way that does not rely on unreasonable manipulation? As much as all storytelling is manipulation on some level, it is possible to emotionally engage but do so in an unauthentic, cynical way that does not further the argument. As we explored earlier in the book, Darren Aronofsky's *mother!* (2017) may have been a high-profile example of the audience's emotions being engaged to no edifying end, but it is also possible for a film to have an edifying conclusion that is not argued in a worthwhile way—through manipulations in ethos, logos, or pathos. Another way to think about it is that the rhetorical stance of the film is out of balance, focused too much on the subject or the audience or projecting the persona of the filmmaker.

This is not always by design. With so many creative and institutional elements to harmonize, mainstream narrative feature filmmaking is a difficult process that requires both a mastery of the craft and stakeholders who share the same vision of the project. If we put to one side the fact that most filmmakers do not conceptualize their practice as film-as-worthwhile-argument, non-filmmaker interference (based on prioritizing external goods) is perhaps the most significant reason why most films fail by varying degrees to meet the internal goods of the practice.

If we take *Toy Story 3* to have a worthwhile conclusion, how could it have been argued in a nonworthwhile way? Sticking with Aristotle, it would be by way of manipulations of emotion and logic or reliance on the credibility of the filmmakers, franchise, or studio to make up for or distract from flawed argumentation. As all tangible and intangible elements of a film are in play, this can take many highly delicate forms. An unjustified happy ending is perhaps the most famous Hollywood manipulation of emotion, allowing the audience to get a perceived desired-for dopamine hit, even if it weakens, compromises, or fully changes the argument. *L.A. Confidential* (Hanson 1997) is a good example of this, with the character of Bud White (played by

Russell Crowe) sacrificing his life for the greater good, only to be revealed in the final moments of the film not to have died after all.

Manipulations of logic often take the form of out-of-character decisions that make sense only for the argument. Romantic comedies are particularly susceptible to this, with the protagonist choosing to be with the object of their affection despite the lack of chemistry or the terrible things this character has done to them. Notable examples are Meg Ryan and Tom Hanks as Kathleen and Joe in *You've Got Mail* (Ephron 1998), where he closes down her business (her beloved bookstore), or *Four Weddings and a Funeral* (Newell 1994). Hugh Grant's character Charles's decision to be with Carrie (Andie MacDowell) despite what could justifiably be thought of as her emotional abuse (not telling him she's getting married / making him shop for wedding dresses with her / inviting him to her wedding / turning up at his wedding telling him of her separation) has led to a whole radical reinterpretation of the film not as romantic fairy tale but as romantic cautionary tale: Charles has clearly made the wrong choice and ended up with the wrong girl.[9] However, perhaps the most egregious and parodied example is from *Batman v. Superman: Dawn of Justice* (Snyder 2016), where Batman decides not to kill Superman (despite his continuing belief that Superman is a credible threat to the planet) purely as their mothers have the same name.

The film also represents a strong example of nonworthwhile use of ethos, by an overreliance on the franchise to make up for flawed argument. Its conclusion is a straightforward variation used by many superhero group films, based around the intrinsic value of cooperation: only then can we reach our goals, be it saving the world or living a well-lived life. It is an uncontroversial assertion that the audience will likely want to accept, but as the argumentation is so flawed it relies on the audience's preestablished love for the characters and potentially other knowledge gleaned from other sources around character motivations to even partially function.[10]

Toy Story 3 as Evidence

As we've already discussed, a hidden power of mainstream feature film—and why it has the capability to change hearts and minds more quickly and efficiently than written or spoken arguments—is its ability to work as both the argument and its evidence in one simultaneously impactful package. It's worth reminding ourselves that for Aristotle, an enthymematic argument is a compelling rhetorical proof in itself.[11] Noël Carroll and his fictional skeptic go so far as to believe that film as evidence is a given, even if the evidence is false—at best representing only the side of the story that suits the filmmaker's agenda.

In this way every event and character reaction in *Toy Story 3* provides the perfect evidence to support the conclusion that friendships and relationships should not be thought of as requiring eternal loyalty under any and all circumstances. But surely that cannot be as powerful as other forms of real-world evidence that support the same conclusion? As emotionally and intellectually invested as the audience may be, knowing suspension of disbelief dictates that they are well aware they are watching fiction, which must weaken the evidence.

This is not necessarily the case. As much as we might like to believe that we are swayed by objective proof alone, desire and emotion are always part of the mix. And what of unwilling suspension of disbelief, where a viewer unwittingly suspends critical thinking and logic to better engage with the viewing experience?[12]

It is one thing to read a peer-reviewed research paper about the various psychological models, dynamics, and life cycles of friendships, but seeing Andy give away Woody to Bonnie, understanding the truth of the moment for all characters, is far more affecting. The filmmakers could just have had Andy give the toys away to Sunnyside, but they invented Bonnie to give the viewer a poignancy, a human representation of the functional relationship over the nonfunctional, the sense of moving on but everything being in its right place.

There is also the impact of the cumulative over the individual. It is not practical to track where we get all our information from, and thus fiction can magically transfigure into fact over time as we don't quite remember the exact details of the evidence that made us believe something. This effect is strengthened if other sources claim the same thing, fictional or otherwise—it all just becomes compelling evidence.

Ultimately, the flaw in saying that film evidence is tainted is that fiction film is not presenting an evidentiary argument (documentaries might; but fiction films like *Toy Story 3* certainly do not). Fiction doesn't present evidence in any ordinary sense of the term, but it does supply reasons to believe a conclusion. How does it do this? Not all reasons require evidence. Some are simply reminders. Some are conceptual, showing what is implied by commitments we already hold, or showing what is possible given the concepts we hold. Some are invitations to imagine or to empathize with others and their fictional situation (from which we learn such things as what it is like to face a situation). All of these are reason generating: they all give us good reason to hold one belief rather than another or make one commitment rather than another.

Toy Story 3 provided the evidence, one example of what could happen when you hold on to nonfunctional friendships. It will impact some viewers more than others, be it in a surface or fundamental way, always dependent on their basic nature, taste, and what other real-life or fictional evidence contributes to their understanding of human relationships.

CHAPTER 6

The Counterexample

Mulholland Drive

TOY STORY 3 is a great illustration of how film-as-worthwhile-argument works in conventional mainstream film storytelling. But what about less straightforward stories? Surely not all films fit the paradigm so neatly. In short, how about we pick a hard one?

This is trickier than first appears. We are making a case not about all film but about all mainstream narrative feature films, which means we cannot use experimental works that would be more at home in an art gallery or nontraditional screen spaces. Film-as-worthwhile-argument does not apply to anything that happens to be filmed, yet should apply to any mainstream movie, no matter how complex.

The criteria have to be as follows: a film that appears to contradict film-as-worthwhile-argument by having all the external markers of fulfilling the internal good of the practice yet does not, by intention or result, move the audience to a worthwhile conclusion in a worthwhile way. This means that filmmakers, critics, and audiences alike must sincerely love the film, and it must be enduringly regarded as an artistic success. This counterexample should be as unconventional as the mainstream allows.

This leads us to *Mulholland Drive* (2001) by David Lynch, as both the film and filmmaker didn't fit the conventional mainstream mold but thrived nonetheless.[1] *Mulholland Drive* is recognized as one of the most significant films of this century by film critics, with a 2016 BBC poll of 177 international film critics judging it the greatest film of the twenty-first century.[2] Lynch both wrote the screenplay and directed the film and was nominated for the American Academy Award for Best Director. Other significant filmmakers and critics such as Richard Kelly (screenwriter and director of *Donnie Darko* 2001), Jaco Van Dormael (director of the Caméra d'Or–winning *Toto le Heros* 1991), and Thierry Jousse (editor in chief of *Cahiers du Cinéma* 1991–1996) cite the film as one of the most impactful they have ever seen.[3]

Yet despite the uniformity of praise for the film, there continues to be debate as to its meaning and even whether the film has—or should have—a meaning. Todd McGowan, a critical theorist known for his work on Lynch, notes that it is a divisive work that "creates a filmic divide between the experience of desire and the experience of fantasy."[4] And if a film has no meaning, how can it have an argument?

Mulholland Drive further serves as an effective counterexample as Lynch's methodology is in direct contrast to that of the ultraconventional Pixar. On Pixar's storytelling pyramid, Lynch arguably sits somewhere in the top third, a less conventional storytelling approach appealing to smaller but still significant audiences. His work as an artist exemplifies what could be considered a mysterian philosophy, one that posits that true understanding of consciousness is beyond the biological limits of human beings. Lynch originally trained as an abstract expressionist painter before studying under František Daniel (formerly of FAMU in the former Czechoslovakia), who specialized in Russian dramatic art and the Slavic storytelling principles of the soul and the irrational.[5] Experimental body-horror film *Eraserhead* (1977) was Lynch's first feature, but he is perhaps most associated with the series of what could be loosely labeled neo-noir films that started with *Blue Velvet* (1986) and continued with *Wild at Heart* (1990), *Twin Peaks: Fire Walk with Me* (1992), a prequel to his *Twin Peaks* (1990–1991) television show, *Lost Highway* (1997), and *Mulholland Drive* (2001).

Lynch is celebrated as a purely instinctive storyteller who specializes specifically in the surreal, his films often presented as dreams to be experienced by the viewer. These film-dreams are evocative yet elusive, and it is this elusiveness that appears not just to be the point but a key part of his global appeal. Lynch is often feted by critics and other practitioners precisely because his films are opaque and full of inconsistencies, with no easily paraphrased meaning or deconstruction possible. This is what makes *Mulholland Drive*, arguably the most celebrated work in Lynch's canon, the best possible counterexample.[6]

Synopsis

The film begins with a montage of 1950s-style jive dancing with various couples moving to the music, although the film score carries a more foreboding tone. The figures dissolve into the smiling face of BETTY (whom we'll meet properly later), dressed glamorously, as if accepting an award. The off-screen crowd cheer. The image dissolves again, and we are in a darkened room. A softly moaning figure—as if in distress—rocks under some much less glamorous bedclothes.

A limousine drives down a dark winding road, revealed by a street sign to be Mulholland Drive. Inside sits RITA, a dark-haired woman in her twenties in a cocktail dress. The car stops, which disturbs her. She says, "What are you doing? We don't stop here." Instead of answering, the driver points a gun at her, but before he can shoot the limousine is hit by a car driven by drunk, high-spirited teens. Rita staggers out and struggles to downtown Los Angeles, sneaking into an apartment to rest. She falls asleep.

At a diner called Winkies, the awkward DAN tells his breakfast companion that he eats at this particular Winkies as he has a recurrent nightmare where he is confronted by a HORRIBLE FIGURE in the parking lot. They go to the parking lot to allay his fears, but the Horrible Figure appears, and Dan collapses in fright.

Rita continues to sleep and we see a middle-aged man in wheelchair, MR. ROQUE, call a mysterious man (we do not see his whole face) telling him, "the girl is still missing." The mysterious man makes a second call, answered by another person whose face we do not see. This person makes yet another call to a seedy motel phone next to an ashtray.

We now see Betty, an aspiring actress, arrive at the airport with an OLD FRIENDLY COUPLE she has met on the plane. When the couple leave her and get into a cab, they continue to smile huge forced fake smiles. Betty arrives at an apartment complex to be met by MRS. LENOIX, but the woman tells her, "Just call me Coco, everybody else does." Coco shows Betty to her apartment (owned by Betty's Aunt). After Coco leaves, Betty is shocked to find Rita there, who claims to be a friend of Betty's Aunt. The two talk, Betty communicating her excitement to be in Hollywood, "this dream place." Rita goes back to sleep.

Meanwhile, in a production meeting, director ADAM has his film taken over by two odd-acting MOBSTERS, and they demand he cast an unknown actress named CAMILLA RHODES as the star (Mr. Roque listens in from his office). Adam storms out.

Across town, JOE, an incompetent hit man, attempts to steal a book full of phone numbers, but keeps killing people by mistake.

Betty speaks to her Aunt and finds out that Rita was lying. Rita reveals she has amnesia (it's now clear that Rita took her name from a film poster in the apartment). To help Rita remember who she is, Betty opens Rita's purse, revealing it contains a large amount of cash and an ODD BLUE KEY.

On returning home, Adam finds his wife cheating on him with another man but is beaten up by him and thrown out of his own house.

Betty and Rita go to Winkies to find out more about Rita's car accident. A waitress called DIANE serves them, and Rita remembers the name DIANE SELWYN. They find Diane Selwyn in the phone book, but she does not answer their call.

After Adam learns his bank has cut him off, leaving him penniless, he agrees to meet a mysterious figure called THE COWBOY.

At the apartment, a "crazy" older neighbor called LOUISE knocks on the door, telling Betty that something bad is happening, but seems confused as to who Betty is and who is in danger.

Adam meets the Cowboy on his ranch at night, and the man calmly suggests he cast Camilla Rhodes.

Rita helps Betty practice for a role, where Betty gives a clichéd, if well-executed performance. Yet when Betty goes to the audition, despite the odd unprofessionalism of the others in the room, she makes a different, more sensual choice and gives an outstanding performance. Everyone is impressed. Betty is taken to the studio where Adam is casting his film, *The Sylvia North Story.* Camilla Rhodes auditions, and Adam resentfully picks her for the role. Adam and Betty briefly lock eyes—and the moment is significant—but Betty bolts before she can meet him, claiming she is late to see a friend.

Betty and Rita break in to Diane Selwyn's apartment. In the bed, they find a woman's body—and she has clearly been dead for several days. Frightened that they are in danger, they go home where Rita disguises herself with a blonde wig. The distress connects them further, and that night Betty and Rita have sex. Rita starts talking Spanish in her sleep and keeps saying "Silencio." Rita wakes and insists they go to a theater club called Club Silencio.

The MC gives a convoluted speech about everything being an illusion. A singer comes onstage and sings Roy Orbison's "Crying" in Spanish. She collapses but her voice continues, revealing it to be a recording. Both women are highly moved and cry, and Betty opens her purse to find a BLUE BOX inside that matches Rita's key. They return to the apartment, but when Rita finds the key she realizes that Betty has disappeared. Rita unlocks the box, and it falls to the floor.

There is a short sequence where Betty's Aunt comes into the bedroom only to find it empty, before we see Diane in her own bed (we do not see her face). The Cowboy tells her to wake up, only to then realize that the body on the bed is dead. He leaves. Then Diane Selwyn wakes up in bed, clearly the same apartment that Betty and Rita broke in to. Diane looks exactly like Betty, but is a failed actress driven into a deep depression by her failed affair with Camilla Rhodes, a successful actress who looks exactly like Rita. Camilla invites Diane to a dinner party at Adam's house—on Mulholland Drive. Diane is driven alone in the back of a limousine, in a variation of the first scene with Rita. The car stops suddenly, and Diane says the same line, "What are you doing? We don't stop here." This time, Camilla comes out of the bushes and leads Diane up to the party via a back way. Diane meets Adam's mother, who looks exactly like Mrs. Lenoix. This version also tells Diane, "Just call me Coco, everybody does."

At dinner, Diane mentions that she came to Hollywood when her Aunt Ruth died and left her an inheritance, and she and Camilla met when they auditioned for *The Sylvia North Story*. A woman who looks like the original "Camilla Rhodes" from earlier in the film kisses Camilla, and they smile awkwardly at Diane. Adam and Camilla try to make an announcement that looks to be about their engagement but can't stop themselves from kissing and laughing as Diane watches, tearful. We then see Diane meet hit man Joe (who looks the same) at Winkies, and it appears that she is paying him to kill Camilla. A stranger, Dan (who also looks the same), notices them. Joe says that when the job is done, Diane will find a blue key in her apartment. When she asks what it is for, he just laughs.

Later, Diane stares at the blue key on her coffee table. Overcome by guilt, she hallucinates as she masturbates, eventually shooting herself after being chased by a cackling, nightmarish vision of the Old Friendly Couple from the airport. The screen dissolves into a backdrop of Hollywood where images of a happy Betty and Rita (in blonde wig) are overlaid. Back at the nightclub, a woman whispers, "Silencio."

The Argument

It is relevant that, as American film scholar Jason Mittell notes, "the most acclaimed American film of this century was a television program."[7] *Mulholland Drive* was originally filmed as a television pilot, a follow-up to *Twin Peaks*. However, the network rejected it, and eighteen months later Lynch raised the money to complete the project as a feature film, shooting an additional eighteen minutes of footage. This is the reason for the mosaic-like structure of the narrative, with multiple characters and scenarios that were originally intended as the basis for longer storylines.

The key question is simple: Is there a worthwhile argument being presented in a worthwhile way? If not, the film represents a significant exception to all that we have been discussing. Yet if *Mulholland Drive* does, despite popular perception, not just have a meaning but argue a meaningful conclusion sincerely, the concept of film-as-worthwhile-argument is significantly strengthened. And—spoiler alert—this does appear to be the case.

If we use the same analytical methods as *Toy Story 3* to detect and justify the argument, *Mulholland Drive* may have a substantially more nuanced presentation than the Pixar film, but it is consistent, comprehendible, and worthwhile nonetheless. It can also be stated in a way that maintains Lynch's mysterian worldview: *even though there is enrichment, humor, and validity in the search for meaning, human memory, identity, and consciousness are of such complexity that only a surface subjective level of understanding of who we are can be achieved.*

The somewhat skeptical conclusion (and even the attempt to find a conclusion) certainly goes against the grain of those who typically embrace and revere Lynch's work. But it could explain why *Mulholland Drive* in particular has grown in reputation over the years, to become a key part of Lynch's canon—as opposed to other works that have been ill received or become more marginalized over time.

Now I may also have cooked the books by choosing *Mulholland Drive* to prove my point, but by all objective measures it is still an elusive work. Let's revisit our four points of analysis. It is far from straightforward to establish:

1. that this is the correct conclusion
2. that this conclusion is worthwhile
3. how precisely the film constructs a compelling argument using cinematic tools

4. how the film does this in a worthwhile way that does not rely on unreasonable manipulation

Obviously, for a filmmaker such as David Lynch proving (1) is problematic, especially as he was actively discouraged from attempting any transparency (whether he desired to or otherwise) by audiences and critics, who constantly cite reticence to even attempt to unravel or articulate any meaning behind his work. Unlike *Toy Story 3*, where there is a reliable objective perspective and great clarity given to every moment-to-moment cause-and-effect sequence, *Mulholland Drive* does not prioritize transparency of storytelling. This means we have to add another level to our inquiry: before the argument can be demonstrated, we must first clarify what precisely the audience is seeing.

Most of the discussions around *Mulholland Drive* are about not the meaning of the film overall but the meaning of the events that have taken place in the narrative. There are essentially two schools of thought, the first and most popular interpretation being that the film is quite clearly made up of two unequal halves. The first two-thirds is the fever dream of an aspiring actress living the perfect fantasy of finding love and being discovered in Hollywood, the final third the reality that she is a failed actress who has been rejected by her girlfriend.[8]

The second, minority school of thought is the base-state reaction to Lynch's work: the reticence to deconstruct. It is championed more commonly by critics than academics who believe the dream interpretation is too easy and that to try to find meaning does not play to the strengths of the screen experience. The point is not that the film makes sense but that it provokes the audience.[9]

The "Betty's Dream" understanding of the narrative is clearly the most justified. Although there is momentary confusion once the blue box has been opened (and we are in the second reality where Betty is Diane), it is a straightforward process to reinterpret and reassemble the previous scenes into a consistent, meaningful narrative. The opening of the jive dancing dissolving into a moaning figure under the bed sheets becomes a conventional framing device when taken with the interpretation of Betty as Diane's fantasy self. It is also a view that takes the Occam's razor approach: other interpretations are of course possible and meaningful but rely on far wider and less justifiable logical leaps.

Now that there is a solid basis on which to deconstruct the argument, we can assess whether the conclusion of (to paraphrase) "true meaning in life is not comprehendible but worth exploring" is the most credible interpretation.

As with *Toy Story 3*, we'll start by seeing which thematic idea is consistently being tested on a scene-by-scene basis. Many abstract concepts are touched upon at various times, including love, sex, jealousy, randomness, romance, fame, talent, self-respect, desire, fantasy, ambition, optimism, feminism, capitalism, corruption, nostalgia, dreams, nightmares, identity, and violence. These can all fit under a vague conception of the nature of "Hollywood itself," and the setting provides opportunity for satire that could also indicate meaning. It is also unsurprising that a high number of themes are embedded in the work, given the television-pilot origins of the project. However, these are all subthematic concepts that complement the main standpoint of the film. Although they have points to make, they represent more of an unfinished flow of ideas and perspectives, none of them the basis for a fully developed argument. The only thematic idea consistently being tested throughout the film is Lynch's mysterian point of view.

Various conceptualizations and manifestations of mystery are present in every frame of the film, whether it is Betty and Rita trying to solve the mystery of Rita's past or the broader mysteries of perception, identity, and reality. In terms of genre, *Mulholland Drive* is set up as a neo-noir mystery with all the necessary tropes and signifiers (femme fatale, amnesia, organized crime, glamorous lives with seedy underbellies), where the initial setup is deliberately conventional: the two main characters attempt to solve a mystery, therefore setting up mystery as a central concept with both the characters and an audience on the lookout for clues. However, unlike *Toy Story 3*, there are no clear discussions of these thematic ideas, with the viewer expected to do more cognitive work to discern thematic point of view.

How the film constructs its argument cinematically is particularly revealing. The events and argument of the film often being opaque to a casual viewer is not due to the absence of a worthwhile argument being made in a worthwhile way but due to the use of unconventional screen storytelling.

Mulholland Drive may be a neo-noir film, but it also functions as an almost perfect exemplar of the mind-game film, a conceptualization developed by film scholar Thomas Elsaesser in 2009. A mind-game film is often referred to as a puzzle film, defined as those that play games with either the characters or the audience (or both), with crucial information being withheld or ambiguously presented. An overriding feature of the films is that they thrive on disorienting or misleading audiences that themselves take joy in the manipulation.[10]

Some mind-game films lean very heavily into the mind and brain aspects of the genre, featuring mentally unstable characters concerned with separating real from delusion: common themes are those concerned with memory, consciousness, and the true nature of being and knowledge. Typical mind-game narration revolves around unreliable narrators, multiple timelines and time loops, obscure and ambiguous flashbacks, and surprising causal reversals. Central characters often suffer from some kind of psychopathology such as amnesia to highlight issues with consciousness, memory, and identity. All these elements are present and accounted for in *Mulholland Drive.*

The mind-game film was originally a genre that used a series of unconventional storytelling techniques, but these have become far more popular in recent years. A potential cause of their increasing prevalence is the need for the modern feature film to exist on a variety of platforms that make them constantly accessible. This requires filmmakers to create work that can sustain multiple viewings by multiple generations, lest the work be deemed basic or simplistic.

In this way, in the period since its release, the storytelling of *Mulholland Drive* has become increasingly conventional and accessible, which may account for the increasing esteem in which the film is held. But how precisely does this puzzle narrative structure relate to the forming of the argument? The answer is that although the general storytelling techniques in the mind-game film have become steadily more orthodox, *Mulholland Drive* continues to argue unconventionally as it is the narrative structure itself that carries most of the weight of the argument—events presented in such a way as to convince us of the conclusion.

This is set up and nuanced by the characters and their interactions (the plot is a mystery, amnesia and identity are key themes), but the shape of the argument dominates the content, quite efficiently organizing the abundance of thematic ideas into a hierarchy. Given the conclusion, that *even though there is joy, humor, and validity in the search for meaning, human memory, identity, and consciousness are of such complexity that only a surface subjective level of understanding of who we are can be comprehended,* it is clear that the puzzle structure is a very efficient form of presentation. Film theorist David Roche believes that Lynch's films are detective stories only in the sense that they turn the audience into detectives in order to understand the narrative. Roche believes that *Mulholland Drive* is a mystery film constructed wholly "by the spectator-detective's desire to make sense" of it.[11]

Toy Story 3 laid out the thematic question in dialogue and answered it in thematic action. *Mulholland Drive* uses only action to communicate both. This makes the thematic question and answer wholly implicit, and in doing so perhaps represents the ultimate enthymematic argument: completely unexpressed but undeniable rhetorical proof. To have the audience to go to the significant cognitive effort to piece together the puzzle, providing their own assumptions and worldviews in the process, only for more mystery to remain is one way to make the viewers uniquely feel the conclusion as well as comprehend it.

Overall *Mulholland Drive* adheres quite strictly to Aristotle's theory of argumentation. Ethos and logos both are applied in typical fashion—David Lynch has considerable credibility as an artist, and the argument is logical, if requiring some assembly. However, when it comes to the intrinsic cinematic strength of pathos, the film takes yet another unusual argumentative approach. Pathos in filmic storytelling is ordinarily used to invoke emotions embedded in narrative and character, rather than senses generated purely through spectatorship. However, the story structure, philosophical themes, and performance style of *Mulholland Drive* make meaningful emotional engagement and/or identification problematic, and instead the film prioritizes the engagement of the senses rather than the emotions.

Let us take the example of the unreliable narrator, not just common to mind-game films but a staple of German Expressionism, itself the main inspiration for the noir genre. The revelation that Betty is not who she first seems comes a full thirty minutes before the close of the film. At this point, over and above the intellectual work of assessing this new identity and reality for stability and permanency, the audience now has to learn about (and potentially care for) this new iteration of the character; what is gained in terms of narrative impact is lost in terms of emotional connection. Audiences may like, or even prefer, this new Betty/Diane, but they had built up a relationship with the previous incarnation that may (or may not) have to be jettisoned. Not only is there a new character to contend with, attention is also split. The use of this technique combined with the psychopathologies of paranoia and amnesia—as well as the motif of the doppelganger—push *Mulholland Drive* away from being just a film noir (in the sense that it is a crime story with visual and thematic roots in German Expressionism) toward a film solidly in the tradition of German Expressionist filmmaking. Essentially the film could be viewed as an homage to *The Cabinet of Doctor Caligari* (Wiene 1920), which covered much of the same ground on the nature of identity and reality (complete with unreliable narrator and twist/reversal ending).[12]

In *Mulholland Drive,* Lynch's argument building relies not on pathos as emotion but on pathos as sensuous (in the Miltonian, nonsexual sense). It's this use of sensation over emotion that allows any loss of emotional connection with Betty to have less impact than with a more conventionally told mystery, such as *Shutter Island* (Scorsese 2010). The arch, deliberately artificial performance style—up to the point of the main plot twist—in *Mulholland Drive* does not encourage empathy. Lynch uses a heightened Brechtian level of performance that goes against the grain of realism as it constantly reminds us that we are watching fiction.[13] Only when Betty is revealed as Diane does the acting mode change to something more akin to screen realism, but again there is limited time in which to connect with the character. In a typical mainstream film, the audience would usually care about the protagonist as their journey embodies the argument. If this does not emotionally engage us, the argument is weakened or lost altogether.

This brings us to the way the argument is made cinematically without relying on unreasonable manipulation. There does not appear to be any dishonorable use of any Aristotelian elements here, as *Mulholland Drive* is presented by a credible filmmaker, takes place in a credible world, and relies on neither emotion or sentimentality nor false presentation of real-world facts to create its argument. Any films with an unreliable narrator can open up accusations of exploitative bait-and-switch storytelling, but here the instability of the narrator augments the argument, rather than being a superfluous twist merely designed to make an impact (as with Aronofsky's *mother!*). The same goes for the use of sensation, the overriding feeling of oddness feeding into the idea of a dream. In the same way that the puzzle structure itself carries substantial weight of the argument, the sensations evoked become evidence of the truth of the conclusion: we are supposed to feel the elusiveness of any complete understanding of consciousness.[14]

Finally, there is the question of whether the conclusion itself is worthwhile. Although it is uncommon in mainstream Western cinema and literature, the mostly unknowableness of consciousness is a relatively familiar science-fiction preoccupation, especially those stories involving robotics, androids, or cyborgs (particularly those written and influenced by Isaac Asimov). It is both reminiscent of and far more optimistic than the answer to the meaning of life, the universe, and everything being the mundane number forty-two, as suggested in Douglas Adams's classic novel *The Hitchhiker's Guide to the Galaxy*.[15] The idea that such a complex question can have such a simple answer is absurd in the extreme. Yet worthwhile does not mean unique. A worthwhile conclusion is largely dependent on social context and can be quite familiar if its restating has value in that historical time and place. The first-wave surge of romantic comedies during and after the COVID-19 pandemic and their love-will-always-find-a-way conclusions provided welcome (if not always sincere) reassurance and comfort in a testing time for much of the world viewing audience. Perhaps less so the second and third waves. The conclusion of *Mulholland Drive* is far from those simple viewpoints on romance, as filmmaker Jaco Van Dormael states: "I think that Lynch's work contributes to the fight against simplification, against a trend of unambiguous movies, which provide answers the way television news does. His work speaks to a different kind of awareness, a different perception, of what we believe to be reality, without knowing what it is. Is it what we perceive through our eyes and ears, or something else?"[16] But what of those who laud *Mulholland Drive* but resist any attempt to find meaning? How can feature filmmaking practice be to move people to a worthwhile conclusion in a worthwhile way if some audiences regard meaning as unimportant yet enjoy mainstream cinema?

The response is twofold: the easy path is to dismiss such an audience as the exception that proves the rule. Even Lynch's most successful cinematic works are seen by relatively modest audiences, with not all members wishing to avoid meaning. This would render the meaning-averse audience as outliers, particularly small and not representative of typical mainstream viewers. In purely numerical terms, David Lynch never made a film that grossed more than US$31 million in American cinemas (*Dune* 1984). With *Mulholland Drive* making US$7.2 million compared to independent comedy *My Big Fat Greek Wedding* (Zwick 2002) drawing in US$242 million, this is a valid position.

However, a more robust but contentious response is that the meaning-averse audience is perhaps unaware or misdiagnosing which elements of the film have triggered their ongoing engagement with it. *Mulholland Drive* continues to be Lynch's most well-received cinematic work, and this could be due to it being his most successful attempt at layering his narrative, deliberately or not, to suit different levels of engagement and, thus, different audiences.

The film, clearly influenced by Lynch's favorites *Sunset Boulevard* (Wilder 1950) and *The Wizard of Oz* (Fleming 1939), has struck a Schrödinger's cat–like perfect balance of being both a solvable and an unsolvable mystery simultaneously.[17] It is at once possible to find an overall interpretation and yet with some—but not equal—validity (due to either extraneous narrative elements or a lack of interest in doing the cognitive work) also possible to swallow whole the Lynchian mysterian standpoint. For those meaning-averse individuals who desire elusiveness, they either consciously or subconsciously resist (or are genuinely unaware of) the presence of the solvable surface mystery that allows for coherent argument.

One way to test this theory is to consider another film from Lynch, one that conveniently shares almost identical narrative and structural elements but is resolutely insoluble. That film is *Inland Empire* (2006). The similarities are unusually precise. It shares with *Mulholland Drive* the Hollywood setting, the puzzle-like structure, the dreamlike/nightmarish atmosphere, the focus on sensation over emotion, the *Wizard of Oz / Sunset Boulevard* homages, and the central character attempting to solve a mystery, as well as featuring regular Lynch actors Laura Dern, Harry Dean Stanton, and *Mulholland Drive* alumni Justin Theroux, Laura Harring, and Naomi Watts. Most of the narrative is concerned with actress Nikki Grace (Dern) starring in a film but becoming confused about what is real and what is fiction. Yet, unlike *Mulholland Drive, Inland Empire* presents no key, metaphorical or otherwise, to help decode the events depicted on-screen. If the audiences, critics, and filmmakers who champion the ability of Lynch's work to defy analysis or even speculation as to the meaning of physical on-screen events (other than a subconscious engagement with the feel and tone of the work) are right, *Inland Empire* should be equally well received.

Yet *Inland Empire* became Lynch's least successful film, so much so that one critic thought the film resembled "the work of an old genius with Alzheimers."[18] Whereas *Mulholland Drive* topped the aforementioned list of best films of the twentieth century, *Inland Empire* does not appear and made only 11 percent of the previous film's U.S. theatrical gross.

In fact, *Inland Empire* is a good example of a film that truly fails as film-as-worthwhile-argument. It is all sensation and mystery and puzzle, but despite what various sectors of the viewing audience might hope for, it is untethered to the internal good of the practice and the film is unable to engage. Momentary sensation may happen, but with no argument to structure the puzzle narrative, sustained engagement does not. The conclusion may be worthwhile, but the argument for it is not made in a worthwhile way; in fact, the mode of storytelling almost completely obscures it.

This indicates a loss—momentary or otherwise—of the creative generosity virtue. As we previously noted with Terrence Malick, another filmmaker who concentrates on difficult topics that will inevitably limit his audience, generosity is maintained only if the filmmaker is genuinely attempting to communicate with their audience. Placed in the context of Lynch's oeuvre (*Inland Empire* was his final feature film), it suggests an increase of self-indulgence, a rhetorical stance focused too much on the ethos of the auteur. The film could be considered to be Lynch's equivalent of Malick's *Knight of Cups* (2015), a film targeted not just for audiences at the top of the Pixar pyramid but purely for Lynch himself. It is worth revisiting the fear of didacticism here, as it seems this is what unites a large section of audiences, critics, filmmakers, and self-styled film gurus. When it comes to David Lynch, a further potential reason why his films appear to work for those groups independent of meaning is that mystery or even incoherence is often preferred over any hint of explanation.

CHAPTER 7

Three Approaches

Brave, Frozen, and *Barbie*

WE'VE ALREADY LOOKED in detail at an exemplar and a counter-example, so with these case studies we're taking a different approach. There are many parallels between *Brave* (Andrews and Chapman 2012), *Frozen* (Buck and Lee 2013), and *Barbie* (Gerwig 2023), but each film takes a different approach to their cinematic argumentation. This results in quite different levels of success financially and critically and the ability to achieve the internal good of the practice.

Synopses

BRAVE

In medieval Scotland, KING FERGUS (huge, unrefined, with a cheeky sense of humor) gives his toddler daughter, the flame-haired PRINCESS MERIDA, her very first shooting bow, much to the disapproval of his wife QUEEN ELINOR (small, elegant, well aware of the subtle nuances of her position as a woman of limited power in a male-dominated society). Merida is a lady and should not be concerned with such brutal things. Merida fires an arrow into the woods, and collecting it sees what she thinks is a WILL-O'-THE-WISP, a small, fast, smokelike creature. Elinor tells her that some believe the Wisp leads you to your fate, but Fergus does not believe in magic. As they leave the forest, they are attacked by a giant bear.

In voice-over, a now teenage Merida tells us that some believe destiny is tied to the land. Others say fate is woven like a cloth, with all destinies intertwined: we search for our destiny, or fight to change it. Some never find it, but some are led to it. Merida tells us that her father lost his leg to the demon bear that attacked them, MOR'DU, and it became legend. She also now has three young mischievous brothers, HARRIS, HUBERT, and HAMISH. They get away with everything, while she cannot get away with anything; Merida has duties, responsibilities, and expectations, her whole life planned out until she becomes her mother, a Queen.

Merida is a natural tomboy, more like her father, naturally uncouth and strong-willed with a love of adventure and the outdoors. Elinor attempts to train her in how to be a lady, how to stand, speak, eat, play a musical instrument—but Merida resists or cooperates reluctantly.

Every once in a while, Merida has a day to herself, where she chooses to go into the forest to ride, climb, and shoot: it is her joy, and she is an expert archer.

At dinner that night, the King and Queen tell Merida that she is to be married. The three other clans are all sending a suitor to compete for her hand in marriage. Merida is angry and storms out; she does not want to get married—it is their plan, not hers. Elinor tries to convince her, reminding Merida of an old legend: there was a much beloved King who when he grew old divided his kingdom among his four sons, so they may be the pillars on which the peace of the land rested. But the oldest son wanted to rule the land for himself; he followed his own path and the kingdom fell. Merida tells her it's not fair, she's not ready, she wants her freedom. The Queen tells her it's marriage; it's not the end of the world. Both feel the other is not listening to their point of view.

The clans arrive and present their suitors. None are impressive, being either vain, simple, or weak. The clans argue among themselves, and a fight breaks out. The King stops it, but quickly his sons prank some of the soldiers and it starts up again. This time the Queen ends it by walking into the fight and pulling the suitors to the front by their ears. She lays out the rules for the games, and Merida chooses archery as the sport her suitors must win for her hand.

By accident, the least talented suitor hits the bullseye, but Merida joins the competition. She has decided that she can compete for her own hand in marriage. She gets three bullseyes, splitting the formerly winning arrow down the middle. Afterward the Queen and Merida have a huge argument, Merida saying she'd rather die than be like her mother. She uses her sword to slice the tapestry on the wall that depicts their royal family. It literally splits Merida from the Queen and King. The Queen retaliates by throwing Merida's beloved bow into the fire. Merida runs away crying, and regretting her actions, the Queen rescues the bow from the flames.

Merida rides her horse into the forest. The horse gets spooked and stops at a circle of stones. Merida gets thrown into the middle of them and sees the Will-o'-the-wisp. It leads her to an old lady wood carver's cottage. When the crow starts talking, Merida realizes the wood carver is a WITCH and asks her to change her fate. The witch resists (too many unsatisfied customers), until Merida offers to pay for everything in the cottage with her locket. Merida wants a spell to change her mother and, in doing so, her fate. The witch mentions that the last time she did the spell was for a prince, and it worked well. The spell takes the form of a small cake she has to give her mother.

Back at the castle, Elinor is relieved to see her daughter safe. She's pacified the clans, and the King is entertaining them. Merida is touched by her mother's concern, but still gives her the cake. The Queen eats it and almost immediately falls ill. Much to Merida's surprise, the Queen transforms into a bear. As a bear, the Queen cannot talk but can gesture and make approximations of words through moans and howls. Merida comes clean and tells her mother about the spell.

They both realize that being a bear in the castle is a death sentence. They attempt to escape and have to rely on Merida's three brothers to help. The boys are totally unconcerned there is a bear in their home. As Merida and her mother leave, she tells her brothers they can have anything they want in the castle. They quickly find the cake.

Merida and the Queen travel to the forest, looking in vain for the Will-o'-the-wisps to guide them to the witch's cottage so she can undo the spell. They find the cottage anyway, but the witch is not there—away at a wicker festival. However, she has left a message for Merida. The witch tells Merida that she forgot to tell her something about the spell. By the second sunrise the spell will be permanent unless Merida remembers these words: *Fate be changed, look inside, mend the bond torn by pride.* Neither Merida nor her mother understands what this means.

The next day they continue into the forest, and Merida teaches her mother how to catch fish straight out of the water. They have genuine fun. But this ends when the Queen goes wild and attempts to attack Merida. It's a momentary episode, but it's clear that the longer that time goes on, the more the Queen is becoming like a real bear. She is mortified by the lapse.

A wisp appears, and they follow it to some ruins on the edge of the water. The ground collapses and Merida falls into a cavern. Unhurt, she realizes she's in an old throne room and speculates that it could be the one from the old legend the Queen likes to tell her. There is a carving of four princes, with one split from the other three. Merida suspects the bear spell has been used before. She has an epiphany—the eldest prince became the bear Mor'du—just as the huge beast sneaks up on her and attacks.

They make their escape. Merida decides that they must get back to the castle. She interprets the witch's words *mend the bond torn by pride* to mean they have to repair the tapestry that Merida sliced with her sword.

Back at the castle, they find the clans on the verge of war with each other. The Queen stays hidden at the back of the room as Merida uses her mother's technique of walking into the middle of the fray. Merida makes a stumbling but rousing speech. She tells them that she has been in conference with the Queen and that once there was an ancient kingdom that fell into war because of one selfish act. Their kingdom is young, their stories are not yet legend. Their clans were once enemies, but when invaders threatened from the sea, they worked together to defend their lands. The story of their kingdom is a powerful one. They have an alliance forged in bravery and friendship. Merida admits that she has been selfish. She tore a rift in their kingdom.

She knows now that she needs to correct her mistake and mend their bond. Merida has decided to do what is right and is about to pick one of her suitors when her mother gestures for her to stop. Prompted by the Queen, Merida tells everyone that the Queen feels in her heart that there should be a break in tradition and everyone should be free to write their own story. They should be able to follow their hearts and find love in their own time. Merida puts it to the heads of the clans to decide—can the young people decide for themselves whom they love? Before they can answer, Merida's suitors voice their opinion—they wholeheartedly agree that they should be able to choose their own fate. It is decided that the boys should be able to see if they can win Merida's heart before they can win her hand.

Merida and the Queen make it to the tapestry. Merida tries to find a needle and thread, but the Queen goes feral again. At the same time, King

Fergus finds Elinor's torn dress, left behind when she transformed, and believes her kidnapped. Searching the castle, he finds Merida—and the bear—and jumps to the wrong conclusion. Merida tries to explain, but the King won't listen. The King and Queen fight, and he is thrown against the wall, momentarily dazed. The Queen comes out of her feral state and is again mortified at her actions. She runs away and is discovered by the clans. Merida tells her father that the bear is his wife, that she used a spell—but he dismisses it as nonsense. Blinded by rage, he declares that he'll avenge her mother, but won't lose her as well. He locks Merida in her room.

As the clans pursue the Queen into the forest, Merida tries to escape. Looking through the door, she sees her three brothers are now little bear cubs. She tells them to get the key. Merida and her brothers ride out of the castle taking the tapestry and needle and thread with them.

The clans surround the Queen, trapped in the circle of stones. They tie her with ropes. Merida finishes repairing the tapestry, and the wisps show her where to go. However, she is not aware that Mor'du is also in pursuit.

The King is about to unknowingly kill his wife, but at the last moment is stopped by Merida. She tells him to stay away from her mother. He doesn't believe her until he sees the three little bears that are clearly his sons.

Suddenly Mor'du arrives, wanting revenge. The clans attack, but they have no chance. Mor'du is about to kill Merida when her mother breaks free and attacks the demon bear. They fight, and the Queen cleverly makes one of the heavy stones fall on Mor'du, killing him. The ghost of the prince rises from the body, silently thanking them for his release from the curse. He becomes a will-o'-the-wisp and disappears into the forest.

The second sunrise is upon them, and Merida puts the tapestry on her mother. But there is no transformation. As the sun rises, the Queen's eyes turn to those of a real bear. Merida is devastated. She tells her mother she is sorry; it is all her fault. The Queen never gave up on her, and Merida just wants her back. She loves her.

Suddenly a human hand strokes her hair. Merida is overjoyed—her mother has changed. The Queen tells her that they both have.

Later, back at the castle, things have further changed. The Queen and Merida are working on a new tapestry, one with Merida holding hands with her mother as a bear. The clans leave, and Merida tells us that some believe that fate is beyond our command, that destiny is not our own, but she knows better. Our fate lives within us. You only have to be brave enough to see it.

FROZEN

We are in Arendelle, a Scandinavian kingdom in the mid-nineteenth century. The film opens with ICE HARVESTERS cutting through a frozen lake. A young boy, who we find out later is KRISTOFF, and his small reindeer SVEN tag along.

At the castle, we meet two young princesses, ELSA (younger, red hair) and ANNA (white-blond hair). In the middle of the night, Anna asks her sister if she wants to build a snowman, and we discover that Elsa has magic powers. In the ballroom she creates snow and ice, and girls have a fantastic time until Anna gets a little too excited. By accident, Elsa hits her sister with a magical ice bolt, and Anna collapses—a lock of her hair turning white. Their parents, KING AGNARR and QUEEN IDUNA rush Anna and Elsa to a village of trolls. Kristoff and Sven, intrigued by the trail of ice from the royal carriage, follow and watch from a secret hiding spot. They are discovered, but the troll who finds them is warm and friendly and decides she wants to keep them. The head troll, GRAND PABBIE, also has magical powers. As Anna was hit in the head, he is able to heal her by removing her memories of Elsa's magic. He warns that if she was hit in the heart, a cure would not be so simple. He tells the King that people will fear Elsa's powers as she grows older, so they should keep her gifts secret.

The King and Queen take the advice and close the castle to all visitors. Anna cannot remember and is never told of Elsa's powers. The two grow up into teenagers almost completely separately. Elsa, scared of her abilities as they grow stronger, becomes cautious and withdrawn. Anna cannot understand why her sister will no longer spend any time in her company, so she grows up lonely and confused although her natural playfulness and spontaneity flourish as she learns to keep herself amused. When the girls are in their midteens, the King and Queen are lost at sea, so it becomes just the two of them.

A few years later Elsa is about to turn twenty-one, so it is CORONATION DAY. Anna is excited about the prospect of opening the castle gates and meeting new people, whereas Elsa is anxious about revealing her powers. Anna meets HANS, a handsome prince from another kingdom visiting for the coronation. They are instantly smitten. He proposes.

At the state ball following the coronation, Anna and Elsa bond for the first time since they were children. Anna asks the new Queen to bless her marriage, but shocked at the suddenness she refuses to allow Anna to marry someone she met only that day. There is an argument, and all of Anna's frustration about her upbringing comes out. Elsa loses her temper and reveals her powers—sharp ice surrounding her.

Aghast at the scared reaction of the crowd, including her sister, Elsa flees the kingdom. Despite it being summer, snow begins to fall.

Everyone is scared, but Anna defends her sister, realizing this is the reason for her isolation. As Arendelle begins to freeze, Anna decides to go after Elsa alone to bring her back and restore summer. She leaves Hans in charge.

Anna quickly loses her horse, who bolts back to the castle, and falls in a freezing puddle. At a rest stop and supply store in the middle of the woods, she meets a grown-up Kristoff and Sven. They do not get on well. Kristoff is now an ice harvester and seller, and the sudden winter is bad for business. He has no money. In exchange for supplies and food, she convinces Kristoff to help take her to Elsa, who she believes is at the North Mountain.

Meanwhile Elsa, initially devastated by the way she revealed her powers, quickly realizes she is free for the first time in her life. She begins to truly test her powers and builds a huge and intricate ice palace on the side of the mountain.

Anna's horse arrives at the castle. Believing her in danger, Hans decides to go after her with a group of soldiers.

Anna and Kristoff start their journey. Kristoff echoes Elsa's reaction when she tells him about Hans: How can she marry someone she just met? How do they know they're compatible? They argue and agree to differ. Pursued by wolves, Kristoff shows his ingenuity and bravery in the escape, although his sled gets destroyed. Anna promises to buy a new one, and feeling guilty lets him out of their agreement to help her. Kristoff knows she has no chance without him and Sven, so agrees to continue. They walk the rest of the way.

Kristoff has doubts about Anna's optimism, but Anna is adamant that Elsa will end the winter as soon as they talk. They enter a beautiful snowy tree-lined grove and meet a walking, talking, fully alive snowman called OLAF. He's incredibly friendly and cheerful and very open about the fact that Elsa created him. He also idolizes summer, seemingly oblivious to the fact that heat will destroy him. Anna is initially terrified but calms down when she realizes he's identical to the snowman that she and Elsa made as kids before the accident. Olaf helpfully knows exactly where Elsa can be found.

When they arrive at Elsa's palace, Kristoff is in awe of the ice and Anna realizes the scale of her sister's powers. She tells Kristoff and Olaf to wait outside. Elsa is worried that Anna is there. It's not that she doesn't love her sister, but she's afraid she might hurt her. Anna is relentless; she has so much to say now that she understands why Elsa had to keep away. She urges Elsa to return home. Believing her people are safer without her, Elsa refuses and tells Anna to go back.

When Anna reveals that Elsa has caused an eternal winter, Elsa is utterly stunned, feeling trapped again. At first Anna is sure her sister can easily undo her magic, and when Elsa tells her she does not know how, Anna continues to be certain that they can solve the problem together. Feeling vulnerable, Elsa panics and loses control of her powers. She accidentally strikes Anna again, this time directly in the heart. Neither realize the implications. Anna falls to the ground as Kristoff and Olaf arrive, still trying to convince her sister. Elsa loses patience and demands they leave. When Anna refuses, Elsa creates MARSHMALLOW, a ten-story snow monster to remove them from the palace.

Marshmallow chases the three of them, and they have to jump off a cliff to escape. No one is injured, but Anna's hair begins to turn white, and they realize it must be Elsa's magic. Having seen this before as a child (not knowing it was also Anna), Kristoff takes them all to the trolls. He reveals that he and Sven were raised by the stone creatures; they're his family. Before he can explain to his adopted mother BULDA, they try to matchmake Kristoff and Anna—but Anna collapses. Grand Pabbie arrives to explain that as Anna was struck in the heart, she can be saved only by an act of true love. Bulda interprets this as a true love's kiss, and Kristoff rushes to get Anna back to Arendelle and her true love Hans.

Meanwhile, Hans reaches the ice palace with his search party. They do not believe that Elsa is unable to undo her magic, and a fight breaks out. Elsa is knocked unconscious and taken back to Arendelle as a prisoner. She awakens in chains.

Kristoff gets Anna safely back to the palace but leaves knowing she no longer needs him. Both he and Sven are heartbroken, as it is clear he now has feelings toward the young princess. Hans rushes to meet Anna, and she tells him what happened: she is in desperate need of a true love's kiss. Hans leans down as if to kiss her, but an evil smile appears at the critical moment.

While putting out the fire and candles to hasten Anna's death, Hans reveals that he never loved her. Too far down the succession line in his own kingdom, he simply wanted to marry into the throne. Originally he had his sights on Elsa, but Anna made—and continued to make—things so easy for him. Now he will blame her death on Elsa, execute the Queen, and rule Arendelle as a true and just King.

Anna is too weak to do anything, and Hans locks her inside the room. He immediately announces to the other royal families trapped in the kingdom by the snow that he and Anna just had time to marry before her death. Hans also tells them that he has no choice but to charge Elsa with treason and sentence her to death.

The weather is directly related to Elsa's mood, and her inner turmoil is reflected by an increasingly severe blizzard. Before the guards come to take her away, Elsa escapes, but her anxiety worsens and threatens to destroy all of Arendelle. Kristoff and Sven notice the storm and, guessing things have gone badly, rush back to save Anna.

Back at the palace Olaf finds Anna and quickly lights a fire to keep her alive. He begins to melt but is happy to make the sacrifice for his friend. Anna admits that she doesn't know what to do now, as she doesn't even know what love is. Olaf tries to explain that it is about putting someone else's needs above your own, unwittingly describing Kristoff's actions. Anna realizes Kristoff loves her and uses her remaining strength to get out of the palace before it is destroyed by Elsa's magic. They get to the fjord, but Olaf is blown away by the wind and Anna's hands freeze.

Close by, Hans finds Elsa. Continuing to play the hero, he tells her that Anna died of a frozen heart—because of her. Devastated, Elsa breaks down, and the storm immediately clears. Now everyone can see, Anna and Kristoff find each other, but Anna can barely move. As she tries to get to her true-love's kiss, she hears a sword sliding from its scabbard. Turning, she sees Hans about to execute her sister. She makes a choice, and with a look to Kristoff, uses the last of her energy to throw herself between Hans and Elsa. The sword strikes Anna just as she finally freezes solid. A shockwave from the contact throws Hans across the ice.

Elsa breaks down in tears at the loss of her sister, realizing how she had been duped. Kristoff, Sven, and Olaf arrive but have no words of comfort. But suddenly, Anna begins to thaw. Her sacrifice for Elsa was the act of true love, breaking the curse. The sisters embrace, finally free of all secrets and concerns. Elsa has an epiphany: love is the key to controlling her powers. In moments, Elsa frees Arendelle from its eternal winter. As the ice melts and color returns to the kingdom, Hans wakes up. Abandoning any pretense of goodness, he is shocked to find Anna alive. She calmly confronts him before punching him in the face, knocking him into the water. Anna and Elsa hug again, and Anna looks to Kristoff with romantic affection.

The film concludes with Elsa taking her rightful place as Queen. Hans and his allies are deported, while Kristoff is given the newly created position of Official Arendelle Ice Master and Deliverer. Anna buys Kristoff a new sled, and although he almost spontaneously kisses Anna, he remembers to ask for consent first. She willingly accepts and they share their first kiss. Elsa permanently reopens the palace gates and celebrates by making the courtyard an ice-skating rink. She vows never to close the gates again. The sisters, Olaf, Kristoff, and Sven skate around the palace grounds with the rest of the townsfolk, excited about the future.

BARBIE

The film opens with a parody of *2001: A Space Odyssey*, where little girls play with baby dolls in a desert landscape. THE NARRATOR tells us that since the beginning of time little girls always had dolls, but they were always baby dolls. This means they could only play at being mothers. Then an oversize BARBIE appears, towering over the girls, dressed in a 1950s-style swimsuit and sunglasses. They try to touch Barbie, then one girl smashes her baby doll into the ground. The others follow suit, becoming feral and enjoying the wanton destruction. One girl throws her doll up into the sky.

We see Barbie dolls throughout the decades as the Narrator explains that Barbie changed everything, again and again. She may have started out in a bathing suit, but she became so much more—with her own money, house, car, career. "Because Barbie can be anything, women can be anything." We see a world map and are told that Barbie's successes have been reflected back onto women in the real world, so girls can be whatever they want to be. Barbie has ensured that the problems of equal gender rights have been solved. However, the Narrator finally adds that this is just what the Barbies think as they live their lives in Barbieland, and she doesn't have the heart to break the truth to them.

In Barbieland, STEREOTYPICAL BARBIE (Barbie) lives in Barbie's Dreamhouse. It is a full-size version of the plastic toy, complete with open walls, no glass in the mirrors, no water in the showers, and no food on the plates. Barbie acts as if everything is both normal and perfect. There are many other Barbies in Barbieland, all looking different but all having a perfect day.

Barbie literally floats down to her car from the top floor of her house. The Narrator reminds us that when we play with Barbies, no one bothers to walk them down the stairs. MIDGE (a pregnant Barbie doll) waves at Barbie, but the Narrator cuts in to ask the film to avoid her: she was discontinued by toymaker Mattel as a pregnant doll is just too weird.

As Barbie drives through the town, we see that all the jobs are done by women, with just the occasional male Ken doll present. BARBIE ISSA RAE, President of Barbieland, signs a bill into a law, BARBIE RITU wins the Nobel Prize in Journalism, and every member of the Supreme Court is a Barbie. Everyone is proud and nice to each other all the time.

Barbie arrives at the beach. KEN is there holding a surfboard. Every Barbie has a Ken, and this is Barbie's Ken. The Narrator tells us that Barbie has a great day every day, but Ken only has a great day if Barbie looks at him. Ken calls out to Barbie and Barbie greets him. Other Barbies arrive and greet their Kens. ALLAN, a weak-looking sensitive type, is also there. We are told there are no multiples of Allan, he's just Allan. Barbie says hello to him too.

To impress Barbie, Ken jumps into the surf with his surfboard. But it's all hard plastic, and he injures himself. Everyone is worried and rush to help. Barbie helps Ken to his feet, but Ken is more concerned if she saw his error of judgment. The other Kens ridicule him, and Barbie has to break it up.

An ambulance arrives and immediately folds out into a hospital room. Ken is laid down and he asks Barbie to stay. Other Barbies in doctor outfits take X-rays and tell Ken he will be fine. Barbie tells him he was very brave, and he points out that his job actually isn't surfer, it's "beach." He asks if he can come around later, and Barbie tells him he can—as she has nothing planned other than an amazing party.

All the Barbies and Kens are at the party. Ken gets jealous when other Kens start dancing with Barbie, but she'd rather be dancing with the other Barbies anyway. All goes well until Barbie suddenly asks if anyone thinks about dying. The music stops—everyone is shocked, including Barbie. She covers up, saying she's just dying to dance. Everything gets back on track, but Barbie is clearly concerned.

Later that night it's just Barbie and Ken. He leans in for a kiss, but Barbie just smiles. He leans back, reacting as if they'd just had a great kiss. She tells him he can go now, but he suggests he stays over because they are boyfriend/girlfriend. Barbie asks what they will do, and he's not sure himself. She tells him she doesn't want him in her house, and he's disappointed. Barbie tells him it's girls' night, and it's revealed that all the Barbies are still there and have watched the whole exchange. Barbie tells Ken every night is girls' night. Forever.

The next morning, something is clearly off. Barbie feels groggy, her breath smells, and she reacts to cold water in the shower that isn't really there. The other Barbies can see her from their dreamhouses, and she makes out that everything is fine. They look at her curiously.

At the beach, Barbie falls over as her feet are no longer arched, ready for high heels. They are now normal flat feet where the heels naturally hit the ground. The other Barbies vomit, but nothing visible comes out. Barbie admits to the other problems that day, and BARBIE ALEXANDRA accuses her of malfunctioning. It's happened before—but is usually just hair related. They suggest she goes to visit WEIRD BARBIE. She is so named as a child played with her too hard in the real world (painted her face, cut her hair) and now her destiny is to help other Barbies while falling further into disrepair herself.

Barbie visits the WEIRDHOUSE, an abstract art version of a worn-out dreamhouse. She's greeted by Weird Barbie, who is doing the splits and has an oddly direct manner. Weird Barbie has never heard of flat feet before and, when she finds out about the other events, tells Barbie that she has opened a portal: a rip in the continuum between Barbieland and the real world. Barbie needs to go into the real world to fix it, or things will get worse—namely cellulite and a personality that will get increasingly sad and complicated. Weird Barbie doesn't know why, but usually it takes two to rip the portal—the Barbie and the real-world girl playing with her. Barbie has become entwined with the girl, so has to help the girl to help herself.

Weird Barbie holds up two shoes (one stiletto, one sandal). If Barbie picks the stiletto, things will return to normal and she'll have no memory of any of this. If she picks the sandal, she'll know the truth about the universe. With no hesitation, Barbie picks the stiletto—but it is a phantom choice. Weird Barbie just wanted her to feel like she had control by making a choice. Barbie has to fix the problem.

The journey to the real world involves taking a sports car, speed boat, rocket ship, tandem bike, camper van, snowmobile, and finally rollerblades to California. Barbie worries how she'll find the girl, but Weird Barbie tells her she'll just know.

Barbie has a "Bon Voyage to Reality and Good Luck Restoring the Membrane That Separates Our World from Theirs So You Don't Get Cellulite!"

party with the other Barbies and Kens. Barbie is apprehensive but is told she'll see all the good Barbies have done to fix the world and be welcomed with a big thank-you and a hug.

As she drives out of Barbieland alone, Ken pops up in the backseat. They crash (no damage to anything), and Ken explains he wants to help as he has a bet with KEN SIMU and doesn't want to look bad in front of him. Barbie does secretly want help and allows him to stay as he has brought his rollerblades.

They arrive in the REAL WORLD, rollerblading down the Venice Beach boardwalk; Barbie wears a bikini, Ken a onesie. Looking very out of place, they get a lot of stares. Barbie begins to get anxious, but Ken is happy there is a beach. He loves all the attention and notes there is no undertone of violence to it. Barbie mentions her attention very much has an undertone of violence. She goes to a construction site to meet all the women who work there, but instead it's all men spouting cheesy pickup lines. The men are not aggressive, and when Barbie informs them neither she nor Ken have genitals, they find it funny. Ken starts to realize everything is reversed in this world, but they are distracted by a poster for the Miss American pageant, which Barbie mistakes as a picture of the Supreme Court. A BEACH DUDE slaps Barbie on the backside, and she punches him in the face.

At the police station, Barbie and Ken have their mugshots taken. Due to more disparaging comments on their appearance by the police, Barbie realizes they need some new clothes. After they are released, she and Ken shop for some cowgirl/cowboy clothing but leave without paying. They are arrested again.

After their second release from the police, they worry how they are going to find the girl. Barbie sits down to focus, to see if she can feel for the girl playing with her. Ken is bored and goes for a walk. He ends up in Century City and sees men in power everywhere—on the street, in the gym, and in adverts showing presidents, sportsmen, and Sylvester Stallone. Barbie sees images in her mind of a girl growing up, first getting introduced to a Barbie doll by her mother, then playing with it, then growing out of Barbie and her mother's overt displays of affection. Barbie cries but feels better for it.

An OLD WOMAN sits next to Barbie on the same bench. Barbie has never seen age before, but she tells the woman she is beautiful. The woman agrees. Ken comes back, excited to share that men rule this world. But Barbie knows where the girl is, so they go to find her.

At the MATTEL headquarters, minor employee AARON gets a call from the FBI that two dolls have gotten loose. We meet GLORIA, an executive secretary who is drawing a series of sketches of Barbie (dressed in Cowgirl gear) crying. She calls them Crippling Shame Barbie, Irrepressible Thoughts of Death Barbie, and Full Body Cellulite Barbie. Next to a picture of her daughter, Gloria has an old Barbie on her desk that resembles the Barbie currently running around Venice Beach.

Gloria takes Aaron to see the CEO of Mattel, a late middle-aged man who constantly pontificates about female agency and empowerment. There is a sense of absurdity about his manner and the interactions with the rest of his executive team, as if they are all overgrown schoolchildren. Aaron asks if he can put the bad news in a "whisper" and quietly tells the news to the CEO. The CEO is panicked—if it got out that there is a Barbieland and life-sized living versions of the dolls could roam around, it would be very bad (especially for business, but that does not seem to be his primary concern). The team need to get Barbie back in the box. Gloria listens at the door, shocked that Barbie is real.

Barbie and Ken arrive at a high school. Barbie wants to leave as soon as possible as she's getting very new and unwelcome feelings of anxiety. Ken loves it in the real world and goes to the library to read while Barbie finds the girl from her vision. Her name is SASHA. She is very popular and sits in the cafeteria with her two friends.

Barbie is all confidence as she approaches Sasha and introduces herself. She thinks it'll be like a movie star meeting her top fan, but everyone just thinks she's clinically insane for thinking she's actually Barbie. The takedown is brutal. Sasha tells her that Barbie dolls have been making women feel bad about themselves since they were invented. They represent everything wrong with the culture: sexualized capitalism, unrealistic physical ideals. Barbies have set the feminist movement back fifty years and are killing the planet with their glorification of rampant consumerism. Sasha calls her a fascist. Barbie bursts into tears and runs away.

Meanwhile Ken runs out of the library excited, holding literature about the patriarchy and how men rule—as well as one book on horses. He now believes men and horses run the world and cannot believe that women respect him. He tries out his new power as a man by trying to get jobs in business and medicine just by being a man. It doesn't work. He tries to get a job at the beach (to do "beach"), but as he is not a trained lifeguard he fails there also. He realizes he needs to start the patriarchy afresh.

Barbie is approached by Mattel employees that look like FBI agents, and she willingly gets in their van, as she hopes Mattel can sort this mess out. Ken sees from a distance and lets her go. He's going to go back to Barbieland to tell the Kens what he's learned. Sasha gets into her mother's car—it's Gloria from Mattel. They see Barbie getting into the van, and Sasha tells Gloria that the woman thinks she really is Barbie. Gloria feels connected to Barbie as she disappears into the van.

On arrival at Mattel, Barbie is treated like a VIP. She asks the CEO what he can do to help her situation, but he's confused. He hides it and tells her if she gets into the life-size Barbie box in his office, all will be as it was. She agrees, and everyone is relieved. But before she goes, she wants to talk to the CEO, which she assumes is a woman. She's unhappy when she finds out that all senior executives are men, but the CEO makes enough random excuses to seemingly pacify her. Barbie gets into the box, but as she feels the plastic ties touch her wrists, she jumps out and says she wants her hair to be factory perfect before she gets in. They allow Barbie to go to the bathroom, but she makes a run for it. The men chase but are comically ineffectual.

Eventually Barbie is trapped, but one door is unlocked. It leads to a MAGICAL 1950'S KITCHEN, where an old lady, RUTH, sits sewing something. Ruth tells Barbie she is safe here. They have tea. Barbie admits that the world is not what she expected. Ruth agrees but believes that's a great thing. They hear Mattel executives nearby, and Ruth tells Barbie how to get out without being seen. Barbie makes her escape.

On the street, Barbie does not know where to go when Gloria drives up and tells her to get in. As they are chased on the roads, Gloria tells Barbie about feeling lonely as Sasha is growing up and seems to resent her. Gloria started to play with her Barbies again, but it made her feel sad and weird. As Gloria could never be like Barbie, she drew versions of Barbie to be like her instead. Barbie realizes she is here for Gloria, not Sasha. She apologizes for messing up the world—she loves women and wants to help them. Sasha doesn't believe her; they all know deep down everyone really hates women—even other women.

They all escape to Barbieland: it's the one safe place for women. They take the journey via camper van and snowmobile, and Gloria loves it, Sasha less so—although she is starting to warm up to the experience. Gloria admits that she never got a Ken, and Barbie explains it is because he is superfluous.

Back at Venice Beach, the Mattel CEO realizes Barbie, Gloria, and Sasha have gone to Barbieland. Humans in Barbieland could affect the real world in unpredictable ways.

As the women arrive in Barbieland, Barbie is convinced this is what she was supposed to do to make everything right. But she notices some odd things—Kens playing volleyball while the Barbies cheer on, and their version of Mount Rushmore is no longer Barbies but horses.

They get to her dreamhouse to discover that Ken has moved in and turned it into a man cave (his Mojo Dojo Casa House). He is secretly thrilled to see Barbie so she can see what he's become, but hides it. Barbieland is now a patriarchy with all the Kens united in their cartoon version of masculinity (although Allan looks miserable) and the Barbies relegated to menial work serving them in different ways. Barbie is outraged.

In the real world, the toy version of Ken's Mojo Dojo Casa House is selling out. The Mattel CEO and his team are on their way to Barbieland, and it's clear that even though Mattel is making money from Ken products, the CEO is more concerned with empowering women.

Barbie tries to convince the other Barbies that this is all wrong, but they seem happy in their new lives where they don't have to think. Ken brags that as soon as he explained the undeniable logic of the patriarchy, the Barbies fell into line. Gloria realizes that it's like the 1500s with Indigenous people and smallpox; the Barbie's have no defense against it. And it gets worse. In forty-eight hours all the Kens will vote to change the constitution to a government for the Kens forever. In a reverse of the earlier scene, Ken dismisses Barbie from his house. She runs away screaming in frustration.

Gloria and Sasha follow, and Barbie blames Gloria for the mess. Sasha defends her mother. Barbie decides just to sit and wait for one of the leadership Barbies to snap out of it and fix things. Gloria and Sasha leave her, but she is picked up by Weird Barbie.

Gloria and Sasha drive the car away from what is now Ken Land, bonding as mother and daughter. Gloria clearly has mixed feelings, then Allan pops up in the backseat. Like the earlier scene, they crash but no one is hurt. He hates Ken Land and wants to escape with them. No one will care if there's an Allan in the real world. But Sasha decides they must go back. She didn't like Barbie, but Gloria believed in them and what they could do. Gloria is not so sure; Barbie gave up and the Kens won. Yet Sasha is convincing—if they can't make it perfect they can at least make it better. Gloria should embrace who she is, weird, dark, and crazy.

They find Barbie at Weird Barbie's Weirdhouse. She's there with the reject dolls, EARRING MAGIC KEN, SUGAR DADDY KEN, GROWING UP SKIPPER, TEEN TALK BARBIE, TANNER THE POOPING DOG, and VIDEO GIRL BARBIE. Teen Talk Barbie and Video Girl Barbie attempt to un-brainwash BARBIE ALEXANDRA. It's not working. Barbie realizes her exposure to the patriarchy in the real world has made her immune but is in the midst of her own existential crisis. She is messy from crying and believes she's not pretty, has no specialist skills, and is not smart enough to be interesting.

This angers Gloria, who launches into the problems of being a woman: unrealistic and contradictory expectations. Women always have to be extraordinary but are always doing it wrong. They have to be thin but not too thin, love their kids but don't talk about them all the time, be pretty for men but not too pretty as to tempt them. They can never get old, be rude, show off, or be selfish. The impossible list goes on, but ultimately everything is always the woman's fault. The impromptu speech snaps Barbie Alexandra out of her patriarchal trance.

Barbie has an epiphany, that by giving voice to the cognitive dissonance required to be a woman under the patriarchy, it's robbed of its power (she expresses it in exactly these terms). Inspired and strengthened by this, she forms a plan. Get the Barbies away from their Kens (by using decoy Barbies pretending to be helpless with movies, sport, technology, or money), then deprogram them and use them to help the other Barbies.

Once all the Barbies are deprogrammed, they decide the best way to stop the vote is to get the Kens to turn on each other. Barbie returns to the house of Ken, who pretends to be surprised to see her. She pretends to want to be his long-term-distance-low-commitment-casual-girlfriend. He says he'll think about it and invites her in to play guitar at her. That night, all the Kens are playing guitar at their Barbies on the beach. Then Barbie pretends to get a text from Ken Simu and giggles at it. She goes over to Ken Simu, and he takes the opportunity to attempt to impress her. Ken is angry—but this dynamic is happening all over the beach with each of the Barbies. That night Ken, KEN NCUTI, and KEN KINGSLEY angrily come up with their own plan to go to war with the other Kens.

The next day on the beach it happens, a farcical fight with singing, suction-cup arrows, and frisbees. The Mattel executives arrive and walk through the fight, getting the occasional ball in the face. Meanwhile, the Barbies vote to keep the constitution. Sasha grabs her mom's hand, a tear running down her cheek. Barbie smiles. This is what she wanted to show them.

The Kens return from the battle to find their houses are back to being Barbie dreamhouses—but the aesthetic is now an attractive mix of dreamhouse, Mojo Dojo Casa House, and Weirdhouse. The Kens are told the constitution has been upheld. They look exhausted and confused, but Ken realizes his folly and is embarrassed. He runs crying into the dreamhouse, and Barbie joins him. They talk, and he admits it was really hard running stuff, and once he realized patriarchy wasn't about horses, he mostly lost interest. Ken also wanted the dreamhouse to be their house. Barbie does not have the same feelings for Ken but apologizes for taking him for granted; not every night has to be girls' night. Ken tries to kiss her, but she rejects it. Ken doesn't know who he is without Barbie, but she tells him he needs to find out. All the Kens realize they were only fighting as they didn't know who they were.

Suddenly the Mattel CEO comes out of the treehouse, clapping and crying. He agrees, it's hard to be a leader. He can now restore everything just the way it was, but the Barbies don't want that. No Barbie or Ken should be living in the shadows. They invite Weird Barbie onto the government and one Ken onto the Supreme Court.

Prompted by Sasha, Gloria suggests to the CEO that there should be an ORDINARY BARBIE, one that just wants to get through the day. The executives run the numbers and believe it will make money. She asks what will happen to Barbie when they restore the portal; what's her ending? The CEO thinks she's in love with Ken, but she is not. The CEO asks what Barbie wants, but she does not know. Then Ruth arrives and tells them that's the point of Barbie—that she doesn't have an ending.

Ruth is revealed to be the ghost of Ruth Handler, inventor of Barbie—and Mattel. She has an office on the seventeenth floor. She and Barbie go for a walk. Barbie admits she's not sure where she fits anymore—and realizes she's not Barbie anymore. Ruth tells her that ideas live forever, but humans have only one ending, and being human can be very uncomfortable. But Barbie wants to be one of the people that makes meaning, rather than the thing that is made. This surprises and impresses Ruth. The older woman cannot let Barbie make the choice without really knowing what it means, so she takes Barbie's hands and shows her life. Barbie has visions of the mess of being human—and a woman. A tear rolls down her face, and she says "yes."

Barbie moves to the real world. She is driven to an appointment by Gloria, her husband, and Sasha. Barbie is nervous, but they all give her moral support. She arrives at the offices, excited and proud. It's her first appointment with her gynecologist.

The Arguments

BRAVE

Let's start with *Brave* (we will nominally look at each film in turn, but the discussion will quickly become about all three films).

This is likely the kind of film that McKee was worried about: a didactic, preachy, and obvious film that resulted in the cardinal sin of being a dull viewing experience. In terms of those external goods and measures of success, the film made US$539 million at the international box office and received mixed reviews.[1] Half a billion dollars is a tremendous amount of money, but the general consensus was that by the Pixar standards of the time, it was a misfire that made enough at the box office not to be considered an embarrassment for the studio. To put the figures into perspective, the box office totals of other Pixar films made before and after *Brave* were as follows: *Up* (Docter 2009)—US$731 million; *Toy Story 3* (Unkrich 2010)—US$1.06 billion; *Cars 2* (Lasseter 2011)—US$560 million; *Monsters University* (Scanlon 2013)—US$743 million. *Cars 2* made more than *Brave* but was actually considered a critical and commercial failure garnering Pixar's first significant negative response.[2]

But more importantly for our purposes, *Brave* is an example of a failure of argumentation. Let's start with the conclusion it is arguing. Despite some clearly stated themes, it's actually unclear as to what precisely it is. The opening voice-over is concerned exclusively with destiny, how we search for it, fight to change it, sometimes never find it, or are led to it. The word "destiny" seems an odd choice here, as by definition destiny is a predetermined course of events. Predetermined fate robs all characters of agency, with no free will, just automatons going through the motions. A better choice here would have been "path," something you can search for, fight to change, be led to, or never find.

Merida wants to change her path, not marry a prince from another clan, but that is merely the setup for the main body of the story. This is the relationship between Merida and her mother Elinor, two women of different generations who cannot understand the other's perspective. This is the thematic idea being tested in the majority of scenes but is problematic as it is not intrinsically concerned with ideas of destiny. Merida and Elinor's relationship is naturally more resonant with ideas of social expectation and tradition than predetermined fate.

This leads us to the conclusion of the film: *Every generation has traditions that have function and value, but traditions need to evolve if each generation is to thrive (especially when it comes to social expectations and pressures on women), and this can be done only with mental and emotional growth and understanding on both sides.*[3]

Let's address the fact that the feminist element is interpreted as a nuance rather than the core of the argument. The mother-daughter relationship is central and sets up the main action of the film—Merida rejecting her role in society as a ladylike princess and political pawn—but the film does not fully commit to an argument specifically about gender. It may be the thematic element that gains the most attention, but strictly in terms of argumentation, gender politics functions as a borderline subthematic nuance. This means that points can be made but there is no requirement to make a full argument, essentially feminism with a small "f." We see Merida's life in comparison to her three brothers, and there is much here to illustrate the restrictions and expectations of women across various cultures, but these ideas are not systematically developed. The main argument is about the need for generational change, learning from history but still evolving in a gender-agnostic way. Neither Merida nor her male suitors have a choice, and all don't wish to have their romantic future decided for them.

In a way the film is the worst of both worlds. On the surface it appears to be a strongly didactic film with overt feminist priorities, inviting the wrath of those who find the topic challenging. Yet the film is actually making a far more general argument, even if it is highly flawed in its presentation. This is in stark contrast with both *Frozen* and *Barbie,* which take quite different approaches. Spoiler alert: *Barbie* is a film that very much commits.

The argumentation has problems functioning as it attempts to serve two linked but separate conclusions—one about destiny, the other about the need for social change, and both told through a feminist lens. This means the scenes, characters, and plotting cannot operate efficiently or, more crucially, convincingly. In fact, some scenes toward the end of the film concerned with the trapping of the Queen-as-bear don't appear to serve either conclusion or gender perspective.

The final voice-over telling us that destiny is inside ourselves, that we just have to be brave enough to find it is especially problematic for two significant reasons. First, the film doesn't really test any ideas of destiny or free will. Second, and this seems to be a particularly fundamental flaw, *Merida is not brave.*

Merida is driven by rage at the injustice of tradition. Her actions during the highland games border on petulance. Her choice to go to the witch and ask for a spell is cowardly. After her mother is turned into a bear, her actions to restore things back to how they were are desperate. Merida does stop her father from killing her mother at the climax, but this is less bravery than a family squabble with swords. Even if we try to transmit bravery to the mother, the fact the Queen battles Mor'du reads more as pure motherly instinct, further obscured at this point by her increasing wild bear instincts.

A key issue with the argumentation of the film is that it resolves at the sixty-nine-minute mark of an eighty-five-minute run time (not including end credits). That's about 80 percent of the way into the film. If the argument completes there, why is there another 20 percent of the story left? This is why the final climactic action feels extraneous. It's pure activity, yet with no argumentative function. The women already appreciate each other, so all that is left is to transform the Queen back from a bear (we'll come back to that bear later). The film seems to be pushing the idea that to mend the bond is for Merida to actually tell Elinor she loves her, yet there was never any suggestion that she didn't love her mother, just that she disagreed with her. Why does she have to say the words? The bond healed almost as soon as the Queen became a bear and Merida realized her mistake.

Another reason the film is badly argued is that the conclusion is indeed telegraphed from very early in the film (not a fundamental flaw, but as we'll see later, not ideal), yet there is very little development of the argument in any meaningful sense. There is an assertion, just not many reasons given to convince of this assertion. The majority of the film attempts to show how the two women bond and see each other's perspective, but in reality they do little more than hunt in the forest and be led to the old kingdom. The epiphany that hits Merida, that the bear transformation has happened before and this selfish act is why the old kingdom fell, is supposed to give insight to both her own mistake and her mother's priorities. But by this time in the story Merida already realizes her act was selfish, even if she only now realizes the impact it will have among the clans. She learns that the legends are based in truth and therefore, as her mother says, provide genuine history lessons, but learning from history is not quite the same as the importance of tradition. These ideas are connected yet not really developed and don't quite align, which makes for a less-than-convincing argument.

These problems are more clearly revealed by the use of the bear.[4] This is a film where the argument would most efficiently be made using the tropes of the body-swap comedy, such as *Freaky Friday* (Nelson 1976 and Waters 2003); mother and daughter swap places, and greater understanding of each other ensues. Yet instead we have Queen-as-bear. This gives a nice dramatic irony and tension as the King is famous for his bear-killing abilities, but it is all surface-level conflict. It is reminiscent of a famous cartoon by director Alan Parker, where a filmmaker draws a set of lines while an irritated friend comments, "Oh no. You're not drawing parallels again."[5] Being a bear may provide great jeopardy for the Queen but does not drive the argument forward. Ultimately, it could have been any fierce animal: Queen-as-lion would have made no stronger or lesser impact on the argument.

Before we move on, we have to decide whether *Brave* is a success in terms of worthwhile argument. If we agree with the conclusion suggested, is it a worthwhile one? Using our criteria, the answer is yes. Generational change provides constant social friction, so what the film suggests is certainly significant and plausible. Does it argue in a worthwhile way, even if flawed? Here it has issues, as although it is not reliant on insincere manipulation of credibility, logic, or emotion, it does not make its case in a compelling way.

This goes beyond a basic clumsiness in articulation. Comparing it to *Toy Story 3*, which laid out its key ideas in dialogue and concluded with action, or *Mulholland Drive*, which laid out both in action, *Brave* does the opposite. In cinematic terms, it works against the principles of enthymematic argument and articulates its key ideas and conclusion explicitly in voice, be it dialogue or voice-over. This will likely always be less impactful.

The film's use of the cinematic medium is fundamentally hampered by these choices, the building blocks of character, story, plot, vision, sound, and rhythm not working in unison. It is essentially an issue of argumentative logic being inefficient rather than unsound, and thus emotions are not engaged in an effective way to make the film the perfect evidence to support the conclusion. We understand it, but we don't feel it. So ultimately, by our standards, it's a failure. A well-meaning one, but a failure all the same.

FROZEN

Frozen, released a year later in 2013, seems to have learned from *Brave*. While it is not quite a thematic remake of the earlier film, it presents many of the same story moments to far greater argumentative success.[6] *Frozen* should not keep McKee awake at night.

The key lesson that *Frozen* appears to have learned, perhaps also from *Mulholland Drive*, is that if you want to make a highly effective cinematic argument, present it as a puzzle. Instead of a conventional verbal debate where each team argues for or against a motion fully known to all at the start, cinematic arguments excel when the conclusion not only provides insight but surprises us. Yet it has to be a surprise that has been carefully, if secretly, been built toward, lest the audience feel cheated. It's the best kind of bait and switch: a conclusion that improves on audience expectation.

To return to the film that gave us our central metaphor of the two-sided headpiece, *Raiders of the Lost Ark* generously provides a particularly famous example of setting up then exceeding audience expectations: the sword fight in Cairo, often claimed to be the greatest moment in modern cinema. We excitedly anticipate an intricate and clever fight scene between our hero Indy and a highly skilled swordsman, only for Indy to simply take out his gun and shoot the man dead. It didn't deliver on our expectation, it topped it with an even better, unexpected, moment. (It was perhaps particularly cathartic as "just shoot" continues to be the war cry of many an audience member in an action or martial arts film.)

David Mamet takes an Aristotelian view of endings, believing the best kind are those that are surprising but inevitable, ones you didn't see coming but when happen you cannot imagine the film ending any other way.[7] It's one of the most critical instances of how the conventions of storytelling shape those of argument: *Ubi fabula, ibi argumentum* (as for story, goes argument). Storytelling relies on conflict, tension, and suspense, so in the same way that predictable plots are dull, so too are predictable conclusions and argumentation. We may know the general direction of travel, but keep us guessing and the final moments will impact far greater.

So what is *Frozen*'s conclusion, and why is it a surprise? It could be about societal expectations (Princesses, Queens) or being too emotionally closed off (Elsa) or too open (Anna). It could circle ideas of honesty, be it about yourself or how others present themselves (Hans and Kristoff). Alternatively, the story could relate to perception—don't judge books by their covers—or focus primarily on identity through issues of social acceptance and the secret self. Musical phenomenon "Let It Go" was a torch song for many who felt the shackles of having to hide a part of who they really are. And what of the intrinsic importance of family? Yet when you consider and reflect on how the film deals with all these themes, it is ultimately a story about fear and love.

My suggestion for the conclusion is this: *Do not let your life be defined by fear, be it of yourself or others, or it will compromise your choices, your sense of self, and those around you—especially those closest. Love (and critically, this does not necessarily mean romantic love) is the only way forward that allows for acceptance, understanding, and the living of a truly fulfilled life.*

Fear is what sets everything in motion, Elsa's fear of her powers and the warning that others will fear them too. It causes everything to be literally and figuratively closed off (Elsa and the castle) and pushes the lonely Anna to open herself up too much; fear has made both girls vulnerable. At the close of the film, love is quite literally the answer to both inner and outer conflicts: love allows Elsa to control her powers and return summer to Arendelle.

But what of *Frozen*'s feminist credentials? I've previously written in the press about how, in terms of social impact, it is perhaps one of the most important feminist films in cinematic history. But how does that reconcile with a conclusion that, as with *Brave*, is primarily non-gender-specific? The short answer is that like with *Brave*, the feminist ideas are presented as specific examples within the overall argument, but unlike with *Brave*, they are far more elegantly delivered to provide maximum impact. A conclusion that seeks to remind us that suppressing your authentic self through fear is certainly edifying but not necessarily impactful. A key to the success of the overall argument is the element that it is not always romantic love that provides the answer, even if we think it does.

The incredible impact *Frozen* made was not simply because it avoided the usual tired trope of representing female characters as damsels in distress, defined by men or romantic love—but did so within a high-profile Disney princess film shaped as a romance.[8] The effect was primarily contextual; released at a different time in history, the film would not have had the same result. If *Frozen* was the first princess movie ever made, there would have been no tropes. If it was released now, we've seen fully self-actualized princesses before. Yet reliance on context does not lessen its impact. In this case, it improves it.

Just like representation in cinema more broadly, specific issues don't have to be addressed within the story to communicate significant ideas within the culture. Part of the skill of the *Frozen* filmmakers is understanding how to best make their argument. They chose to disguise it and let context take much of the strain. This returns us to the puzzle and bait-and-switch approaches to argumentation.

Unlike Elsaesser's mind-game films that overtly present their plots as puzzles for the audience (and often the protagonist) to solve, presenting a film's argument as a puzzle is different. As with most screen techniques, it works best when the method is not foregrounded. This is argument in elegant disguise that avoids the sense of didacticism that McKee and others fear. *Frozen* provides us with many uncertainties that resolve only in the final moments of the film, and it's all the more satisfying for it. We mostly know what is coming, but there are various elements that could go either way and still satisfy genre expectations. For instance, cute snowman Olaf could live or die—remember imaginary friend Bing Bong from *Inside Out* (Docter 2015)? We don't even quite know who the main character is. Elsa was originally written as the villain of the piece, and it's quite possible this is a dual protagonist film as the unreliable algebra used to evaluate is often not decisive. Here, both sisters learn the same lessons, but although Anna has more screen time, she goes through less of a character arc: strong foundations for a robust postscreening discussion.

Besides avoiding didacticism, there is another benefit of disguising the argument: we can't resist if we don't yet understand. The film may ask its key thematic question in dialogue, but its importance is truly clear only at the close of the story. All elements that will finally be understood as evidence are accepted through the drama, which makes them more powerful. But to do this successfully is far from straightforward.

This is where the bait and switch comes in. There must be viable alternatives within the story, key moments that could go either way, for the argument to be effectively disguised. In *Frozen*, the bait and switch is the genre (or more accurately, the subgenre). If we regard the film primarily as a princess-adventure movie, these are usually princess-adventure-romance movies. *Frozen* presents itself with a love triangle at the center: will Anna choose Hans or Kristoff? The reason Elsa runs away is due to a disagreement with Anna about marrying Hans. Yet the final moments reveal the film was not a romance but a family drama: a sister movie. The women in the film do not define themselves in terms of their relationships with men, and their reconciliation solves both the inner problem (self-suppression) and the outer (the eternal winter). This provides the Mamet surprising-yet-inevitable ending.

Compare this with *Brave*. It foregrounded what appeared to be its argument from the outset (in fact, even before the release of the film, as the first teaser trailer was of Merida winning the archery competition against the suitors). It also attempts the same twist, that it is really a story about mother-daughter love, but this too had been signposted the whole movie, putting the audience far ahead of the characters. It's presented as a plot reveal rather than a thematic one and does not feel like a revelation at all, especially as the women healed their relationship earlier in the film.

Could the idea of disguising the argument cause *Frozen* to fall foul of the standards of worthwhile argumentation? Is it all not just a bit manipulative? The answer to both is no, the film merely represents sophisticated argumentation. Mainstream cinematic technique is designed around the idea of invisibility. The audience is not supposed to notice the mechanics of screen stories, so argumentation should be no different. *Frozen* comes from a credible source, the world building is consistent, the argument is built logically, and there is no unreasonable provoking of emotion (it's not the only example, but Olaf does not die). *Frozen* is the epitome of successful film-as-worthwhile-argument.

BARBIE

Barbie makes a mockery of the "go woke, go broke" criticism of films with an obviously inclusive agenda. At the time of writing, its worldwide gross stands at US$1.447 billion. Unlike *Brave*, *Barbie* does very much commit to its feminist soul. It actually shares as much with *Brave* as it does with *Frozen* in terms of skill of argumentation but still became a cultural phenomenon that financially outperformed both.

As with the other films, *Barbie* ultimately argues and provides evidence for a conclusion that is not primarily gendered. It appears to assert this: *Without genuine empathy and awareness of the experience of others, those in power (in Western society, this is men and sometimes other women who have knowingly or unknowingly absorbed patriarchal values) will always shape a society that serves primarily their interests and, deliberately or not, oppress and diminish those they deem "other" or a threat to their control (often by limiting career paths or creating impossible expectations of acceptable public behavior or body image).*

Like with *Brave* and *Frozen,* the gendered elements are in parentheses. They are part of the overall fabric of the conclusion but do not carry the full weight of the argument itself. A case could be made that the feminist element of Barbie is actually subthematic and not part of the core conclusion at all, but the sheer ubiquity of the discussions of gender throughout the film makes it intrinsic to the overall assertion the film is making.

Is this conclusion the most justified? Let's look at how the film makes its argument. On a fundamental level the film is a literal Bechdel Test.[9] This test is often used in fiction to assess whether female characters are represented and active in a meaningful sense. It asks three questions: (1) Are there at least two female characters in the story important enough to have names? (2) Do they talk to each other? (3) Do they talk to each other about anything other than a man? It's an indicator rather than a decisive measure of valid representation, as it's quite reasonable to have no women in a film set exclusively in an all-male prison. This test may appear unnecessary, even if many films fail it. But reverse it, as *Barbie* did, and its importance quickly becomes clear; in fact it becomes almost embarrassingly absurd. As the vast majority of Western mainstream feature films contain at least two male characters important enough to have a name and talk to each other about something other than a woman, the test becomes meaningless.

Barbieland is a matriarchy. It's telling that the image of a Supreme Court of only women is played as knowingly ridiculous—yet it's a trap. If you laugh along without understanding the wider implications, it may be time to take a good hard look at yourself. Barbie and the other Barbies are presented as the oblivious oppressors—well-meaning but utterly self-absorbed—and the negative impacts are clear. Ken can have a good day only if Barbie notices him, and the Kens live quite stressful, competitive lives defined by the Barbies. The boys have meaningless jobs where they do little else than hang around looking pretty; they can't even swim, so can only stand around on the fake sand and do "beach."

In a very clever move by screenwriter/director Greta Gerwig and screenwriter Noah Baumbach, the Barbies are presented as both good and bad for women, which allows the film to both critique Barbie while simultaneously promoting her (critical when the film is partially funded by Mattel, corporate owner of Barbie). It discusses her problematic nature: undeniably a fun doll, but both inspirational role model and unrealistic physical aspiration for most women. This is foregrounded in most scenes of the film—subtle, unstated enthymematic argumentation this is not; the argument is set out and concluded quite explicitly in both direct and indirect thematic dialogue.

At times this makes the argumentation feel quite clumsy, as there are many lines of dialogue in the film that are great examples of Aristotle's "thought" or "reasoning," where one character within the drama attempts to convince another of a point of view using only words (this does not have to be the same point of view of the film itself). Gloria's monologue on the impossible standards applied to women is one, Barbie having the ideological epiphany that articulating an issue robs it of its power another.

Barbie might lack elegance of argumentation at times, but unlike *Brave*, it offsets its blatancy with self-awareness, often using the Narrator to break the fourth wall to collude with the audience. Unlike *Frozen*, which presented its argument as a puzzle to great effect, *Barbie* takes a different approach. It takes the view that attempting to Trojan horse its argument would be patronizing, so better to own it, make it obvious, and have a lot of playful fun at the same time. Other recent films that took a similar approach (albeit with less humor) and met the same resistance were the Adam McKay films *Don't Look Up* (2021) and *The Big Short* (2015), which tackle climate change and the global financial crisis of 2008.[10]

It's not a body-swap film, but *Barbie* uses a walk-in-their-shoes story dynamic, as both Barbie and Ken get to understand how the other experiences the world. We start with Barbieland being an obliviously oppressive matriarchy, which Barbie doesn't think to question, then see it turn into a more obviously oppressive patriarchy, before finally becoming a more understanding and inclusive matriarchy. The message is clear—we need to follow Barbieland and make our real-life patriarchies far fairer, especially in terms of gender (it's tacit that this should also mean fairness to other communities also). At the point in history in which it was released, with ongoing issues in the United States concerning abortion that mean many women have lost control over their own bodies, it seems a very worthwhile conclusion to argue.

As to the question of whether the film relies on unreasonable manipulation to make its case, this takes a little more unpacking. Who is the primary author of the argument? Is it Greta Gerwig as screenwriter/director, Warner Brothers, or Mattel? Gerwig has huge credibility as a female film creative, especially when it comes to overtly feminist issues. Warner Brothers is a film studio that has a strong track record of quality but is still ultimately an institution that is focused on external goods (money) rather than internal reasons for the practice. Mattel is neither a filmmaker nor an entertainment company but an international toy conglomerate whose purpose is to sell more toys. This compromises the perceived credibility of the author, which can be crucial in whether or not an argument is persuasive.

In this case it appears that Warner and Mattel took the view that the best way to make money and sell toys is to empower a credible filmmaker to make a film with integrity. The film does not shy away from common criticisms of Barbie, but the characterizations of the Mattel CEO and executives are perhaps an instance where corporate needs conflicted with the storytelling. The men are represented as buffoons more tonally consistent with Barbieland personalities than the real-world humans of the rest of the film, which damages the world building. As with Barbie herself, lack of awareness is key: the executives can't be seen to be bad, with either a hidden agenda or understanding of the damage their dolls cause, but the contrivance weakens the argument overall by presenting unconvincing evidence.

This leads us to whether the film has built a logical argument based on true premises. Notwithstanding the above inconsistency, it does so, as it uses a conventional structure that debates both sides of the Barbie problem before landing on an uncontroversial conclusion. As to whether *Barbie* cynically engages emotion or sensation over and above the demands of the narrative, tonally everything is light with no lapse into sentimentality or gut punches simply to make an impact.

So, would Barbie pass the McKee test of didacticism? Not even close. The film's argument is extremely overt and verbose, even if it leans into its clumsiness. The agenda is predictable, allowing resistance that reduces the impact of the conclusion, whether or not you agree with its worldview. In this way,

Barbie is closer to *Brave* than to *Frozen* in terms of effective argumentation. It's important to note that it has not failed by the internal standards of film-as-worthwhile-argument, but it's not a shining example either. So why was it so critically and financially successful?

The truth is that film-as-worthwhile-argument is what we all strive for: the gold standard. And as with all aspirations, realistic or not (looking at you, Barbie), most of the time we inevitably fail. The same goes for mainstream feature films. Most don't make the grade. But we still need an industry, the audience still needs something to make their viewing experience satisfying, even if their lives are not fundamentally enriched by the time the lights go up.

They need some compensation.

PART III

NOW ON RELEASE AND COMING ATTRACTIONS

CHAPTER 8

Why Failures Succeed

The Cinema of Compensation

It is a quirk of mainstream feature filmmaking that the majority of films fail its internal standards of excellence. Yet the industry survives. How can this be?

Let's clarify our definitions of failure. So far, we have been concerned with failure only in terms of film-as-worthwhile-argument, yet clearly external goods are crucial—especially financial success; without it there would be very few feature films at all.

Typically, a film that is well argued should lead, at the very minimum, to critical success. Yet it is quite possible, even necessarily common, to achieve financial and critical success despite flawed or simply bad argumentation. So although *Barbie* stumbled as it moved its audience to a worthwhile conclusion, it enjoyed huge box office receipts and mostly positive reviews. The film did this as it provided the audience artistic compensations that outweighed or distracted from its problems meeting the internal goods of the practice.

The Cinema of Compensation

Below is a list I've developed that itemizes and systematizes how mainstream narrative feature films can achieve financial and/or critical success despite having flawed or nonexistent arguments.

It is important to note that it is not a summary of tangible techniques and intangible choices that filmmakers can employ. Often the same elements would exist in a version of the film that was without flaw, so their application is a matter not simply of inclusion (although it can be) but of combination and emphasis.

To use a culinary example, let us say that a mainstream narrative feature film is a chicken pizza. And for purposes of simplification, the ingredients of a chicken pizza are a pizza base, tomato sauce, cheese, chicken, and pepper. It was always conceived to be a chicken pizza, and if the qualities of the ingredients are good, it will be a flawless chicken pizza. This obviously represents film-as-worthwhile-argument at its best. But what if there is a problem with the logic of the argument? Perhaps due to influence from the institution, changes are made to the story that are not in the best interests of the production. What are the choices for the filmmaker? Can the flaws be disguised? Can the audience be guided to focus on other things? Or if not, can other elements work harder to compensate for what is an identifiable fault? Using our analogy, if the tomato sauce is bad, can more cheese disguise it? This is where emphasis is key. To take a film comedy, this could mean that if story logic is lacking, the gags will need to be funnier; not ideal, but a likely satisfying compensation. For *Barbie*, franchise power certainly did much of the heavy lifting.

But what if, going back to our pizza, the extra cheese is not helping, the chicken is not making up for it, and the pepper is making no impact? Then new ingredients will have to be added. Now it becomes a matter of both emphasis and inclusion. Perhaps the chef now adds high-quality ground beef, pepperoni, and bacon to make it a meat feast. The pizza now tastes wonderful, and in one way is a successful dish. But as it was never intended to be a meat feast, it still represents a failure to the chef (and other chefs), namely that the great meat feast is really just a failed but artfully disguised chicken pizza.

Returning to our hypothetical comedy, if the story logic is lacking and the gags are not compensating (be it at the script or shooting stage), this might mean adding new cast members who are particularly famous—perhaps now making it an ensemble comedy. If these new high-profile actors make the necessary impact, it means that even if the film is both critically and commercially successful, for the filmmakers it really represents a failed nonensemble comedy. *Annie Hall* (1977) is an example of a significant hit that was nevertheless a disappointment to the writer and director Woody Allen. The original cut didn't even feature Annie Hall as a central character.[1]

Determining whether an aspect of a film is compensatory requires a subtraction test. In a well-argued film there is nothing to compensate for, with all elements integral to the storytelling. If the argument is considered inadequate, it is a question of whether it is further weakened or indeed undermined if the aspect were removed or substituted with a noncompensatory equivalent.

To use the celebrity cameo (sometimes referred to stunt casting) as an example, it does not mean that the role disappears when the element is removed, just the celebrity playing it. For instance, veritable superstars Harrison Ford, Liam Neeson, Jim Carrey, Marion Cotillard, Kirsten Dunst, Vince Vaughn, Sacha Baron Cohen, Will Smith, Tina Fey, and Amy Poehler all appeared in the "clash of the news anchors" scene at the end of *Anchorman 2: The Legend Continues* (McKay 2013). While it was necessary to have other news anchors in the scene, it was not necessary for them to be played by celebrities; therefore, it is an example of compensation by emphasis. If the roles themselves were not necessary for purposes of argument, then it would be compensation by way of addition. However, if the humor of the film were based around the idea of celebrity cameos, such as the TV shows *The Larry Sanders Show* (Shandling and Klein 1992–1998) or *Extras* (Gervais and Merchant 2005–2007), then the celebrity element would be simply a core part of the storytelling.

I've attempted to be as exhaustive as possible with the following list, endeavoring to define the meaningful atoms of a mainstream narrative feature film. An element is included as a compensation if, however intangible, it can be isolated and potentially leveraged to compensate for flawed argument. There are currently twenty in total.

1. HAPPY ENDINGS

In his book *Happy Endings in Hollywood Cinema: Cliché, Convention and the Final Couple*, James MacDowell comments, "The Hollywood 'happy ending' is among the most overutilized and underanalyzed concepts in discussions of popular cinema."[2] As MacDowell notes, although happy endings are clearly not limited to Hollywood, the term "Hollywood ending" is primarily used pejoratively, implying that the end to the narrative has not merely ended happily but at the expense of logic and realism.

Herein lies the difference between a justified happy ending and compensatory one—the former is fully integrated, the latter an addition that lacks

TABLE 1. Compensations: A complete list

No.	Compensation	Description	Main reference film(s)
1	Happy endings	Where the hero gets what they want, often at the expense of what the story needs	*Risky Business* *Get Out* *LA Confidential*
2	Franchise	The power of previous connection	*Planet of the Apes* franchise *The Matrix* franchise
3	Genre conventions	The enjoyment of the expected: tropes that need to be met or subverted	*Scream* *No Time to Die*
4	Casting and performance	The intrinsic strength of stardom, attractiveness, and ability	*Dallas Buyers Club* *American Pie* series
5	Author	The ethos of the auteur or institution	*Star Trek: The Motion Picture*
6	Visual pleasure	Core to the cinematic medium, it can be found anywhere in the frame	*Fifty Shades of Grey*
7	Spectacle	Visual pleasure at scale	*Eternals* *The Marvels* *Inception*
8	Sensation	Primal reactions, both positive and negative	The *Saw* series *Saltburn*
9	Wish fulfillment	Can be satisfied on various levels, independently or simultaneously: narrative, character, world, emotion, or sensation	*Knocked Up* *Westworld*
10	Music	An art form of emotional information that can be enjoyed on its own merits	*Mama Mia!* *Jaws*
11	Puzzle solving	Storytelling predominantly through enigmas	*Memento* *The Sixth Sense*

TABLE 1. (cont.)

No.	Compensation	Description	Main reference film(s)
12	Promise of the premise	The payoff that must be delivered	*How to Lose a Guy in 10 Days* The *Fast* series The *Rocky* series
13	Recognition of self	Be it a look, a gesture, or a phrase, they could be us; often we want them to be us	*Malcom X* *American Psycho* *To All the Boys I've Loved Before*
14	Dialogue	A verbal and rhythmic joy in itself	*The Social Network* *Crimson Tide*
15	Strong sequences	Sections of the film that contain their own internal gratifications, usually not reliant on the rest of the narrative	*Titanic* *A Few Good Men*
16	"Based on a True Story"	It really happened, so you must doubt nothing	*The Wolf of Wall Street* *Fargo*
17	Novelty	The power of first-mover advantage	*Boyz n the Hood* *Thank You for Smoking* *From Dusk Till Dawn*
18	Homage	A sincere allusion to another artist or artwork, it can be a complete filmmaking mode or just moments of reference	*Far from Heaven* *Ready Player One*
19	Fan service	Audience-focused homage and wish fulfillment, based on clearly articulated—or perceived—fan desires	*Star Wars: Episode VII—The Force Awakens* *Ghostbusters: Afterlife* *Ghostbusters: Frozen Empire*
20	Obscurity	Fascination with the impossible puzzle	*Inland Empire* *Primer* *8½*

consistency. This returns us to the David Mamet / Aristotelian view of inevitable yet surprising endings.

Examples of Hollywood institutions interfering with endings are well catalogued. The original ending of Tom Cruise's *Risky Business* (Brickman 1983) sees his character Joel suffering for his dalliance with a prostitute: he is found out by his parents and does not get into Princeton. The ending was reversed at the studio's behest: Joel gets into Princeton with his parents none the wiser.[3] Yet it does not necessarily follow that a sad or bittersweet finale converted eleventh hour into a happy ending is necessarily a Hollywood ending; it could be just the right course correction that gives the film the Mamet/Aristotelian finish. Happy does not always mean Hollywood. In this case the change was successful, perhaps due to being a conventional choice more consistent tonally with the exciting, aspirational story that preceded it. The new ending may have given the film a more logical argument, even though it was not one the filmmakers initially set out to make.

Oscar-winning horror-satire *Get Out* (Peele 2017) also changed its sad-but-fair ending, on this occasion due to what was perceived as very trying political times for the audience. In a comment on issues of institutionalized racism within the North American penal system, the African American lead Chris originally defeats the evil antagonists but goes to jail. In the release version, justice is served cleanly with no prison time. The thoughts were that the target audience needed a bit more cathartic joy.[4]

These compensatory endings are of note, as the compensation itself destroys the original argument in pursuit of wish fulfilment. It compensates, not necessarily for a flawed argument but perhaps for a difficult truth, by turning it into a comforting lie. However, it is also possible to change to a happy ending without undermining the initial argument. Little Red Riding Hood initially died along with her Grandma at the hands of the Wolf, the Woodcutter rescue being written only centuries later. But both versions constitute a cautionary tale about not trusting strangers, as being eaten is never a nice experience even if the more deadly ending makes a stronger impact.

We've previously mentioned that *L.A. Confidential* (Hanson 1997) has a false happy ending, but it is also a high-profile example of another variation: the double-finish. This is a film that has an honest then happy ending. Here, Bud, the antihero played by Russell Crowe, is shot multiple times in the penultimate sequence. There is little doubt that a human could survive and is the necessary act of sacrifice for a character on a redemptive path. The villains are caught and duly punished, the tone deliberately melancholic and undeniably final. Yet the real closing (and surprising) image is of Bud in a car, so heavily bandaged to be almost comedic. It is clearly an addition inconsistent with story logic.[5]

So why the fascination with the happy ending at all costs? In perhaps the ultimate piece of meta-casting, Spike Jonze's *Adaptation* (2002), about a screenwriter struggling to write an adaptation, casts Brian Cox as Robert McKee. He gives the screenwriter some mentorly advice: *"Wow them in the end, and you got a hit. You can have flaws, problems, but wow them in the end, and you've got a hit. Find an ending, but don't cheat."* Here, the character of McKee explicitly explains that a stunning ending can literally compensate for everything else. Yet "wow" does not necessarily mean happy—just impactful. This ending is not additive or compensatory (not "cheating") but hardwired into the DNA of the argument.

You might think that the happy ending is the ultimate act of creative pragmatism: if a film is to have an unconvincing ending, a happy one is preferable to an unhappy one. But it is just one tool and forms part of an overall set of genre expectations. In a children's adventure, an action film, or a romance, the happy ending is a foundational element of the fiction. However, in a drama, especially a tragedy, the happy ending would be out of place. This is especially true of filmmakers such as Alejandro G. Iñárritu (*The Revenant* 2015) and Bela Tarr (*Werckmeister Harmonies* 2000). In these cases, a happy ending could never be on the menu.

2. FRANCHISE

Based on their primary source of income, cinemas are often considered as sweet shops with screens.[6] In the same way, it would take very little reorientation to consider the traditional Hollywood studios and large global streaming services as being in not the film industry but the franchise industry.[7] At the time of publication, *Titanic* (Cameron 1997) is the only film in the top ten grossing films of all time not to be part of a franchise.

Franchise is one of the most effective compensations, as the film in question can fail to work on any creative level, yet there will always be market interest that may result in financial success. We've already noted how franchise likely saved *Batman v. Superman: Dawn of Justice,* despite its fundamental storytelling flaws. *Barbie* is currently a standalone movie, but one based on multigenerational globally successful intellectual property. Would the film have performed so well if based on an unknown fictional doll?

Although it appears some film franchises do die, in reality they are merely dormant until rebooted a generation or generations later (such as *The Matrix* series 1999–). Sometimes these reboots, reimaginings, or belated sequels return quickly to the mire (*The Lone Ranger,* Verbinski 2013; *Charlie's Angels,* Banks 2019), while others receive a new lease of life (The *Mission: Impossible* series 1996–). And if they do fail, another attempt can always be tried in the unspecified future, as the *Planet of the Apes* franchise demonstrates. Based on Pierre Boulle's book *La Planète des singes,* the first film was released in 1968, with four more sequels released to ever diminishing budgets and returns until 1973.[8] There were two television series screened between 1974 and 1976, but the franchise effectively shuttered at the close of 1976. In 2001 the franchise attempted a return with Tim Burton's reimagining (essentially a reworking of the source material not consistent with the universe building of the original films) also titled *Planet of the Apes.* But following dismal reviews and box office performance, again the franchise was abandoned. Ten years later Rupert Wyatt directed the latest return with *Rise of the Planet of the Apes,* this time to far better success, and more sequels followed: *Dawn of the Planet of the Apes* (Reeves 2014), *War for the Planet of the Apes* (Reeves 2017), and *Kingdom of the Planet of the Apes* (Ball 2024).

Obviously, if the franchise is strong enough it represents the ultimate insurance for any film financier. This is clearly the rationale behind Disney's aggressive acquisition of the most proven and financially successful franchises—if not mythologies—in modern cinema history: the Star Wars and Marvel universes, as well as the studios Pixar and Fox, with resulting character, story, and merchandising subfranchises too numerous to list.

Can franchise ever exist as a minor element of a film? It is rare, but yes. Franchise functions as the twist in the M. Night Shyamalan film *Split* (2017). What is essentially a conventional psycho-inspired serial-killer film is revealed in the final scene to be the origin story of a villain from the world of *Unbreakable* (Shyamalan 2000). This sets up a new franchise from what was previously a standalone film. As the revelation comes at the close of the film, if the argumentation was flawed it could function as both a franchise and happy ending compensation.

3. GENRE CONVENTIONS

Genre is essentially an organizing structure containing tropes and expectations that need to be met and/or subverted if the film is to qualify for that category.

The compensation formula here is quite simple: the more flawed the argument, the more genre expectations need to be met. This usually means certain events have to be present but can also mean events avoided (such as the happy ending in an otherwise challenging European art house film). The more expectations are met and tropes well executed (in a horror, the scene-by-scene jump scares are genuinely jumpy and scary), the more they will compensate. If quality execution of the conventions is not possible, then a clever subversion of these conventions is allowable, especially if they provide something new or unique to the genre. Horror film *Scream* (Craven 1996) is an effective example of this, the freshness the fact that the film was actively self-aware of its own genre conventions, even if now this has become yet another genre convention.

The James Bond franchise has become almost a slave to those expectations, beyond the usual spy-action-thriller tropes that it helped to establish. Imagine a Bond film without the meeting with M, the seduction of the "Bond girl" (usually two, divided into good and bad varieties), the exposition of the chief villain, and the big explosion at the end—but at the budget those films require, financial security is a key concern. Bond did attempt to significantly subvert expectations in *No Time to Die* (Fukunaga 2021) by (spoiler alert) doing the unthinkable: killing Bond, a character defined by his indestructability. However, the choice was more tolerated than well received, largely due to the death not being necessary or deserved. It is clearly a compensation as is a stunt ending, impactful but not part of the argument of the film. To be so, it would require the film to make a coherent and consistent argument about sacrifice rather than, as is typical for a Bond film, natural justice prevailing. A similar ending was also attempted with *Glass* (Shyamalan 2019), the third part of the aforementioned *Unbreakable* trilogy, which also garnered the same reaction for the same reason.

4. CASTING AND PERFORMANCE

This compensation is split into three closely interrelated categories: level of star, level of attractiveness, and level of performance. The level of star is perhaps the simplest to quantify as statistics exist to prove scale of media attention and fees commanded. Although highly subjective, attractiveness and performance can also be quantified in a similar way: perception of beauty and talent as defined, rightly or wrongly, by media (and social media).

Use of a star is perhaps the most well-known of industry insurances. The equation is straightforward: as long as the star appears in the film, there will be interest (and sales) even if no element in the film works. It is the primary reason fees for genuine stars are so high. A genuine star in this context is one where the star operates as the genre (where an audience member will primarily refer to the star, not the genre of the film: a Jennifer Lawrence film, for instance).

The case could be made that use of a star or high-profile cast member is always a compensation, as it is a purely contextual benefit, with nothing within the story world requiring that particular character to be played by anyone other than a competent actor. The only exception to this would be if the star were playing themself, such as John Malkovich in *Being John Malkovich* (Jonze 1999) or the entire cast of *This Is the End* (Rogen and Goldberg 2013). Did *Barbie* need Margot Robbie and Ryan Gosling to play Barbie and Ken? Of course not. But did the audience go to see the film just because they were in it?

Alternatively, the compensation can be based purely on the perceived level of attractiveness of an actor. We'll look at general visual pleasure later, but all actors' careers are based on their looks, whether they are Danny DeVito or Zendaya. Actors are traditionally split into two categories: lead or character actor (the latter often used as a euphemism for someone who is not conventionally attractive enough, by whatever cultural standards that dominate, to be considered as a lead). However, it is possible to move categories depending on genre, as actors such as Octavia Spencer and Paul Giamatti regularly demonstrate.[9]

Teen comedy is a genre that is not star-dependent but does rely largely on the overall attractiveness of its cast to appeal to critics and audiences. The epitome of a successful teen franchise is the *American Pie* series of films (1999–2020). Unlike previous teen comedy franchises, such as *Porky's* (1981–1986), whose casts consisted of more realistic looking people, the *American Pie* actors are clearly scaled up in terms of physical appeal. Clearly the story is not predicated on the teenagers in the film being hyperattractive, so potentially it is a clear-cut case of attractiveness as compensation. The only way the strategy could be viewed otherwise is for it to be a core teen comedy trope, therefore the film is merely playing by genre rules.

The reverse can also be true: lack-of-beauty-as-compensation. In horror, often it's the grossness of certain characters that impacts, such as the iconic Pinhead in the *Hellraiser* series (1987–) or Freddy Krueger in the *Nightmare on Elm Street* franchise (1984–2010). The famously confronting Tod Browning horror-drama *Freaks* (1932) is not in this category as the nature of his cast was intrinsic to his argument.

Another subset is the transformative role, usually a particularly handsome or beautiful actor making themselves less attractive for the part. Robert De Niro's transformation in *Raging Bull* (Scorsese 1980) is arguably the most well-known example when he gained large amounts of weight (shutting production down for five months) to play boxing legend Jake LaMotta. Former Batman actor Christian Bale lost what would be considered a dangerous amount of weight to play an insomniac in independent psychological thriller *The Machinist* (Anderson 2004), as did Matthew McConaughey in *Dallas Buyers Club* (Vallee 2013).

McConaughey won the American Academy Award for Best Actor for the role, yet his transformation could very well be considered a compensation due to the sheer amount of weight he lost. Performance is one of the most established compensations on our list, with individual portrayals commonly detached from the films they appear in for separate comment and critique. However, it is possible for an actor, through either transformation or performance style, to exceed the needs of the story. Instead, they become a distraction, a breaking of the fourth wall, a modern version of the star over-performing or "hamming" it up onstage as they constantly demand center stage at the expense of the overall storytelling. In McConaughey's example, the role could have been played equally well if he appeared very skinny, as opposed to a veritable walking skeleton. If the part were played by an actor unfamiliar to the general public, it would not have formed a compensation as the audience would have no previous image for comparison—but with a star of McConaughey's profile, the extreme transformation adversely affected the storytelling.

5. AUTHOR

Usually applied to the director, writer, producer, and occasionally even the institution ("from the production company / studio / distributor that brought you . . .") the author compensation relies on previous achievement. It is very much an extension of Aristotle's concept of ethos: the credible source of the work.[10]

As with actors, employing a previously critically or commercially successful filmmaker can always be viewed as a compensation as it is not strictly about the material. This is the strength of the auteur in any field. The alternative, sans marketing hook, would be to have a filmmaker equally capable in terms of skill but not renowned in any way. The reverse can also be considered true, that by definition the filmmaker can never be a compensation as they are part of the DNA of the film, their track record responsible for developing both their skills and their status.

Again, it is a matter of emphasis, as any of Aristotle's three pillars of persuasion could be used as compensations. In this case, if the logos is flawed and the pathos inadequate, the author needs to have significant gravitas to convince (perhaps be even a God of some kind).

Perhaps the test here is to consider emphasis in context. If the filmmaker is heavily marketed in the promotion of the film to the exclusion of most else, this could indicate compensation. Alternatively, if the storytelling is clearly substandard compared to the filmmaker's previous work, or if they are obviously not a good fit for the material—or even no longer fully functioning due to either illness or age—then this could be considered a compensatory use. An example of an awkward fit is Robert Wise, a director who achieved his most notable successes as the director of large-scale musicals (*West Side Story* 1961 and *The Sound of Music* 1965), being given the task of directing the first big-screen outing of the *Star Trek* franchise with *Star Trek: The Motion Picture* (1979). While the appointment certainly brought a sense of significance to the production, the result was tonally at odds with the original series, a slow-paced epic rather than a fun adventure.

6. VISUAL PLEASURE

Theories on how visual pleasure works are likely to be debated ad infinitum, yet there is general agreement across the critical, academic, and professional fields that visual pleasure is core to the cinematic experience on any platform.[11]

As all audiences are made up of individuals with their own nuanced tastes and desires, a definition is necessarily fragmented; what one finds pleasing another may not. Therefore, visual pleasure can be found in a variety of ways, be it the pleasure in seeing actors, performance, composition, editing, locations, design, props, light, color, or even choreography.[12] Much satisfaction can be had from the way that screen storytelling can juxtapose angle and motion, with movement long since held up as intrinsic to the form, literally "moving pictures." Such seemingly minor factors such as the film stock or codec used to encode the image can also provide a greater sense of joy for some.

The *Fifty Shades of Grey* film franchise (Taylor-Johnson 2015–2018) is a good illustration of visual pleasure as compensation, perhaps understandably so, as the filmmakers had to make some high-stakes creative choices with the source material. Originally erotic fan fiction based on the *Twilight* books and films (2005–2012), the novel was released in 2011 and became a publishing phenomenon, selling 15.2 million copies. The budget for the first film was US$40 million, which meant that it would have to make back approximately US$120 million just to break even.[13] This put great pressure on the project, especially as the books were borderline soft-core pornography, a genre unlikely to generate the amount of income needed.

As the ubiquity of pornography demonstrates, there is considerable visual and other pleasures to be had from showing explicit sex acts, but this is not an option for a conventional film studio. So it appears there was a transference of visual pleasure: if the actual sex was to be minimized in a story ostensibly about sex, then every other element needed to be beautified beyond the needs of the narrative, especially people and production design. It could be thought to be a strategy of prioritizing the sensual over the sexual.

It certainly worked financially, with *Fifty Shades of Grey* making a huge profit. Not so critically, as Joanna Weiss remarked in the *Boston Globe* in 2015, "There are several kinds of porn in 'Fifty Shades of Grey': house porn, clothes porn, closet porn, helicopter porn, all of them more interesting than the sex scenes that have caused so much breathless anticipation. Those come across as stiffly academic, a cataloguing of body parts and equipment. The passion is largely missing. The real appeal is the stuff."[14]

7. SPECTACLE

There is nothing suspect about the use of spectacle in mainstream narrative feature films; Aristotle explicitly talked of its justified use in drama in *Poetics*. Yet McKee is right to warn that "flawed and false storytelling is forced to substitute spectacle for substance, trickery for truth. Weak stories, desperate to hold audience attention, degenerate into multimillion-dollar razzle-dazzle demo reels."[15]

Spectacle is visual pleasure at scale. It can certainly be a primary genre convention, as any big-budget action-adventure will demonstrate. This is typified by the MCU (Marvel Cinematic Universe), where Disney/Marvel has used these separate film spectacles to create one overall extravaganza. The strategy does not always result in financial or critical success (as *Eternals* [Zhao 2021] and *The Marvels* [DaCosta 2023] illustrate) and has attracted some high-profile criticism from legendary directors Martin Scorsese and Francis Ford Coppola. Scorsese notes that the film series no longer resembles cinema: "Honestly, the closest I can think of them, as well made as they are, with actors doing the best they can under the circumstances, is theme parks. It isn't the cinema of human beings trying to convey emotional, psychological experiences to another human being." Coppola goes one stage further, commenting, "When Martin Scorsese says that the Marvel pictures are not cinema, he's right because we expect to learn something from cinema, we expect to gain something, some enlightenment, some knowledge, some inspiration."[16]

Examples of noncompensatory spectacle can be found in classic epics like *Ben Hur* (Wyler 1959) and *Cleopatra* (Mankiewicz 1963). Not only is spectacle a convention of the epic genre, but scale and awe are needed to communicate the power and reach of the respective emperors and empresses. *Inception* (Nolan 2010) uses its signature spectacle scene (the literal folding up of a city street) to underline the malleable nature of even the most permanent fixtures in a dream; it would not have worked anywhere near so well if all the character could manipulate was an apple.

8. SENSATION

Sensation as compensation is most commonly used in horror, action, and erotic/explicit thrillers and dramas. These primal reactions that exceed narrative necessity can be provoked in the direct visceral sense with use of imagery and sound that are intrinsically confronting, such as in the iconic body-shock work of John Carpenter in *The Thing* (1982) or Clive Barker in *Hellraiser* (1987), which attempt to trigger guttural feelings of disgust and fear. The sensations can also be triggered by plot moments, such as the execution of children in Lars von Trier's *The House That Jack Built* (2018), which inspired walk-outs at the Cannes Film Festival. Perhaps the ultimate sensation scene would be an objectively repulsive creature engaging in horrendous violence on an innocent who has just had explicit sex. If this scenario sounds familiar, it is because it is a staple of exploitation films.

However, extreme sensation can certainly be a genuine genre expectation of a mainstream film. The *Mad Max*–inspired *Saw* films (2004–) helped usher in a new genre of mainstream horror called "gorenography," named for terror built around graphic torture. The name implies that the genre should exist only in the exploitation world, but there is no doubting that the franchise exists very much in the mainstream (so much so that there is a *Saw*-themed rollercoaster at Thorpe Park in the United Kingdom).[17] These films exist in conventional cinema as the sensation is at the service of the story.

The alternative is violence or imagery that becomes an end in itself—the freak show—that may be a great talking point or meme (and thus perhaps financial success) but reduces the film to a needy look-at-me child, pushing outrageous limits simply to get attention. The critically acclaimed *Saltburn* (Fennell 2023) contains very specific gross-out moments clearly designed to get noticed. This is not to say these moments don't need to be shocking or repulsive, just a question of how shocking or how repulsive: a highly subjective artistic choice. Perhaps David Mamet provides a means test with his lament on modern cinema, "Films have degenerated to their original operation as carnival amusement—they offer not drama but thrills."[18]

9. WISH FULFILMENT

Similar to happy endings, feature film storytelling is particularly effective in creating and fulfilling desires. Whether the wish is formed by the film itself or was already something yearned for by the viewer, the story universe offers a fantasy where any dream can come true. These desires can be narrative-led (viewer wants the hero to get what they want), character-led (viewer wants to be the hero), world-led (viewer wants to place themselves in the fictional universe), or sensation-led (viewer wants the voyeuristic pleasure of the image).

A modern version of narrative wish fulfilment is demonstrated by *Knocked Up* (Apatow 2007), credited as launching not only writer/producer Judd Apatow's career (although he had previously enjoyed significant lower-profile success) but a whole new mode of American comedy. This modern take is notable in that, atypically, the hero does nothing deserving to get the girl yet gets her anyway. This is usually due to a plot contrivance (or more accurately plot ellipsis) that functions as pure wish fulfilment and fits neatly into the millennial zeitgeist.[19]

Wish fulfilment as compensation is typified by films like *Futureworld* (Heffron 1976), the sequel to writer/director Michael Crichton's original film version of *Westworld* (1973). Both stories deal with the heady wish-fulfilment "what if" premise of a theme park where you can live out your wildest fantasies with androids indistinguishable from humans. Yet whereas *Westworld* explored the dangers of humans relying too much on computers, *Futureworld* used them merely as a surface-level plot device. The film's antagonists executed a plan to replace politicians with robot doubles, yet this would have worked equally well with clones or plastic-surgery-altered humans. The former used the wish fulfilment as a fundamental thematic story element, the latter as a hook to carry a by-the-numbers thriller.

10. MUSIC

Aristotle believed that to make language pleasurable it must possess rhythm and melody: essentially be a song.[20] Here we refer to all uses of music—nondiegetic, diegetic, individual tracks, and score. Film takes strength from its ability to blend many art forms, with music a particularly potent tool as it comprises primarily emotional information. The canonical literature on directing focuses predominately on visuals, as if the art were still silent films and the interrelation of sound, music, and picture was not a core skill of the director. This may be as the incumbent view is, as composer Ennio Morricone comments, "While good music cannot save a bad film, even bad music cannot ruin a good film."[21]

So how is music used as a compensation? And how does this function with musicals?

The musical is a useful example as the genre expectations are explicit: a musical without music is not a musical. It is also expected that the performers sing, even if within the world of the film the characters do not. Yet as with assessing cast as compensation, it is a case of removing not the music but the emphasis, to see what remains.

Mama Mia! (Lloyd 2008) is one of the most financially successful live-action musicals of all time. It is sometimes referred to as a jukebox musical, as the songs come exclusively from preexisting chart-friendly tracks (in this case the back catalogue of Swedish supergroup ABBA). A jukebox musical is typically a nonintegrated musical, where the songs (and dances) don't advance the plot: music confirming a moment rather than creating one.[22]

The plot of *Mama Mia!* is remarkably similar to that of *Buona Sera, Mrs. Campbell* (Frank 1968), where the tension comes from a mother unsure of who is the father of her grown-up daughter. It comprises an all-star cast, including Meryl Streep, Colin Firth, and Pierce Brosnan, although none are notable singers. In the film, no songs drive the narrative—which puts them firmly in the sphere of compensations.

This is not to say that all songs in nonintegrated musicals are compensatory. Focusing on whether the songs in *Mama Mia!* (as opposed to the musical score) are functioning as compensations, it is not the tracks that have to be removed but ABBA. Does the film require the franchise power of the songs to tell its story effectively? Would it function just as well with music of equal quality but from an unknown source? The answer seems to be no. Another test is purely quantitative: Just how many songs were used? The more songs used, the more likely they are compensations.

A potential objection may be that the intention was always to construct a film around ABBA music, but this means only that the compensation was a deliberate act, not that the film functions in a different way. The choice makes perfect institutional sense as insurance against financial failure, as even if all other elements of the film fail, the audience is still guaranteed to see celebrities singing famous songs. In these cases, compensatory nonintegrated musicals (and similarly compensatory nonintegrated martial arts films) could be considered a subcategory of exploitation films tolerated by the mainstream due to their mild tone.

As Morricone mentioned, a musical score is more problematic to use as a compensation for the whole film, although it can certainly (and quite commonly) be used to compensate for momentary flaws. Take *Jaws* (Spielberg 1975), where the music was used as very conscious compensation for a nonworking mechanical shark. Yet ironically, despite the intention, the music does not qualify as compensatory as reliance on John Williams's score ultimately improved the storytelling.

11. PUZZLE SOLVING

This relates directly to Thomas Elsaesser's mind-game films, essentially a film that plays in any of a variety of different ways with its audience. The puzzle could be related to plot or theme. It could be that the character is being played with by others with good or bad intentions or that the audience is being played, by information withheld or obscurely presented. Elsaesser puts Jonathan Demme's *Silence of the Lambs* (1991) and Peter Weir's *The Truman Show* (1998) into the former category, and Bryan Singer's *The Usual Suspects* (1995) and David Fincher's *Fight Club* (1999) into the latter.[23]

Humans are meaning-making machines, and puzzle solving is a key narrative joy. In *S/Z: An Essay*, linguist Roland Barthes outlines his five codes of meaning that weave through every narrative (proairetic, semantic, symbolic, cultural, and hermeneutic),[24] and it is this last code to which the puzzle-solving compensation relates. The hermeneutic code is essentially storytelling through a series of enigmas, both major and minor. Noël Carroll developed his own "erotetic" model, which views the micro question-and-answer model as "the most characteristic narrative approach in movies," as the implication is that the film will answer a major enigma at the close, through the answering of the minor enigmas throughout the narrative.[25]

Some directors specialize in this mode of storytelling. If Alfred Hitchcock is considered the master of suspense, then filmmaker Christopher Nolan could be regarded as the master of the narrative puzzle. His films typically play with nonlinear structures that require some reassembly by the viewer, be it telling a story largely backward in *Memento* (2000) or characters moving simultaneously forward and backward in time as the palindromic title suggests in *Tenet* (2020). This approach can sometimes frustrate audiences, especially if the puzzle appears too difficult to solve: *Tenet* came in for much criticism on its impenetrability. On the awards-trail press tour for *Oppenheimer* (2023), which ultimately rewarded Nolan with his first Best Director Academy Award, Nolan took the surprising step to claim that his films are not puzzles to be solved where everything is meant to be understood. "I think that where people encounter frustrations with my narratives in the past is sometimes I think they are slightly missing the point. It's not a puzzle to be unpacked. It's an experience to be had. . . . I have to have my idea of it [a plot point] to be a valid, productive ambiguity, but the point of it is it's an ambiguity."[26]

This view is surprising as his films are undeniably presented as puzzles to be solved (as opposed to the deliberately obscure David Lynch mysteries) and implies a (false) separation of puzzle solving from the overall cinematic experience. Nolan's films can sometimes infuriate not because they can be ambiguous but because clarity is presented as possible, even probable; they fall foul of the principle outlined by director Alexander Mackendrick that there's nothing wrong with ambiguity as long as it's clear that it's ambiguous.[27]

But how does film as puzzle work as a compensation? It relates to how reliant the film is on mosaic-style storytelling. If the mystery is intriguing enough, if the solution is original, bold, or ingenious enough, it could compensate for flaws in argumentation. Put another way, once the trick is revealed, is there anything functional left behind?

Both macro and micro puzzles contribute to puzzle as compensation. There is significant pleasure not just in tracking the main puzzle but also in observing (and speculating) how the smaller puzzles lead up to the big reveal. The quality of this final revelation is obviously key, where puzzle as compensation functions in the same way as spectacle; if the impact is strong enough, if it is "water cooler" worthy, it compensates.

M. Night Shyamalan's *The Sixth Sense* (1999) is a great example of this effect. The story of a psychiatrist attempting to help a child who can "see dead people," it hides information from both main character and audience. Another spoiler alert: the final twist that the psychiatrist has been dead for most of the film has made it one of the more memorable plot twists in recent cinema.

Yet once this reveal has been made, the film does not pass scrutiny from even the most cursory of reflections. Only the moments that work for communicating the mystery of the narrative are shown to the audience. The internal rules of the world give the psychiatrist substantial issues: For instance, despite being in public, did he not wonder why he could not interact with anyone else but the boy? It is certainly a story-logic flaw, but is it an allowable one? Is the puzzle of the film an intrinsic part of the storytelling or just a trick?

To apply our subtraction test, if you present the film in a straightforward way (either by making the audience aware of the protagonist's postmortem character from the start or by removing the twist altogether so he simply isn't dead), does it weaken the argument? Obviously, it depends on how you characterize the argument, but if we agree that it is making a case about the need to face your fears, then it is certainly augmented by the emotional reveal that the main character personifies this more than anyone else. All his decisions have not been simply to help another but to avoid what he most dreads. Using this rationale, the puzzle and twist structure may not have been perfectly executed, but they are not acting as compensations.

12. PROMISE OF THE PREMISE

In *Save the Cat: The Last Book on Screenwriting You'll Ever Need,* screenwriter Blake Snyder discusses the idea of the promise of the premise and the related theory of the obligatory scene. In a high-concept romantic comedy, such as *How to Lose a Guy in 10 Days* (Petrie 2003), the premise is that, for the purposes of a feature story, a female reporter starts dating a man (who doesn't know she's a reporter) specifically to make every possible dating mistake until he has no choice but to break up with her. Unbeknownst to her, the man has a separate running bet with his boss that he can make any woman fall in love with him. Both set a deadline of ten days. The promise of the premise comprises sequences that take full advantage of the guy-tolerating-outrageous-dump-worthy actions from the reporter. These are a logical extrapolation of the premise, and their absence would represent a major disappointment in the eyes of the audience. The obligatory scene(s) are a scene or scenes that are not just those that fulfil the promise of the premise but are significant plot points: the falling in love (for real) scene, the scene where he finds out she is a reporter, and the ending up with each other scene.

When do these elements function as compensations? The definition of premise here is as a plot hook only, not a thematic idea or a fully developed argument. In a film series such as *The Fast and the Furious* (2001–), the promise of the premise is to have superfast, ultraglamorous car chases with outrageously expensive customized vehicles. The concept would function as a compensation only if the film was almost exclusively composed of these sequences with very little narrative motivating them (much like a nonintegrated musical). The obligatory scene would be the final, biggest chase sequence and would qualify as a compensation for the same reasons: nonintegrated and/or the glamour exceeding the needs of the narrative or genre conventions.[28]

The *Rocky* franchise (1976–) supplies a striking example of this kind of compensation. The promise of the premise is the fight at the end of the film, and a key obligatory scene the training montage. In the first two films, the training montages were joyous and very much at the service of the story, yet by the time of *Rocky IV* (Stallone 1985) the montages (albeit not all training montages) had a combined running time of twenty-nine minutes and ten seconds, constituting just under 32 percent of the entire running time of the film.

13. RECOGNITION OF SELF

Aristotle talks of recognition in *Poetics*, but his form was concerned with tragic characters moving from ignorance to knowledge.[29] This variant of recognition is linked to what he believed moved an audience from pity to fear: the sense that the character could be them.

As we've noted previously, Sinnerbrink suggests that audiences can derive meaning from engaging with fictional characters and their perspectives through either emotional connection or estrangement.[30] Audiences can experience enhanced engagement if they recognize themselves in a character or recognize in them an element of themselves they identify with or wish to hold.

For recognition of self to function as a compensation there must be significant alignment between audience member and character, but what element creates this alignment is almost impossible to predict; this makes the compensation less likely to be an encoded insurance when the film is developed. What connects the viewer to the character also does not require much screen time: it could a jacket the character wears, a gesture they make, their voice, a turn of phrase, an attitude, hair, a look, a sense of humor, a personality, a character flaw, a fashion sense, or life or work circumstances. For instance, in *Malcolm X* (Lee 1992), connection to Malcolm X can be through aspirations to his determination or simply how he physically conducts himself moment to moment. Yet once impact has been made and maintained, the compensation can be absolute.[31]

Recognition of self and the consequent connection between audience and character is highly dependent, not just on the writing or staging of the film but on the energy and charisma (or lack of it) of the actor. This connection will always function as a compensation, as the film clearly does not require this strength of feeling from the audience in order to function—yet if it is present most flaws of a film can be overlooked or forgiven.

14. DIALOGUE

Aristotle devoted entire sections of *Poetics* to the importance of what he termed diction, understandable as he was primarily discussing forms of drama that relied far more on the spoken word. For Aristotle, a sign of impressive diction was the appropriate use of metaphor. He believed it could not be taught and was a sign of natural talent.[32]

Dialogue serves many functions in a film narrative: provides thematic nuance and gives the audience a sense of time, place, character, and plot information. Some filmmakers attempt to stay away from dialogue, creatively leaning mostly on image and music (see any of Sergio Leone's Spaghetti Westerns). Others push dialogue into a realm where it becomes a key joy of the film experience itself (Aaron Sorkin and Quentin Tarantino are perhaps the most famous current Hollywood examples of this, almost to the extent of self-parody). Their dialogue is expansive and dominates the picture to such a degree that minimal camera movement is used so as not to distract from the voices. David Fincher, a director known for virtuoso movement of the camera, kept it particularly static for *The Social Network* (Fincher 2010) to allow Sorkin's dialogue to take center stage.[33] It is likely a compensation when not a genre expectation (although arguably Sorkin and Tarantino are now genres in their own right) and the deliberate verbosity serves no dramatic purpose.

15. STRONG SEQUENCES

Although these sequences are usually manifestations of the promise of the premise or the obligatory scene—think the sinking of the Titanic in *Titanic* (Cameron 1997) or the final courtroom confrontation in *A Few Good Men* (Reiner 1992)—it is not necessary for them to be expected or demanded by the audience. A strong sequence is simply an extended sequence that justifies, both literally and figuratively, the admission price alone, providing enough satisfaction to sustain flaws in other areas.

Many contemporary Hollywood directors, especially action directors, appear to be more masters of the sequence than the overall film. The aforementioned *Titanic* is a relatively uninflected upstairs/downstairs romance, but the hour-long sequence of the ship sinking is (by most accounts) breathtaking. A film that comprises three or four of these sequences is likely to perform well critically and commercially, however problematic the overall storytelling.

16. "BASED ON A TRUE STORY"

In *Film Adaptation and Its Discontents: From "Gone with the Wind" to "The Passion of the Christ,"* Thomas Leitch notes that films predicated with a "Based on a True Story" logline are "authorless, publisherless, agentless. Because the description may be claimed or not at the filmmakers' pleasure, it appears only when it is to the film's advantage."[34]

For Leitch, the strategic benefits are initially issues not of fact or truth but of authority. He acknowledges film's ability to persuade and sees the "Based on a True Story" tag as a targeted way to strengthen the argument. It aims to take judgment away from the audience, to present the fiction as fact, not argument, in a way that mimics Bakhtin's authoritative discourse, one that invites not a response, just agreement or obedience.[35] Leitch further acknowledges that the tag functions as "a support for stories that might well have trouble standing on their own."[36]

Therefore, by a simple appeal to real life, the claim that "this really happened" can be a compelling compensation. It can make up for almost all flaws: character inconsistencies, plotting inconsistencies, or lack of argumentative logic. For instance, would *The Wolf of Wall Street* (Scorsese 2013), a completely derivative story of an amoral stock trader, really have been taken as seriously by both critics and audiences if it had merely been classed as pure fabrication? *Fargo* (Coen and Coen 1996) also traded very strongly on the idea that the plot was based on a real case, but the filmmakers subsequently admitted that it was just another element of the fiction.

This compensation also directly relates back to Aristotle's ethos. What better source is there than objective truth?

17. NOVELTY

In marketing, the Unique Selling Point (USP) dominates. What about your product separates it from others? Are you the first to market? In business, the first mover advantage applies to individuals and companies moving into a new market—the earliest entrant can establish market dominance and brand recognition in their field.[37] While films, being a single product (as opposed to a single type of product, such as Velcro), cannot dominate a market in the same way, first to market is nonetheless a demonstration of uniqueness.

Take *Boyz n the Hood* (Singleton 1991). Released not long before the 1992 LA riots, it is credited as the first film to really present the Black South Central LA experience, without the use of stereotype or caricature. Not only was it a huge financial and critical success, but also heralded as having a significant impact on American culture. Singleton went on to become the first Black (and overall youngest) Academy Award nominee for Best Director.

This newness can apply to the whole film or a single element. *Thank You for Smoking* (Reitman 2005) was the first commercially prominent film to show the big tobacco lobbyist world from the inside (and with a lobbyist as the hero); most of the film's running time and inventiveness are spent establishing this reality to the audience. There is very little actual drama present, and if there had been another film set within the same world, perhaps it would not have fared so well financially (making back over six times its budget in cinemas) or critically (an 86 percent score on Rotten Tomatoes). Consider, by contrast, a minimally dramatic film set among the familiar world of a jury, for instance.

From Dusk Till Dawn (Rodriguez 1996) was the first mainstream American film to emphatically and self-consciously switch genres halfway through its running time (crime thriller to horror comedy), an oddity but also an attempt to explore a new method of filmic storytelling. *Bullitt* (Yates 1968) was the first mainstream film to show an extended car chase, at ten minutes and fifty-three seconds, and the first to use the San Francisco streets as a location for the chase (which has been so often repeated now it has become a trope of its own).

As the concept of novelty is contextual rather than textual, it follows that a film manifesting it will always survive if it is removed—yet this is not always the case. As always, emphasis is key, and a level of extremity or boldness is necessary to indicate compensation: a character wearing black shoes for the first time on-screen will hardly function as compensation, but the first film to feature 3D, IMAX, or (as in the case of 1950s American cinema) "smello-vision" may find that this element compensates for other significant issues.

18. HOMAGE

Homage is a sincere allusion or imitation of one artist or artwork by another, with respect or sometimes even reverence given. In film terms, it is usually achieved by the inclusion of props, characters, production design, dialogue, or direct mimicking of shots. This intertextual doffing of the cap to a previous master or masterful film can be self-indulgently obscure or used to create a shared sense of connection with the audience (see Fan Service, below).

At the extreme end of homage is pastiche and parody. Pastiche is the making of an entire film in the mode of an older film or genre, such as *Far from Heaven* (Haynes 2002), a romantic drama set in the 1950s and made as if in the 1950s, probably by Douglas Sirk. Its director, Todd Haynes, returned to pastiche with *Carol* (2015). By contrast, parody is the lampooning of genre tropes (either affectionate or otherwise) for comic effect, perfected in modern cinema by Mel Brooks (see the Western *Blazing Saddles* [1974], classic horror *Young Frankenstein* [1974], Hitchcockian thriller *High Anxiety* [1977], and science-fiction adventure *Spaceballs* [1987] for the best examples). A film such as *Ready Player One* (Spielberg 2018) sits between the two extremes, being neither a pastiche nor parody but nostalgically constructed almost entirely of references to other films, computer games, and pop-culture ephemera.

The test for compensation cannot simply be to remove the references, as this will almost immediately fall foul of the appeal to genre conventions: you cannot remove what makes a film a pastiche or parody and have it remain within genre. A better test is to think of pastiche and parody as multigenre (sci-fi-comedy parody, horror-pastiche) and then to remove knowledge of the original referenced work(s): Does *Far from Heaven* succeed as a drama and in its argumentation if the audience is not aware it's a pastiche? If the answer is yes, it is not a compensation. Yet paradoxically the answer can also be no, and it will not be a compensation if key argumentation is genuinely reliant on the pastiche. This is often the case with satire, but there is a difference between authentic satire and meaningless genre trope references.

Ready Player One presents an interesting conundrum. The film still functions for audiences unaware it is referencing other popular media, but these references are strongly emphasized, present in most scenes of the film. The scale of those callbacks provides compensation for what is a relatively straightforward action-adventure, a genre that does not require homage.

19. FAN SERVICE

In "Superhero Fan Service: Audience Strategies in the Contemporary Interlinked Hollywood Blockbuster," Bart Beaty defines fan service as a series of narrative "rewards" that are established in the film.[38] Fan service has its origins in the Japanese world of anime and manga, where catering to clearly articulated fan desires was initially oriented around gratuitous titillation.[39]

However, the entry of fan service into mainstream cinema has broadened the definition, which now includes any intertextual references that the perceived audience desires, the wish fulfilment compensation on a micro scale. Beaty delineates fan service into five distinct categories, including post-credit scenes, Easter eggs, and crossovers. Each category is designed to reward the audience and create a hierarchy of fandom based on their level of engagement with and knowledge of the source material. This is key, as a primary goal is to deepen the engagement of casual viewers.[40]

Fan service is primarily the domain of franchises, as there first must be fans to service. Almost any film from the MCU would serve as a case study, but *Star Wars: Episode VII—The Force Awakens* (Abrams 2015) is perhaps the epitome of fan service as compensation. For the first Disney production from one of the most successful film franchises in history (and the first not to be overseen by series creator George Lucas), failure on any level was unthinkable. The story, taking place thirty years after the original *Star Wars* trilogy (1977–1983), concerns the next generation of heroes fighting against a resurgence of the old, ruthlessly totalitarian Empire.

From the broadest possible perspective, any sequel(s) can be considered a form of fan service, and there was much public discussion alternately berating and praising the film for making it a clear priority over the needs of the storytelling.[41] The emphasis on the fan service elements was viewed to be excessive and so, by our terms, compensatory. In no particular order the fan service included the use of legacy cast members and key props (Han, Luke, and Leia and the Millennium Falcon), introduction of a new cute droid BB8 (servicing both fan and merchandising needs), overreliance on contrived light saber duels and space battles, and various Easter eggs such as hidden celebrity cameos from film stars Daniel Craig and Simon Pegg.

In fact, the entire film is essentially an homage to the original *Star Wars,* even down to the precise visual look, with the choice of grading and mise-en-scène contributing to the sense of both pastiche and remix. The two *Ghostbusters* reboots, *Ghostbusters: Afterlife* (Reitman 2021) and *Ghostbusters: Frozen Empire* (Kenan 2024) also fall foul of fan service as compensation for similar reasons: flawed argumentation not successfully disguised by the appearance of legacy cast members, props, echoes of previous scenes, and cynical merchandising opportunities. In their cases the films are direct homages to the original films, but with an almost devout reverence for the lighthearted source material that creates a tonal disconnect even though they are set in the same fictional universe.

20. OBSCURITY

The final compensation is the least used with the highest chance of failure. It is essentially compensation by confusion, based on the logic that it is preferable to be obscure than to showcase obvious issues. This is problematic as a compensation usually provides joy to distract from a fault, so covering the defect with a larger deficiency seems an inevitable misstep. However, as we noted with David Lynch, a section of the audience can delight in the impenetrable.

In this way, the compensation could function as a subset of puzzle solving, but in reverse—not satisfaction from solving a puzzle but enjoyment from wrestling with an enigma that can never be fully understood, be it Lynch's *Inland Empire* (2006), Shane Carruth's *Primer* (2004), or even Fellini's *8½* (1963). The usual test of subtraction still stands: Would the film's argument be weakened or undermined if the aspect of the film in question were removed or substituted with a noncompensatory equivalent? This would mean clarity of presentation and/or meaning, so the only films that could answer yes would be those where obscurity is central to the conclusion or the making of the argument.

CHAPTER 9

The End

TO JUMP RIGHT in and embrace the meta, this book has been an argument about arguments: making the case that feature filmmaking is the practice of making cases. Did it convince you? Or did you dismiss it out of hand? Perhaps you require more evidence before you make a decision, whether you choose to find it from filmic or other sources. Either way, thank you for reading and engaging in the debate. I'd like to think it has stimulated or galvanized your own thoughts on the fundamentals of feature filmmaking. As noted earlier in the book, my own journey to film-as-worthwhile-argument started with an outright rejection of another set of ideas.[1] Yet perhaps there is a third way: you broadly agree with the underlying theories but have spotted some flaws in the argument. So you'll evolve the concept yourself, take on some of the concepts we've discussed to mold into your own approach.

This book is, unfortunately, not a feature film (although I'd be utterly fascinated to see what a fictional adaptation would look like), so alas this final chapter will provide no big plot twists, nor a surprising yet inevitable ending to wow you. But it can still adhere to some storytelling conventions, such as coming full circle, the mythical coming back home, hopefully with some insight.

To return to our central metaphor, the double-sided headpiece could very much be the motif for the entire book. There is a strong dual nature to this work. It serves two masters: the filmgoer who wishes to improve their appreciation of the form and the filmmaker who wishes to improve the quality of their films. The heart of the book is unapologetic in its spiritual alignment with the filmmaker, but even within that priority there is a split. As flagged on the first pages, this is not a conventional book on creative film technique. In fact, it has a distinct Schrödinger's cat quality, simultaneously being and not being a book on how to make successful mainstream feature films.

If you are a filmmaker, it has clearly not told you what types of events should happen to trigger the story, precisely on what page the first act should shift into the second, nor how to create nuanced characters that will live forever in the collective imagination. Conversely, it has told you many technical and conceptual ways that will make your films function successfully, much like any other conventional "how-to" guide. It has shown how to structure your stories using the fundamentals of argument, how they manifest in character and situation, and how to present your overall case for maximum impact.

Aristotle and Feature Filmmaking

I stand by my belief that there can never be too much Aristotle. But it is worth clarifying if film-as-worthwhile-argument represents a new understanding of the form or the rediscovery of an old one.

Obviously, Aristotle was working in a time before cinema, so his concepts and analysis could not be applied specifically to feature filmmaking. He does invoke his *Rhetoric* in *Poetics*, but as we have explored, his intentions and use of it were very different from ours. As with all research into the great philosopher, as much of his work is suspected lost, we can never be sure if there isn't some missing piece that will align with our current thinking.

To go by his existing works, with the assumption that they have been correctly translated, we can confidently claim that film-as-worthwhile-argument is based on fundamentally Aristotelian ideas drawn directly from his work on drama, argument, and ethics. These ideas have been further developed into the defining working methodology of feature filmmaking and applied for the first time in this way to this form.

Danger Danger

What is undeniably clear is that the mainstream film industry does not officially conceive of feature films in this way, so the ideas represent a substantial shift in received wisdom—perhaps even a dangerous one. If filmmakers do decide to adhere to the film-as-worthwhile-argument principles, will it unleash a nightmare wave of filmic didacticism, of obviously agenda-led and hopelessly dull features? Or if the industry openly admits that films are intrinsically mechanisms of persuasion, would it open the door to litigation, strict regulation, and censorship, perhaps even an existential threat?

To first address concerns of an unwelcome flood of preachy films, the short answer is that if there was an (improbable) full revolution, with film-as-worthwhile-argument instantly absorbed into conventional thinking as a valid and practical understanding of the process, then yes there will be a period of readjustment, even if only on the individual level. The work may initially suffer, but this will most often be in private. Inexperienced writers and directors may create obvious work, but this is simply a question of craft, talent, and skill and will inevitably improve.

As for the industry becoming more accountable for its influence, even if it was accepted that film-as-worthwhile-argument was the sole underlying purpose of the practice, it should remain business as usual. Even with research such as Green and Brock's, it will never be possible to definitively prove the impact of any media on human behavior.[2] Studies will always be able to discuss the contributions of media and their cumulative effects (especially social media, whose main creative professionals are literally called influencers), but no one film or form will take the blame.

To put any remaining anxious minds fully to rest, there will be no revolution. The more realistic question is whether or not filmmakers and the industry at large will embrace the ideas outlined here at all. As with all new ways of thinking, not everyone will be convinced, and unless the concepts somehow go viral (unlikely, alas), at worst the gatekeepers can expect a trickle rather than a surge. Some natural resistance is also highly probable. Film-as-worthwhile-argument is certainly not the only way to understand the process, even if there is extensive evidence to support it, but we are also making the claim (without prejudice) that filmmakers either have misunderstood and/or are largely unaware of the essential nature of their practice, a minor but uncomfortable truth that will inevitably face some opposition.

So what else can we offer a potentially reluctant industry to persuade and even reassure them that film-as-worthwhile-argument is beneficial to their practice and not simply a matter of making obviously woke-style or partisan films, whatever their personal, social, or political agenda?

The ongoing benefit of self-awareness is clear and significant, as it would be in any field. How can you do your best work when you don't understand the fundamental nature of what you do? Incognizant practitioners spend resources in the wrong areas, and successes are overly dependent upon luck. It is not enough to simply have the innate virtues of a great filmmaker, as the very concept of internal goods shows that these are no guarantee of excellence. A filmmaker can be brave, honest, curious, creatively compassionate, and generous—yet still fail.

Virtues allow for success, but skills development is critical for filmmakers to reach their full potential. What is rare about the film industry is that we buy the product before we see it, and if it is obviously defective we don't expect a refund. Ask yourself how many bad films you've seen this year, however you define quality. How many truly impacted you that you'll see again or will make it into your personal all-time top fifty? We live in a cinema of compensation and tolerate a very low hit ratio for movies. This should not be the case.

The sell to the industry is both financial and creative. Understanding film-as-worthwhile-argument should mean a higher percentage of screen stories connecting with their audiences, allowing for consistency of product: those mythic repeatable, returnable, and predictable successes.

Cinematic Darwinism

All social practice evolves over time. Film-as-worthwhile-argument is a description of the process at this precise moment in history. But the screen industries are currently in a period of great flux. Both large and small institutions, especially the streamers, are continuing to disrupt, changing not just how mainstream feature films are financed and made but how they are seen. Since the rise of television and home video, it has been a long time since feature films were seen by most in the cinema, and this will continue to fragment.

The recent rise of generative artificial intelligence (Gen AI) is yet another disruptor. It is affecting every field, and we are at the start of what could be a significant evolution of how all humans live their lives on a day-to-day basis. It has already had a seismic impact on the screenwriting profession and will inevitably change the way we create and tell screen stories. There are already companies, such as software giant Adobe, pushing the idea that soon we'll just be able to write a few prompts and push a "make movie" button.[3]

It may seem dispiriting, but we are likely to see some films in the near future conceived of, written, and visualized completely by machines, featuring wholly Gen AI actors. Based on the history of the human race and its relationship to technology, I have no doubt this will happen, including all hybrid variations (films written by machines but featuring real performers, and vice versa). But I also know these new Gen AI films will represent just one more creative path among others already established or yet to be invented. To temper any potential distress, consider these films more as hybrid animations than typical live action: Gen AI is far more likely to generate whole new genres rather than replace existing ones. Human audiences still crave human connection, and a balance will be found with these new tools.[4]

So to frame this another way, I hope the impact of this book is such that it affects both the hearts of minds of a new generation of human filmgoer and filmmaker, even if the ultimate sign of success would be integration into all future Gen AI screenwriting and image generation programs (maybe with a "make argument" subroutine?). It's both exciting and terrifying that the impact in the medium and long term is completely unknown.[5]

So barring a full Terminator or HAL takeover by the machines, what next for film-as-worthwhile-argument? There is still much work to be done. Just as you, the reader, might wish to take some of the component parts to formulate your own version of the theory, it will continue to develop.

One path is to deep-dive into specifics. We have not examined precisely what arguments are being made to isolate any potential tendencies and, if trends can be found, if there is an explanation for them. This belongs in the realm of scholarship sometimes referred to as literary Darwinism: research into the evolution of narratives, why some stories survive, some thrive, and others diminish. Anthropologist Daniel Smith has tracked specific stories and found evidence to support their significant (but not decisive) impact on human behavior.[6] Such research would extend our analysis by providing hard data to illustrate any potentially dominant arguments told and retold in a cinematic context and their levels of internal and external success.

Genre also has a huge impact on the kinds of cinematic arguments made. In *The Screenwriters Taxonomy: A Roadmap to Creative Storytelling*, Eric R. Williams provides a phenomenally exhaustive account of the possibilities of feature film genre. He systematizes various categories and levels and how their combinations and permutations result in diverse and innovative film stories. When talking about audience test screenings, film and television director Ken Kwapis (*The Office* 2005–2013) notes that audiences are more likely to apply the word "excellent" to "films of an edifying nature" than to a genre film. He cites *Schindler's List* and *12 Years a Slave* (McQueen 2013) as examples and broadens the usual meaning of genre film to include comedy as well as typically horror, action, fantasy, and science fiction.[7] In the same way that films are particularly well suited to enthymemic arguments that attempt to convince us of original conceptual points, it should be possible to fully categorize what arguments (and kinds of arguments) are most common or effective in which genres.

We have also only touched quite lightly upon the idea of presenting cinematic arguments as puzzles, but this technique is highly complex and deserving of further exploration.

This leads to a return of the notion of worthwhile, a word so fundamental to our understanding of feature filmmaking that the theory uses it twice. We've currently defined worthwhile filmic argumentation as that which does not rely on unreasonable manipulation or the compensations. But it does currently allow for a broad range of inclusions. To argue in a worthwhile way includes fulfilling the social contract with the audience by both meeting general cinematic obligations and sincerely dealing with genre expectations. This includes things such as visual pleasure, basic engagement, and entertainment. The latter is often accounted for by these expectations (a comedy that does not seek to entertain is not a comedy), but a more nuanced definition that relates to specific genres may be of use.

Perhaps Aristotle will continue to guide and inform us. Or new thought leaders will emerge. In other words, and in keeping with the dual nature of the book, this is the end. But also not the end.

ACKNOWLEDGMENTS

THE IDEA THAT authoring a book is primarily a solitary writing experience is, to keep the dual nature theme going, both true and not true. There is much time spent alone at the keyboard (or lying on the bed) typing or, as often, not typing. But there are also so many who have contributed in a myriad of different but critical ways to the completion of this work.

First, thank you to my wife, Lucy: life advisor, book advisor, proofreader, rock, inspiration, my outsourced second brain (the one that remembers all the names). I am also so very grateful to my children, mostly for not complaining when I was obviously not as present as I should have been or would somehow quietly disappear, only to be found at the computer. Heartfelt thanks to my editor Nicole Solano from Rutgers University Press, for both believing in this book and being particularly kind with deadlines. I'd like to thank my fellow colleagues in the department of Film, Screen and Creative Media at Bond University, with special mention reserved for Damian Cox, whose wise counsel was always gratefully received; I always feel smarter after our conversations. Gratitude also to Bren Simson, Billy Frolick, Felix Thompson, Ted Geoghegan, John Sweet, Ivan Vukusic, and Sam Timms for their support and encouragement at various steps along the way.

I'd like to recognize the many renowned and unreasonably generous filmmakers and academics who gave their valuable time and insight to help test and refine the ideas, especially Paul Thompson from NYU Tisch School of the Arts, Richard Walter and Wendall Thomas from the UCLA School of Theater, Film and Television, and Jamal Joseph and Ira Deutchman from

Columbia University School of the Arts. Even though we have never met, my warmest appreciation also to the many thought leaders referenced here: the film gurus, philosophers, academics, critics, and journalists who have spent their lifetimes researching and expressing just how films work; what they can, should, and do mean to all of us. I hope that even when I disagree with a point or perspective, my respect and admiration (and sometimes awe) is clear: it has been a pleasure immersing myself in your worlds.

This book would also not have been in any way possible without the thousands of students I have been fortunate to teach over the years. Early on in my career I had the epiphany that I was as happy in the classroom as I was on set and that the two inevitably inform the other. Students have been instrumental in developing the ideas for this book: the ultimate alpha testers.

Just before the final thanks, I'd also like to make a slightly different acknowledgment, one that I may not be able to make again: that this book has been completed end to end without any use of artificial intelligence whatsoever, whether it be embedded into a search engine or used to brainstorm or copilot. This is not meant to be taken as a statement of defiance, as I am always keen to see how new tools of all kinds can help us, but it feels important to mark the moment.

So, finally, to Aristotle. Just thank you. In this book, as in life, I find there's always something to be gained from just a little more Aristotle.

NOTES

Chapter 1 What's the Big Secret?

1. Famous for giving one of the most popular TED talks of all time, Simon Sinek outlines his Golden Circle concept in his 2011 book *Start with Why: How Great Leaders Inspire Everyone to Take Action*. The logic is based in neuroscience, using the principle that people respond best when messages connect with the limbic area of the brain, which controls trust, loyalty, emotion, behavior, and decision-making. It's also referred to as an inside-out approach to business. Outside-in would be starting with the product rather than the mission statement of the company (the vision, the story, the reason the company exists). The order should be purpose (why), process (now), result (product). To apply this directly to film-as-worthwhile-argument, the breakdown would be as follows:

Why: to enrich the lives of others by giving them insight into the human condition through our personal perspective
How: by moving them to a worthwhile conclusion in a worthwhile way using argumentative methodology
What: using mainstream narrative feature films

According to Sinek, the "what" element engages the rational area of the brain, the least likely to influence behavior.

2. One of the best examples of this is John Yorke's 2015 book *Into the Woods: A Five-Act Journey into Story*. It makes the case that five acts, rather than the more common three, constitute the unifying shape of all stories, screen-based or otherwise. Unlike Sinek, Yorke begins with what constitutes a story and ends with why we tell them.

3. In addition to MacIntyre's explanation-by-purpose teleological approach, his theories have been chosen due to their ubiquity across multiple disciplines. Their impact is such that when discussing educational theory in his 2011 article "Refurbishing MacIntyre's Account of Practice," Paul Hager begins with the question, "Why have MacIntyre's views on practice enjoyed such pre-eminence amongst philosophers of education, seemingly to the exclusion of other writers on the topic?" In over three decades since his publication, MacIntyre has experienced relatively little contestation to his fundamental concepts. Critics, typified by Hager and David Miller ("Virtues, Practices and Justice"), focus more on the application of these concepts to specific practices, tending to discuss what qualifies as a practice and evolving MacIntyre's definitions and tacit implications rather than attacking the underlying principles. Lacey ("MacIntyre, Feminism and the Concept of Practice") applies a feminist analysis of social practices and a defense of the notion of evil practices.

4. This definition of a social practice is more complex than those offered by Bourdieu (*Outline of a Theory of Practice*) and Giddens (*New Rules of Sociological Method*), both more conventional sociological theorists.

5. MacIntyre, *After Virtue*, 191.

6. Aristotle, *Poetics*, x.

7. MacIntyre, *After Virtue*, 188–189.

8. MacIntyre, 190.

9. Aristotle, *Nicomachean Ethics*, 2.

10. According to MacIntyre, Homer believes virtues are secondary to a social role, Aristotle believes they are secondary to the good life for man (conceived as the telos of human action), and Franklin believes they are secondary to utility (*After Virtue*, 186).

11. MacIntyre, 192.

12. These virtues are based on my own reflective practice as a professional screenwriter and director for the past three decades, including observation, interaction, and working relationships with those filmmakers who are generally well regarded by their casts, crews, peers, and audiences.

13. Leigh, "What Is David Lynch's Inland Empire About?"

14. The Spider-Verse sequels may come in two halves, but as the many public discourses surrounding the film indicate, that does not mean it is a well-received tradition of the practice. At a public screening of *Across the Spider-Verse* that I attended, the film received boos from an otherwise placid audience when the "to be continued" graphic appeared on the screen.

15. Mittell notes that the television serial "is less of a linear storytelling object than a sprawling library of narrative content that might be consumed via a wide

range of practices, sequences, fragments, moments, choices, and repetitions" (*Complex TV*, 7).

16. Plunkett, "Breaking Bad Creator Vince Gilligan." Such autonomy is still notably scarce, often the case of either having tremendous immediate success or flying under the radar long enough (and being able to be produced cheaply enough) to build an audience that provides some hope of longevity. Yet this does not mean that a planned ending is necessarily satisfying: the abrupt finish of *The Sopranos* (Chase 1999–2007) was not uniformly praised.

17. One high-profile case was the firing of celebrated screenwriter and director Frank Darabont as showrunner of *The Walking Dead* (Darabont 2010–2022) despite being the series creator (Patten, "'Walking Dead' Lawsuit Settled"). The resultant lawsuit was eventually settled in Darabont's favor.

18. It should be noted that the difference in these terms is purely marketing-based, with head of the U.S. television network FX John Landgraf explaining that the term "mini-series" is tainted as "it became synonymous with big, cheesy melodrama" (quoted in Rose and Goldberg, "Executive Quiz").

19. Stefansky, "How TV's Demons, Aliens and Dragons Are Getting More Cinematic."

20. For a rhetorical analysis of how arguments may be presented visually and aurally, see Alcolea-Banegas, "Visual Arguments in Film."

21. Novelist and screenwriter Roald Dahl said of film director Lewis Gilbert, "What I admired so much about Lewis Gilbert was that he just took the screenplay and shot it. That's the way to direct: You either trust your writer or you don't" (Pulver, "Spy Who Loved Me Director"). In *On Directing Film* (1992), playwright and filmmaker David Mamet is even more blunt about the art of directing, stating that the director is but a Dionysian version of the screenwriter (xv) and further, as somewhat of Kuleshov-effect fundamentalist, that directors tell the story through "a juxtaposition of images that are basically uninflected" (2).

22. Mateer, "Directing for Cinematic Virtual Reality." Mateer refers to Melanie Green and Timothy Brock's 2000 study, "The Role of Transportation in the Persuasiveness of Public Narratives," which provides the definition of transportation as absorption into a narrative world. Green and Brock believe that audiences "may show effects of the story on their real world beliefs" (701). Mateer defines transportation as "presence."

23. Mateer, "Directing for Cinematic Virtual Reality," 18.

24. It is worthy of note that most current film directing literature adds very little to any overall conception of mainstream feature filmmaking as a social practice due to the primarily translative nature of the work.

Chapter 2 The Other Half of the Story

1. In a recent example of fact following fiction, in 1997 the major credit card companies began using the same technique and introduced CVC numbers on the reverse of their cards to combat online fraud.

2. Brenes, "Quoting and Misquoting Aristotle's 'Poetics.'"

3. Paraphrased from Glinda, the Good Witch of the South in *The Wizard of Oz* (Fleming 1939).

4. One of the pioneers of film as philosophy was Stanley Cavell. His 1981 book *Pursuits of Happiness: The Hollywood Comedy of Remarriage* was groundbreaking, the Cavellian tradition the idea of film being able to embody philosophical thought. Gilles Deleuze was another theorist with a strong interest in the intersection of film and philosophical thought (although not specifically philosophical argument), naming his study of images and thought "noology" (Deleuze, *Negotiations*). He never stated that film is or is not capable of a complete argument, but did allow that some, but not all, films are capable of thought through image, noting that director Jean-Luc Godard transformed cinema by introducing thought into it (Deleuze, *Desert Islands*).

5. These theses are succinctly laid out by Damian Cox and Michael Levine in their book *Thinking through Film*, 8–10.

6. Cox and Levine note that "films can sometimes be better at presenting certain kinds of philosophical material than standard philosophical genres are. This is not just because film can be more emotionally engaging and entertaining" (10).

7. Cox and Levine, 16.

8. Mulhall, *On Film*, 2.

9. See both Carroll, "Philosophizing through the Moving Image," and Wartenberg, "Beyond Mere Illustration."

10. Wartenberg, "Beyond Mere Illustration," 30.

11. In his *Film Studies* article "Film as Argument," Wartenberg demonstrates how film can function as philosophical argument using *The Eternal Sunshine of the Spotless Mind* (Gondry 2004). Perhaps the ultimate enthymematic argument is the internet meme (in this case the term "meme" meaning more than just simply imitation): a single picture that could compose a whole argument, even if most of it is supplied by the viewer.

12. Plantinga, *Rhetoric and Representation in Nonfiction Film*, 70.

13. Bordwell, Staiger, and Thompson, *Classical Hollywood Cinema*, 38.

14. Aristotle, *Art of Rhetoric*, 67.

15. Although he was not a film philosopher and did not publish widely in this area, academic Laurence Behrens applied rhetorical theory to film criticism in

1979, with the goal to better describe and evaluate the rhetorical choices of the filmmaker. Behrens expresses surprise that more work had not been done in this area, as films are clearly both rhetorical as well as dramatic constructs. He believes that films can argue both inductively and deductively but defines them in a very different way to Wartenberg. For Behrens, an inductively argued film takes us through the steps used to develop the ideas, which don't obviously point to a foregone conclusion. By contrast, a deductively argued film is one that is very clearly created to demonstrate the truth of its assertion. As well as applying Aristotle's principles, Behrens also references Wayne Booth (*Rhetoric of Fiction*) to apply other common literary rhetorical theories to film. These describe the different rhetorical stances a film can take, always a balance between attitude (to the subject), tone (relationship to the audience), and the sensibility projected by the artist. When these elements are out of sync, they result in films that are too focused on the subject matter, audience, or charm of the filmmaker. See his full exploration in "Argument in Film."

16. Carroll, "Philosophizing through the Moving Image," 176.

17. This user-friendly point is very supportive of film-as-worthwhile-argument. As enthymematic argument demonstrates, just because the work is not explicit does not mean there is no argumentative work being done. In an example of theories of argument aligning (consciously or not) with theories of screen storytelling, it is a main tenet of feature films that it is far better to let the audience do the work and come to the (right) conclusion than to tell them explicitly. In his book *Conversations with the Great Moviemakers of Hollywood's Golden Age at the American Film Institute* (2006), George Stevens Jr. reports that Billy Wilder, director of *Some Like It Hot* (1959), had ten story commandments, of which number seven was "let the audience add up two plus two. They'll love you forever" (320).

18. See both Sinnerbrink, *Cinematic Ethics*, and Sinnerbrink, "Emotional Engagement and Moral Evaluation."

19. Sinnerbrink sets out the four dimensions as follows:

(a) Ethics within cinematic representation
(b) Ethics of cinematic presentation
(c) Ethics of cinema as a medium of cultural-historical/ideological perspectives
(d) Aesthetic of cinema to evoke ethical experience/expressing ethical meaning

Sinnerbrink further delineates ethical experience in the cinema into three strands:

1. The shared cinematic experience of engaging with the perspectives of other (fictional) characters depicted in complex situations

2. The viewer moved to reflect ethically on what they are seeing through emotional engagement and moral sympathy
3. Responses to the cinematic experience brought about by the aesthetic means, often by questioning the viewer's beliefs, that can involve broadening the viewer's ethical horizons of meaning and deepening their moral understanding ("Emotional Engagement and Moral Evaluation," 196–198)

20. See Smith, "Film Art, Argument and Ambiguity," 34.

21. Smith notes specifically about *All of Me* that "the film has an epistemic dimension—we might well be brought to reflect on personal identity by the film and learn something from it—but it is subsidiary to its comic imperative" (39).

22. Smith, 35–39.

23. From Livingston, *Cinema, Philosophy, Bergman*, 7, 60–121.

24. We've already noted that, more than any other role, the film director embodies feature film practice. Currently, feature film is widely considered to be a director's medium—but that is due to perceptions of control, rather than creation, of the story. In this way, it might be more accurate (and contentious) for feature film to be considered a producer's medium, and there is currently industry lobbying underway to recognize Creative Producer as a bona fide credit. As directing is understood to be primarily a task of interpretation, adaptation, and transformation (and execution), books in this area tend to focus on those elements that dominate the shoot itself: blocking, shot design, and working with actors.

25. Statistics supplied from Brenes, "Quoting and Misquoting Aristotle's 'Poetics.'"

26. In her 2014 paper, "Gurus and Oscar Winners: How-To Screenwriting Manuals in the New Cultural Economy," Bridget Conor lists "a representative sample of popular and classic manuals," namely screenwriting manuals. The list is compiled as part of a "broader qualitative research project involving labor market analysis, interviews and observations of screenwriting as labor, practice, and pedagogy" (125).

27. Macdonald, *Screenwriting Poetics and the Screen Idea*. Macdonald notes that based on his analysis of popular screenwriting manuals in 2002 and 2012, "most manuals present the industrial orthodoxy; the dominant conventions of the doxa" and that "the extent of the consensus of the manuals on offer reveals the coherence of their orthodoxy" (39–46).

28. Field, *Screenplay*, 3. As Field, like most of the film gurus, does not go into much detail when it comes to theme or what could be considered cinematic argumentation, all further references made to the book can be found in the introduction, the first two chapters, and chapter 5.

29. Macdonald, *Screenwriting Poetics and the Screen Idea.*

30. The key passages from Linda Seger's *Making a Good Script Great* can be found between pages 120 and 134.

31. It is worthy of note that the Sam Goldwyn quote, although clearly included to illustrate the point, is actually apocryphal (Berg, *Goldwyn*). In reality, it was highly likely that Goldwyn, as an experienced producer, was well aware of the practice of narrative feature filmmaking. In fact, he was almost always misquoted for comic effect—usually by his own press department at his behest—as it made him a very marketable brand. Other famous yet apocryphal quotes include "our comedies are not to be laughed at" and "the next time I send a damn fool for something, I'll send myself" (Boller and Davis, *Hollywood Anecdotes*).

32. Currently in its nineteenth edition, the book has been translated into twenty languages. Perhaps the most visible indication of McKee's impact on the industry was when director Spike Jonze included McKee as a character (played by Brian Cox) in *Adaptation* (2002), his film about a screenwriter struggling to adapt a novel for the screen.

33. McKee, *Story*. McKee talks more extensively, if euphemistically, than the other film gurus about theme and the potential for cinematic argument, but as it is not the focus of the book, the key passages can be found in a limited number of pages: 7–12, 21, 33, and 110–130.

34. McKee, 113.

35. McKee, 121.

36. Green and Brock, "Role of Transportation in the Persuasiveness of Public Narratives."

37. Here, McKee invokes not Aristotle but Plato: "Authoritative personalities, like Plato, fear the threat that comes not from idea, but from emotion. Those in power never want us to feel. Thought can be controlled and manipulated, but emotion is willful and unpredictable. Artists threaten authority by exposing lies and inspiring passion for change. This is why when tyrants seize power, their firing squads aim at the heart of the writer" (130).

38. Joseph Campbell's *Hero of a Thousand Faces*, first published in 1949, has itself become somewhat legendary in the world of narrative research, becoming the de facto mother text of the hero's journey. However, many industry professionals and those who aspire to the industry likely access the original material via other work based on it, such as Vogler's.

39. Vogler, *Writer's Journey*. The key references used from Vogler can be found in four passages on pages 1–15, 84–99, 111–112, and 248–266.

40. From Vladimir Propp's *Morphology of the Folk Tale*, originally written in 1928. We are using the 1968 translation. The Russian formalists were a loose collection of early twentieth-century Russian theorists. They created a branch of

literary criticism that focused primarily on devising scientific methods to describe and analyze poetry and prose, rejecting the more prevalent cultural, historical, or psychological approaches of the time. Propp was a prominent member of the group.

41. As Vogler's euphemisms directly relate to film-as-worthwhile-argument, it's worth reproducing them verbatim here to provide full context: "*The mythological approach to story boils down to using metaphors or comparisons to get across your feelings about life* [his emphasis]" (*Writer's Journey,* 84); "Of course, if your dramatic point of view is that life isn't fair and you feel justice is a rare thing in this world, then by all means reflect this in the way rewards and punishments are dealt out in the return" (253); "The needs of your story and your attitude may dictate ending with the feeling of a period, an image or line of dialogue flatly making a declarative statement such as 'Life goes on'" (259); "Many stories fall apart in the final moments. The Return is too abrupt, prolonged, unfocused, unsurprising, or unsatisfying. The mood or chain of thought the author has created just evaporates and the whole effort is wasted" (257).

42. Aronson, *Screenwriting Updated,* 29.

43. Although Aronson presents it as merely a potential point of view, she seems to feel that audience expectation of a moral is limiting the art form: "Most audiences complain that while the films are often extremely good, they fizzle at the end and it is hard to know what they were 'about' or what 'the point' was. . . . Another way to see it is that audiences seem to be seeking, effectively, a 'moral,' even if that moral is bizarrely surprising (as in *Pulp Fiction*), immoral (as in *Crimes and Misdemeanors*), or depressing (as in *City of Hope*). Some would say that audiences need to be re-educated in their expectations so that they do not expect a moral or closure, but instead believe that travelling the journey of the film is enough. . . . But at present (and this could change) most audiences come to film, as to all art, for a parable or conclusion of some kind, and feel disappointed when none is given to them" (187).

44. Aronson, *Screenwriting Updated,* 35.

45. Aronson, 8.

46. As the most influential writers on screenwriting don't discuss film as argument explicitly, it is difficult—but not impossible—for them to explore ways to argue effectively. Aronson's lateral thinking is the most developed technique in the literature to combat didacticism, with McKee (*Story,* 111) referencing but not further developing a notion of the irrational that could be harnessed to improve screen storytelling.

47. Maras, *Screenwriting,* 154.

48. Dancyger and Rush, *Alternative Screenwriting,* 79.

49. Phillips and Huntley, *Dramatica Dictionary,* 6.

50. Phillips and Huntley, 20–21.

51. Phillips and Huntley, 18.

Chapter 3 What and How Films Argue

1. As with many concepts first developed by Aristotle, precise definitions of enthymematic argument vary, but all refer to a lack of something, typically either a premise or a conclusion. David Hitchcock's 1985 "Enthymematic Arguments" gives an instructive overview.

2. Carroll, "Philosophizing through the Moving Image," 176.

3. In my opinion, the book that currently comes closest to exhaustively analyzing English-speaking Hollywood-centric feature film stories is *The Screenwriters Taxonomy* by Eric R. Williams. It's a terrific and particularly thorough classification of the various genres and subgenres and how they have historically been combined.

4. At the risk of destroying our visual metaphor of the headpiece of the Staff of Ra, there is a case to be made that there are not only two sides to it but three: the need to add Aristotle's *Ethics* to his *Poetics* and *Rhetoric*. Yet although his *Ethics* is certainly relevant, as it doesn't provide a working methodology for film-as-worthwhile-argument our elegant visual is safe. If there is a strong desire to include it, *Ethics* can be thought of as the material that makes the headpiece: the living of a good life is the foundation of what it means to be human and comes well before story.

5. See both Sinnerbrink, *Cinematic Ethics*, and Sinnerbrink, "Emotional Engagement and Moral Evaluation."

6. Main, "Even in the Middle Ages."

7. In the Butcher translation of *Poetics* (1907), the concept is referred to as "thought," and as "reasoning" in the Heath translation (1996). My preference is for the Heath, with reasoning most fully outlined in section 9.1.

8. Aristotle, *Poetics*, 31.

9. Aristotle, *"Art" of Rhetoric*, 17.

10. Cox and Levine have written extensively on film's ability to emotionally engage and note in *Thinking through Film*, "Just as we often believe what we want (or would like) to believe rather that what we have good reason to believe, we often believe things because we feel a certain way. Emotions influence belief, as do desires. This is a fact that cinema often exploits, and one that largely accounts for its ability to engage an audience" (5).

11. This view is typified by Murray Smith and Christopher Falzon. See both Smith, "Film Art, Argument and Ambiguity," and Falzon, *Philosophy Goes to the Movies*.

12. From Linda Seger's *Making a Good Script Great*, 130.

13. From Robert McKee's *Story*.

14. Seger, *Making a Good Script Great*, 132.

15. Propp, *Morphology of the Folk Tale*.

16. It's worth delineating the difference between sensual and sexual here, as the two terms are often used synonymously. It is believed that sensuous was a word specifically invented by John Milton in 1641 to mean invoking or gratifying the senses in a nonsexual way.

17. Sinnerbrink, "Emotional Engagement and Moral Evaluation."

18. At the time of writing, film directing is currently a role exclusively performed by humans, but the speed at which generative artificial intelligence is progressing in all areas of society, especially the creative arts, may mean significant elements of this role could soon become automated. Advances in text to video may make digitally real Mamet's belief in the director as mere extension of the screenwriter.

19. This is the reason that film is often referred to as the seventh art, viewed as a combination of the previous six: architecture, poetry, painting, sculpture, dance, and music. The most significant cinematic techniques include strategic implementation of shot size, composition, blocking, lenses, camera movement, lighting, production design, color palette, editing, transitional effects, sound design, casting, and performance.

20. Eisenstein, *Film Form*. An Eisensteinian intellectual montage attempts to create coherent and typically complex intellectual meaning or ideology within a contained sequence.

Chapter 4 Alternate Conceptions

1. Wetstein, "One Girl Chorus."

2. Dyer, *Only Entertainment*, 19.

3. Morrison, "Life after James."

4. McKee, *Story*, 12.

5. Silver quoted in Lovell and Sergi, *Cinema Entertainment*.

6. Another film that fit the category of edifying without providing delight or joy is the first British film to win an Oscar for Best International Feature Film (Best Foreign Language Film until 2020), *The Zone of Interest* (Glazer 2023). Potentially most Holocaust or war dramas could be considered to be in this group, as well as any confronting drama that does not provide any elements of relief (comic or otherwise).

7. Fear et al., "25 Best Modern Exploitation Movies."

8. Contemporary filmmakers such as Quentin Tarantino were so influenced by what they termed Grindhouse films (the term used to describe a cinema that

showed mostly exploitation films) that he, along with fellow Miramax filmmaker Robert Rodriguez, made two pastiche exploitation films in 2007 to be released as a double feature under the joint name of *Grindhouse*, although they were also released separately as *Death Proof* (Tarantino) and *Planet Terror* (Rodriguez). These modern exploitation films should not be confused with traditional exploitation films as they are postmodern, self-referential works that are in no way as extreme in their treatment of sex and violence as their original referents and therefore meet the "deemed releasable" clause in our definition of mainstream narrative feature films.

9. In what is a typical screen agency comment, in 2011 a *Screen Australia* report highlighted the fact that 79 percent of the Australian public agreed that Australian screen stories are vital for contributing to their sense of Australian national identity. Most national governments certainly don't subscribe to the "just entertainment" conception and have always been aware of—and often utilized—the power of the moving image as a tool for propaganda. There may be an expectation that this is confined to factual content, where clear political approaches are common, but it is mainstream fiction that can perhaps more effectively influence hearts and minds. The Hollywood Hays Code was, in part, created in the 1930s not just to classify films but to specifically stop suspected propaganda in American cinema (Bennett, "Film as Argument"). A very high-profile example of real-world impact is the fact that the action-romance film *Top Gun* (Scott 1986) is routinely credited with significantly increasing U.S. naval recruitment (Novelly, "'Top Gun' Boosted Recruiting").

10. "We just tell stories" is a particularly common phrase among feature filmmakers and not always used defensively to close down further thought or investigation. Sometimes, as in the case of Hollywood screenwriter and director Robert Zemeckis, it is used to conflate the writer/director roles. As Zemeckis puts it, "This idea of a director and a writer is only created by the unions and the guilds, because we're both just storytellers and we're making this film as a collaborative thing" (Mellor, "Robert Zemeckis Interview"). Other times, such as in the case of screenwriter and director Darren Aronofsky, it is used to highlight the visual element of the medium. Aronofsky says, "We're not just storytellers, we're visual storytellers" (Aronofsky, "Master Class"). The claim is also made in a reductive sense. For example, Australian actor, screenwriter, and director Mel Gibson claims, "We're all just storytellers, right?" (Belloni and Galloway, "Director Roundtable").

11. The term "narratology" is widely credited to Tzvetan Todorov, first coined in his book *Grammaire du Décaméron* (1969). Todorov was working in the Russian formalist tradition but was not part of the original movement, working a few generations later in Paris. Narratology is not to be confused with narrative

paradigm, a communications theory developed by Walter Fisher that states that all meaningful communication occurs via humans telling stories to each other, as outlined in *Human Communication as Narration*. This theory aligns very much with film-as-worthwhile-argument as it contends that stories in all their forms are more persuasive that conventional arguments. For a comprehensive overview, see Genevieve Liveley's *Narratology*.

12. Bordwell, "Common Sense + Film Theory."

13. Bordwell.

14. Yorke, *Into the Woods*, 205–209.

15. Here Yorke quotes Nassim Nicholas Taleb, a scholar who specializes in randomness and risk analysis: "The more orderly, less random, patterned and narratized a series of words or symbols, the easier it is to store that series in one's mind" (207). Essentially, the story becomes an epistemic database.

16. Yorke, 214.

17. Shanley, "Darren Aronofsky Responds."

18. Hooton, "Darren Aronofsky Defends Mother!"

19. Gleiberman, "Film Review."

20. See both Beugnet, *Cinema and Sensation*, and Beugnet, "Cinema and Sensation."

21. Bordwell, Thompson, and Smith, *Film Art*, 59.

22. Mackendrick, *On Film-Making*, 11.

23. Yorke, *Into the Woods*, chap. 6.

24. Falzon, *Philosophy Goes to the Movies*, 56.

25. Metz, *Imaginary Signifier*, 42–56.

26. Mulvey, "Visual Pleasure and Narrative Cinema." Mulvey is widely regarded as the inventor of feminist film criticism, with this considered the founding document. Based on the works of Freud and Lacan, it was the first to combine feminism, film theory, and psychoanalysis.

27. A recent film to fall significantly foul of this contract is writer and director Taika Waititi's *Thor: Love and Thunder* (2022). Following the considerable critical and commercial success of *Thor: Ragnarok* (2017), there were huge expectations for the next installment for the Thor character. Although it was not a complete financial disaster, the film was regarded as a universal disappointment, with some viewers not just disgruntled but angry. The extreme reaction was likely due to a film that clearly promised lighthearted action and romance but began with the extended death of a child from thirst and malnutrition, followed immediately by revealing a romantic lead having stage 4 cancer. It was a betrayal of emotional trust with the audience, especially as those story elements were not present in the promotional trailers, so it came as an unwelcome shock to many. Since its release, both the director Waititi and star Chris Hemsworth have

distanced themselves from the film, not quite apologizing but noting their dissatisfaction with the tone of the piece that was never quite solved.

28. Keegan, "Jordan Peele on the 'Post-racial Lie.'"

29. Suggitt, "Five Record-Breaking Book Facts."

30. As their grosses are so close, there is currently a battle between Cameron's *Avatar* (2009) and *Avengers: Endgame* (Russo and Russo 2019), where they have switched places as numbers one and two due to cinema rereleases. However, if inflation is taken into account, *Avatar* is the clear winner.

31. Conan Doyle, *Complete Sherlock Holmes*.

32. Even if you take the view that most whodunnits are actually whydunnits, the final exposition typically deals with both simultaneously, so the structure and experience are unchanged.

33. Between them *CSI: Crime Scene Investigation*, *NCIS: Naval Criminal Investigation Service* and *Law & Order* have thirteen spin-off television series and one spin-off television film. This does not include other television series set in the same fictional universes. *NCIS* was actually a spin-off of *JAG* (Bellisario 1995–2004), where two episodes in season 8 were used as a "backdoor" pilot to test and launch *NCIS* with less pressure than a traditional television pilot.

34. Alesi, "TV Watchers around the World."

35. From Mark Hartley's 2008 feature documentary *Not Quite Hollywood: The Wild, Untold Story of Ozploitation!*

36. Sinnerbrink, "Emotional Engagement and Moral Evaluation."

General Notes on the Case Studies

1. Sinnerbrink, *New Philosophies of Film*.

2. Very few film directors working within a mainstream studio system ever reach a level where they are given final cut. This means that the director has final say on all creative matters, selecting what they regard as the best version of the film to release to the public. Most casual cinemagoers would assume that this is always the case, but it represents the exception rather than the rule. This is why the director often only symbolically embodies filmmaking practice, as they are not wholly in control of the process. Typically, a film director's job is complete when they deliver their version of the film to the producer, production company, or distributor, depending on the particular financial structure of the production.

It is rare for a film director to have final cut as it means other stakeholders have no legal control over the material, able only to cancel release rather than modify the work itself. Prior to the final cut, even a distributor (who, even if they are not the principal production company, usually puts finance into the production budget of the film to secure the release in their national territory) may have a say over the material. A distributor will accept delivery only once they are satisfied with the work. This is a legal position, as once the distributor accepts delivery, they are liable to pay for it. Delivery can be rejected for either technical reasons (the film master has physical glitches) or creative concerns. These creative rejections can range from the head of the distribution company not liking certain elements personally to poor test screening ratings (if the distributor engages in test screenings).

A very public example of final cut complications is the Alan Smithee director credit. In the United States, as part of Directors Guild of America (DGA) rules, if a director is unsatisfied with the final cut they are able to remove their name from all credits—and until the year 2000 the name of the director would be credited as "Alan Smithee." This credit is no longer in use as the audience became aware of the practice, so presently a director is still able to take their name from the credits with a range of different alternatives now available.

In most cases, a film can be redelivered any number of times. In Hollywood, guild officials have recognized that institutional interference is problematic, so to protect the director DGA rules allow them to ban everybody from the editing suite for ten weeks in order to deliver their first cut of the film. If the stakeholders do not like this cut, they are within their rights to ask for changes, and this process can be repeated until they are happy with the final product. This process may include the original director, or a new director may be hired to oversee changes, which may include reshoots.

As the precise delivery process for each film is typically unique to that production, and often filmmakers have to sign an NDA (non-disclosure agreement), it is difficult to unpick precisely what the director first delivered (even on small-scale independent films). Therefore, to fully demonstrate feature filmmaking practice as a whole, it is necessary to select case study films that were clearly under the control of the filmmakers (and not external or arm's-length stakeholders). In practical terms, this means the director had final cut or complete autonomy over the course of the entire production.

3. Barthes, "Death of the Author," 148. Barthes makes the claim that "a text is made up of multiple writings, drawn from many cultures and entering into mutual relations of dialogue, parody, contestation, but there is one place where this multiplicity is focused and that place is the reader, not, as was hitherto said, the author."

4. See both Wolff, *Social Production of Art*, and Burke, *Death and Return of the Author*. Wolff argues that the "birth of the reader" restricts the authority of the author rather than marking an outright "death," and Burke demonstrates more wide-ranging problems with structural linguistics, believing the abolition of the author is philosophically unsound.

5. For perhaps the most notable use of this method of analysis, see Kristin Thompson's *Storytelling in Film and Television* (36–73). Thompson believes that the most significant research questions in the study of screenwriting are concerned with what screenwriters think they were doing rather than the final result of the filmed work, which represents another intellectual property altogether. It is a similar approach to that taken by Ian W. Macdonald in his *Screenwriting Poetics and the Screen Idea* (2): "Even if an element is likely to be true, such as a loud and sudden noise creating a startling effect in the viewer, it is not perhaps the noise that is significant, but the fact that the screenwriter chooses this moment in the narrative as the appropriate moment to startle you, and to use a specific means to do so."

Chapter 5 The Exemplar

1. Pixar still has an incredibly strong track record, but it is no longer flawless. This may have been complicated by the impact of the COVID-19 pandemic on cinema attendance numbers, release strategies, and the accelerated rise of streaming platforms, but both *Onward* (Scanlon 2020) and *Toy Story* spin-off *Lightyear* (MacLane 2022) were notable misses.

2. This dogmatism is not completely formalized, existing as a series of articles and unofficial (but not disavowed) mission statements. In 2011, Pixar storyboard artist Emma Coats put together a list of twenty-two Pixar storytelling rules she observed during her time working for the studio, as detailed in Cavna, "Pixar Tips." Two are of note: one mentions that "trying for theme is important" (but not integral), the other asking the writers to express "the belief burning within them," from which their story feeds. Although this idea of belief could be viewed as a conclusion, at no time is the idea of film as argument articulated, which while not decisive, is a strong indicator that this is not a practice they consciously follow. This is not a criticism, as Pixar, perhaps rightly so, is more concerned with perfecting the form than interrogating the practice.

3. McKee, *Story*, 112.

4. McKee, 119.

5. Often, whether or not a film contains genuine dual protagonists is hotly debated. Other high-profile examples include *Lethal Weapon* (Donner 1987), *Thelma and Louise* (Scott 1991), and *The Prestige* (Nolan 2006).

6. It is important to note that all these modes are based on the assumption that the film meets the minimum requirements of suspension of disbelief, a process where the audience allows themselves to fully commit to the story. Before a film can convince an audience of an assertion, it must simultaneously convince the audience in all other areas of story: that the world, characters, situations, and

resolution (or nonresolution) are authentic. Failure in any area weakens the argument. Suspension of disbelief relates directly to genre, with comedies (especially animated ones) given more latitude than domestic drama. The film must convince the audience that the film world is believable enough for them to invest their intellect and emotions and that the characters, situations, and outcome(s) are believable. If each element of the film is convincing, then the argument may convince.

7. Seger, *Making a Good Script Great*, 129.

8. As film philosophers Cox and Levine point out, it is cinema's ability to invoke feelings that makes it so superbly efficient at making impactful arguments (*Thinking through Film*, 5).

9. As is common, the internet is abound with fan theories. The Reddit thread "Is Carrie from Four Weddings and a Funeral the Most Unlikable Female Love Interest Ever to Be Seen in a Beloved Romcom?" is indicative of this particular reading of the film.

10. Films such as these often rely on transmedia storytelling to meaningfully work, rather than the stories in other media augmenting an already functional film. This is obviously problematic, as there is no guarantee the audience will have seen what can be critical story information spread across other films, television shows, books, and comics, often going back decades.

11. Aristotle, *Art of Rhetoric*, 67.

12. It is worth restating here that Cox and Levine make the case that "belief is more often than not a function of desire and emotion as well as reasons and evidence" (*Thinking through Film*, 16). Unwilling suspension of disbelief is a relatively new theory, put forward by Peter Kivy (*Once-Told Tales*, chap. 7). Suspension of disbelief was a term originally invented by Coleridge to describe reading epic poetry (*Biographia Literaria*, chap. 14), and he believed it a willing suspension where the reader consciously surrendered to the text. Kivy makes the case that the audience can believe a character or world is both fake and real simultaneously, the latter unwillingly as they know rationally that those elements are fictional. In his essay "On Fairy-Stories," literary great J. R. R. Tolkien believes that any conscious dealings with disbelief are problematic, as they take the reader out of the story. Tolkien prefers what he calls secondary belief, a state provided by a fully consistent and detailed fictional universe in which the reader or viewer can engage.

Chapter 6 The Counterexample

1. Honorable mentions go to notable filmmakers Yorgos Lanthimos (*The Lobster* 2015), Nicolas Winding Refn (*The Neon Demon* 2016), Julia Ducournau

(*Titane* 2021), Lynne Ramsay (*You Were Never Really Here* 2017), and Charlie Kaufman (*I'm Thinking of Ending Things* 2020), who also successfully navigate the delicate space of challenging conceptual feature films in the mainstream.

2. Buckmaster, "Why *Mulholland Drive* Is the Greatest Film since 2000."

3. The filmmakers talk quite extensively of their love of *Mulholland Drive* and Lynch more generally in interviews as part of the 2010 short documentary *In the Blue Box*, available on the 2017 Australian Blu-ray release of *Mulholland Drive*.

4. McGowan, "Lost on *Mulholland Drive*," 67.

5. For more background on Lynch's education and his creative approaches, see Hilarie Sheets's 2014 *New York Times* article "David Lynch, Who Began as a Visual Artist, Gets a Museum Show," and Olga Tabachnikova's 2016 book *Russian Irrationalism from Pushkin to Brodsky*.

6. In fact, Lynch's 2018 autobiography, a hybrid of biography and memoir, is named *Room to Dream*, and he famously believed in using transcendental meditation as a creative tool. His 2006 book *Catching the Big Fish: Meditation, Consciousness and Creativity* is named for the central metaphor he used to express his understanding of the nature of ideas: if you stay in the psychological shallows you will catch only little fish; bigger fish require deeper waters. In 2018, Xan Brooks's *Guardian* review of *Room to Dream* noted that Lynch had the appearance "of a corn-fed American dreamer who simply likes to show his nightmares to the world."

7. Mittell, "Haunted by Seriality."

8. This view is typified by Todd McGowan ("Accumulation and Enjoyment on *Mulholland Drive*"; "Lost on *Mulholland Drive*"). In his 2014 book *Subjective Realist Cinema: From Expressionism to Inception*, Matthew Campora offers an explanation of the film that "is drawn from a growing consensus of commentators who view the film's first movement (and all its various strands) as a dream and its second as a waking frame that provides clues to making sense of the dream" (69). Tom Charity, a film critic from *Time Out*, says, "For me the first half is the dream of a failed starlet idealising herself as a talented ingénue with a beautiful young woman who loves her. Then, about two-thirds of the way through, she wakes up and is faced with reality: she is a failed actress who has been dumped by her lover and is working as a waitress" (in Lewis, "Nice Film"). In his interview for *In the Blue Box*, Belgian film director Jaco Van Dormael is quite explicit: "The film was crystal clear to me, because of its very bold time structure. Two-thirds of the film is but a dream."

9. This interpretation of the film is epitomized by cultural commentators such as Stanley Kauffman and the BBC's Jane Douglas, who defers all judgment as to meaning: "I'm not a subscriber to the theory that the first half of the film is a dream and the second half reality because I think it's too easy. . . . I do believe

that in some ways it is better to just watch it without constantly trying to work out what it means" (in Lewis, "Nice Film"). Kauffman claims that "sense is not the point: the responses are the point" ("Stanley Kauffman on Films").

10. See both Elsaesser, "Mind-Game Film," and Panek, "Poet and the Detective."

11. Roche, "Death of the Subject."

12. *The Cabinet of Doctor Caligari* parallel is suggested by Campora (*Subjective Realist Cinema*, 68). The works that we discuss throughout this book have a heavy English-language Hollywood bias, but their influences are global. Although Lynch's films might appear to be unconventional in terms of classical Hollywood cinema, he adhered quite closely to other national storytelling traditions, in this case obedience to the traditions of Slavic storytelling imparted to him during his student years. One of Frank Daniel's exercises included writing three versions of the same scene—a poetic version, a comedic version, and a tragic version—with a final version having to include all three elements. The goal was to engage the senses of the audience, not their intellect.

13. From an interview with actress Naomi Watts, featured on the 2017 Australian Blu-ray release of *Mulholland Drive.*

14. The intrinsic satisfaction that Lynch's use of sensation brings is often cited by audiences who either cannot or will not attempt to find overall meaning in his films. In their interviews for *In the Blue Box*, French director Guillaume Nicloux (*Valley of Love* 2015) comments, "What I like in films is to be very much disturbed and lost, like when you're looking at a painting you don't understand," and screenwriter Michaël Souhaité (*Roxane* 2019) notes, "Lynch really works on creating a feeling. He keeps titillating the audience with lots of sounds, which put them into a trance, a dreamlike state." Peter Travers of *Rolling Stone* magazine sums up the position well in his review of the film, that "*Mulholland Drive* is all of a dark, dazzling piece, and lapses in clarity seem a small price to pay for breathtaking images like these" ("Mulholland Drive").

15. Adams, *Hitchhiker's Guide to the Galaxy.*

16. Van Dormael, in *In the Blue Box.*

17. Fox, "David Lynch."

18. Leigh, "What Is David Lynch's Inland Empire About?"

Chapter 7 Three Approaches

1. *Brave* was by no means critically savaged but received widespread lukewarm reviews, most notably from the *Hollywood Reporter.* Todd McCarthy noted a "sense of letdown due to the lack of adventurousness" ("Brave").

2. Barnes, "It Wasn't a Wreck." In contrast to *Brave, Cars 2* was rather politely savaged, such was the affection for Pixar and their track record.

3. This is a remarkably common argument and family dynamic in Disney princess films. A few specific examples are *Moana* (Muster and Clements 2016) and both animated and live-action versions of *The Little Mermaid* (Muster and Clements 1989, Marshall 2023).

4. The idea of transforming into a bear is not unique to *Brave*. It appears across many mythologies, fairy tales, and adventure stories involving magic. Precise details vary, but in Greek mythology the nymph Callisto was transformed into a bear by either Artemis or Hera. Her story is certainly highly relevant here, as it is both a gendered and a highly distressing one. She is tricked by Zeus into bearing his child, the discovery of which angers—depending on the account—either her patron or Zeus's wife. Her fate is to be transformed initially into a bear and then finally, in what is disturbingly related as an act of kindness by Zeus, into the star Ursa Major—the "Great Bear."

5. Parker, *Will Write and Direct for Food*, 79.

6. Many of these moments are highly derivative across decades (and sometimes millennia) of storytelling, but one directly recycled moment is the resurrection beat where Merida-believes-her-mother-is-fully-transformed becomes Elsa-believes-her-sister-is-fully-frozen. Of course, both almost instantly are proven wrong.

7. See Aristotle's *Poetics* (18) and Mamet's discussions in *On Directing Film*. Mamet further claims that it doesn't matter whether the ending is good or bad, happy or sad, just the right ending as defined by the "grain" of the creative piece. Every story has a natural grain, and as with planing a piece of wood, the artist has a choice of planing either with or against the grain. If you go against it, the wood is destroyed (66). This is all another way of saying that the close of the film works for both the drama and the argument. The surprise supplies the necessary impact that drama requires, the inevitability indicating a wholly logical argument, which once laid out is deemed logically faultless.

8. Before *Frozen*, Disney had certainly started to move away from these gendered stereotypes, but as much as we can credit the studio for the film's social impact, it was largely a problem Disney itself created by relying on and encouraging outdated characterizations and attitudes for so many years. Yet only a blockbuster could decisively overturn these tropes. The huge commercial success of *Frozen* proved that these stories make money, influencing the mainstream to generate similar tales. Just look at the current output of Marvel and DC. The idea of women not defined by men has become a given, part of the intellectual fabric of an entire generation of girls and boys, something a challenging independent or art house film could never hope or expect to achieve. *Frozen* closed the door on those old damsel-in-distress characterizations, perhaps forever, in the same way that *Dances with Wolves* (Costner 1990) forever closed the door on the representation of Native Americans as one-dimensional savages (noble or otherwise).

9. Mueller, "What Is the Bechdel Test?" The Bechdel Test is actually a misnomer and should actually be credited as the Bechdel-Wallace Test. In 1983 Alison Bechdel started a satirical weekly comic strip named *Dykes to Watch Out For,* which ran until 2008. It was one of those strips published in 1985 that went viral decades after publication. The actual idea for the test came from Liz Wallace, Bechdel's friend, and was given a credit in the original strip. Bechdel notes that the test quite literally started as a joke, where Mo, the main character of the comic strip, outlines the rules she uses to watch a film. This is why the test is sometimes also referred to as Mo's Movie Measure.

10. McKay's films were both heavily and obviously satirical, exceptionally loud and proud with their politics, with neither trying to be as fun or lighthearted as *Barbie. The Big Short* is not a comedy but playful with its directness and structure, and *Don't Look Up* is perhaps the bleakest of black comedies. Both films have a sharp, biting edge—perhaps as they use no hint of metaphor. They share a confrontational attitude that echoes Aronofsky's howl, as if they know they won't convince any hearts and minds but still want to frustratedly scream their arguments into the void nonetheless.

Chapter 8 Why Failures Succeed

1. The film was originally *Anhedonia,* meaning a lack of interest or pleasure from life. For a comprehensive background to the creative development of the film, see *When the Shooting Stops . . . the Cutting Begins* by *Annie Hall*'s editor Ralph Rosenblum and Robert Karen.

2. MacDowell, *Happy Endings in Hollywood Cinema,* 1.

3. Crowe, "Hot Shot in Top Gun." In an interview with music journalist turned film director Cameron Crowe three years after the film's release, star Tom Cruise shared that the studio decided the film had to be more "upbeat and commercial."

4. From Jordan Peele's director's commentary on the 2017 Australian edition of the *Get Out* Blu-ray.

5. Perhaps the most unique application of the double ending is that of director F. W. Murnau's German Expressionism masterpiece *The Last Laugh* (1924). In this case, the hero's logical yet wholly depressing demise is faithfully rendered, only for a title card to appear (twelve minutes from the end), stating, *"Here our story should really end, for in actual life, the forlorn old man would have little to look forward to but death. The author took pity on him, however, and provided quite an improbable epilogue."* This Brechtian breaking of the fourth wall, the admittance from the "author" that in real life the character would have a miserable end, the admission that with fiction they have the power to give them a happy ending (he

wins the lottery), is a very rare cinematic example of the honest double ending, albeit one that involves a radical change of storytelling strategy.

6. Tuttle, "Movie Theaters Make 85% Profit at Concession Stands."

7. This is a commonly used maxim within the industry. For concise but useful breakdowns of how franchises generate income, see both Arnold, "Economics of Movie Making," and Yeo, "Will the Superhero Films Ever End?"

8. Kaye, "Human See, Human Do."

9. Both tend to be leads in dramas and support players in big-budget actioners. For instance, Spencer starred in *Hidden Figures* (Melfi 2017) and supported in *Insurgent* (Schwentke 2015), and Giamatti starred in *The Holdovers* (Payne 2023) and supported in *San Andreas* (Peyton 2015). Both Spencer and Giamatti were nominated for Oscars for *Hidden Figures* and *The Holdovers*, respectively.

10. The institution as auteur is not just the realm of the major studios. It is simply branding and open to the usual market forces of disruption and rapid rises (and falls). Recent players to be successful in this sphere are A24, which quickly built a following around original, diverse, and artistically authentic filmmaking, and Blumhouse, which specializes in high-concept horror.

11. See almost any discussion inspired by Laura Mulvey's "Visual Pleasure and Narrative Cinema," whether based around aesthetic or psychoanalytic theories of satisfaction.

12. Some examples of visual pleasure through various elements available to film include the following:

Location—the rural fields from *Stealing Beauty* (Bertolucci 1996)
Machinery—the Transformers from *Transformers* (Bay 2007)
Light—the ethereal magic-hour feel from *Days of Heaven* (Malick 1978)
Color—the vibrant greens, yellows, and reds in *Amélie* (Jeunet 2001)
Design—the theatrical staging of *The Grand Budapest Hotel* (Anderson 2014)

13. Alcorn, "'Fifty Shades' Trilogy Takes First Three Spots."

14. Weiss, "In 'Fifty Shades of Grey,' It's Not the Sex."

15. McKee, *Story*, 13.

16. In 2019, journalist Catherine Shoard reported the filmmaker's comments in the *Guardian* over a period of a few weeks, such was the interest in the (very well-mannered) debate. Scorsese's and Coppola's views give weight to ideas of both spectacle as compensation and film as argument. They also echo McKee's words, made some twenty years earlier, referencing film spectacle in general (*Story*, 24): "Spectacles of this kind replace imagination with simulated actuality. They use story as an excuse for heretofore unseen effects that carry us into a tornado, the jaws of a dinosaur, or futuristic holocausts. And make no mistake,

these razzle-dazzle spectacles can deliver a circus of excitement. But like amusement park rides, their pleasures are short-lived."

17. The theme park ride is billed as the world's first horror-movie-themed rollercoaster. It opened in 2009 and is still in operation today.

18. Mamet, in Cousineau, *Painted Word*, 59.

19. Queenan, "Dumb and Dumber." When *Knocked Up* was first released, journalist Joe Queenan expressed concerns with this kind of wish fulfillment fantasy, in terms of both social values and filmic trends.

20. Aristotle, *Poetics*, 10.

21. Alberge, "Ennio Morricone."

22. More recent examples of this are the romantic comedy *Yesterday* (Boyle 2019), which used the back catalogue of the Beatles, and the biopics *Bohemian Rhapsody* (Singer 2018), about Queen front man Freddie Mercury, and *Rocketman* (Fletcher 2019), Elton John's life story.

23. Elsaesser, "Mind-Game Film," 13–14. The term "mind game" was coined by Elsaesser, who took the phrase from director Lars von Trier. In 2006, von Trier made *The Boss of It All*, a film he ensured played "mind games" with the audience by including about half a dozen out-of-place objects, called "Lookeys," he wanted to be noticed. Von Trier offered a prize to the viewer who could spot them all and tell him the rationale for their inclusion.

24. Barthes, *S/Z*, 18.

25. Carroll, "Power of Movies," 97.

26. This is Nolan talking in an interview on *The Late Show* with Stephen Colbert on February 4, 2024. Although the show is often lighthearted, this is clearly a sincere interview about his process, designed to build momentum for his awards campaign.

27. Mackendrick, *On Film-Making*, 33.

28. It is interesting to note that the *Fast* series started with cars, but now every form of vehicle is involved (cars, planes, boats, trains, helicopters), with the marginal sense of realism of the original films abandoned by the later sequels.

29. Aristotle, *Poetics*, 18.

30. Sinnerbrink, "Emotional Engagement and Moral Evaluation," 198.

31. These characters need not be archetypal heroes, nor in any way aspirational. Antiheroes can have impact, as can secondary characters. As recognition is so personal to each viewer, objective examples are problematic, but characters that certainly captured the imagination of their respective zeitgeists are those such as Patrick Bateman (Christian Bale) from *American Psycho* (Harron 2000) and Lara Jean (Lana Condor) from *To All the Boys I've Loved Before* (Johnson 2018).

32. Aristotle, *Poetics*, 37.

33. For a significant period of his work, in terms of personal style Tarantino deliberately cultivated a trademark for not just the way in which his characters speak but what they speak about (usually new interpretations of pop-culture references). The dialogue is usually so distinctive that viewers can often tell what rewrite work he has done—most notably *Crimson Tide* (Scott 1995)—be it credited or uncredited.

34. Leitch, *Film Adaptation and Its Discontents,* 282.

35. Bakhtin, *Dialogic Imagination.*

36. Leitch, *Film Adaptation and Its Discontents,* 288. Leitch breaks these claims down into eight categories: "Don't blame us; Isn't this sad/inspiring/heroic; Stranger than fiction; Now it can be told; Behind the headlines; Explaining the inexplicable; Not just another movie; You need to know this."

37. Kerin, Varadarajan, and Peterson, "First-Mover Advantage."

38. Beaty, "Superhero Fan Service," 324.

39. Russell, "Glimpse and Fan Service," 105. Russell denotes fan service as "the random and gratuitous display of a series of anticipated gestures. . . . These gestures include such things as panty shots, leg spreads (spread legs) and glimpses of breasts."

40. Beaty, "Superhero Fan Service," 322.

41. Perez, "'Star Wars: The Force Awakens.'"

Chapter 9 The End

1. Smith, "Film Art, Argument and Ambiguity." Smith raised some very well-considered doubts on narrative film's ability to argue, citing a clash of priorities where the art would always win out over the argumentation. Yet if we agree that film-as-worthwhile-argument is the practice, there is no conflict: creative choices are also choices of rhetorical approach.

2. Green and Brock, "Role of Transportation."

3. The Writers Guild of America (WGA) strike in 2023 was unique, as although it was not the first time the Hollywood writers have found it necessary to strike in order to get what they believe to be equitable pay and rights, it was the first time that the unsanctioned use of Gen AI was a significant item on the negotiating table. Essentially the WGA did not want the studios to be able to use Gen AI in the creation of scripts without regulation, with any use requiring permission of the writers, who would also have complete power of veto. Writers should also not be asked to redraft a preexisting script written by Gen AI. In a very real sense this was a strike of existential stakes, fighting for the survival of the screenwriting profession globally. Policy set here would inevitably constitute guidelines for its professional implementation elsewhere.

A few months after the writers' strike began, they were joined on strike by the Screen Actors Guild (SAG), which had similar concerns about Gen AI from an image and performance-rights perspective. Both strikes have since ended and were deemed victories for the guilds, but there is no doubt that despite the new safeguards and assurances, both professions are forever changed.

Currently Adobe's Gen AI systems are not yet powerful enough to allow for a "make movie" button, but technology evolves at an exponential rate. Perhaps in the next few years there will be a Directors Guild or Cinematographers Guild strike over Gen AI's usage. In a fascinating demonstration of prescience, the great director Alfred Hitchcock ironically hated the actual film shoot itself. He yearned for a machine that could do it for him. Talking with famed French New Wave director/actor François Truffaut for the interview book *Hitchcock*, he declared, "I dream of an IBM machine in which I'd insert the screenplay in one end, and the film would emerge at the other end, completed, and in color" (330–331).

4. We are not too far away from an actor having a two-tiered career—one greater fee for the actual physical actor to come to set and perform, with another lesser fee for the right for a production to use the actor's digital twin. This twin is an avatar that uses machine learning to generate different and authentic performances based on the actor's previous acting choices in a variety of circumstances. A director would be able to do multiple takes, knowing that each digital performance would be unique.

5. Speaking on *The Tonight Show* in 2024, Yuval Noah Harari, the best-selling author of *Sapiens: A Brief History of Humankind,* warns us that Gen AI is the first technology in human history that can make decisions and create new ideas by itself. He also notes that most generations think technology moves faster for them than in any other period, only this time it's true. It's the first time that we have no idea what to teach our children that we are certain will be relevant in twenty years.

6. Smith, "Why Do We Tell Stories?"

7. Kwapis, *What I Really Want to Do Is Direct,* 276.

FILMOGRAPHY

Motion Pictures

Adaptation. 2002, Sony Pictures Releasing. Produced by Jonathan Demme et al., written by Charlie Kaufman, directed by Spike Jonze. Columbia Tri-Star DVD ed. 2003.

Alien. 1978, 20th Century Fox. Produced by Gordon Carroll, David Giler, and Walter Hill, written by Dan O'Bannon, directed by Ridley Scott.

All of Me. 1984, Universal Pictures. Produced by Stephen J. Friedman, written by Phil Alden Robinson and Henry Olek, directed by Carl Reiner.

Amélie. 2001, Canal Plus. Produced by Jean-Marc Deschamps and Claudie Ossard, written by Guillaume Laurant and Jean-Pierre Jeunet, directed by Jean-Pierre Jeunet.

American Pie. 1999, Universal Pictures. Produced by Warren Zide, Craig Perry, Chris Weitz, et al., written by Adam Herz, directed by Chris Weitz.

American Psycho. 2000, Columbia Pictures. Produced by Edward R. Pressman et al., written by Mary Harron and Christian Halsey Solomon, directed by Mary Harron.

Amour. 2012, Canal Plus. Produced by Margaret Menegoz et al., written and directed by Michael Haneke.

Anchorman 2: The Legend Continues. 2013, Paramount Pictures. Produced by Judd Apatow et al., written by Will Ferrell and Adam McKay, directed by Adam McKay.

Annie Hall. 1977, United Artists. Produced by Charles H. Joffe, written by Woody Allen and Marshall Brickman, directed by Woody Allen.

Avatar. 2009, 20th Century Fox. Produced by Jon Landau and James Cameron, written and directed by James Cameron.

Avengers: Endgame. 2019, Walt Disney Studios. Produced by Kevin Feige, written by Christopher Markus and Stephen McFeely, directed by Anthony Russo and Joe Russo.

Badlands. 1973, Warner Bros. Pictures. Produced, written, and directed by Terrence Malick.

Bad Lieutenant. 1992, Aries Films. Produced by Edward R. Pressman, written by Zöe Lund and Abel Ferrara, directed by Abel Ferrara.

Baise Moi. 2000, Canal Plus. Produced by Philippe Godeau, written and directed by Virginie Despentes and Coralie Trinh Thi.

Barbie. 2023, Warner Bros. Pictures. Produced by David Heyman, Margot Robbie, Tom Ackerley, et al., written by Greta Gerwig and Noah Baumbach, directed by Greta Gerwig.

Batman v. Superman: Dawn of Justice. 2016, Warner Bros. Pictures. Produced by Charles Roven and Deborah Snyder, written by Chris Terrio and David S. Goyer, directed by Zack Snyder.

Being John Malkovich. 1999, USA Films. Produced by Michael Stipe et al., written by Charlie Kaufman, directed by Spike Jonze.

Ben Hur. 1959, Metro-Goldwyn-Mayer. Produced by Sam Zimbalist, written by Karl Tunberg, directed by William Wyler.

Big Bird Cage. 1972, New World Pictures. Produced by Cirio H. Santiago and Jane Schaffner, written and directed by Jack Hill.

The Big Short. 2015, Paramount Pictures. Produced by Brad Pitt, Arnon Milchan, Dede Gardner, et al., written by Charles Randolph and Adam McKay, directed by Adam McKay.

The Big Sleep. 1946, Warner Bros. Pictures. Produced by Howard Hawks, written by William Faulkner et al., directed by Howard Hawks.

Blazing Saddles. 1974, Warner Bros. Pictures. Produced by Michael Hertzberg, written by Mel Brooks et al., directed by Mel Brooks.

Blue Velvet. 1986, De Laurentiis Entertainment Group. Produced by Fred Caruso, written and directed by David Lynch.

Bohemian Rhapsody. 2018, 20th Century Fox. Produced by Graham King and Jim Beach, written by Anthony McCarten, directed by Bryan Singer.

The Boss of It All. 2006, Canal Plus. Produced by Meta Louise Foldager et al., written and directed by Lars von Trier.

Boyz n the Hood. 1991, Columbia Pictures. Produced by Steve Nicolaides, written and directed by John Singleton.

Brave. 2012 Walt Disney Studios. Produced by Katherine Sarafian, written by Mark Andrews, Brenda Chapman, Steve Purcell, et al., directed by Mark Andrews and Brenda Chapman.

Bullitt. 1968, Warner Bros. Pictures–Seven Arts. Produced by Philip D'Antoni, written by Alan R. Trustman and Harry Kleiner, directed by Peter Yates.

Buona Sera, Mrs. Campbell. 1968, United Artists. Produced by Melvin Frank, written by Melvyn Frank et al., directed by Melvyn Frank.

Butch Cassidy and the Sundance Kid. 1969, 20th Century Fox. Produced by John Foreman, written by William Goldman, directed by George Roy Hill.

The Cabinet of Doctor Caligari. 1920, Decla-Bioscop. Produced by Rudolf Meinert and Erich Pommer, written by Carl Meyer and Hans Janowitz, directed by Robert Wiene.

Carol. 2015, The Weinstein Company. Produced by Elizabeth Karlsen et al., written by Phyllis Nagy, directed by Todd Haynes.

Cars 2. 2011, Walt Disney Studios. Produced by Denise Ream, written by Ben Queen, directed by John Lasseter.

Charlie's Angels. 2019, Columbia Pictures. Produced by Elizabeth Banks et al., written and directed by Elizabeth Banks.

Chennai Express. 2013, UTV Motion Pictures. Produced by Gauri Khan et al., written by Yunus Sajawal, directed by Rohit Shetty.

Child's Play 3. 1991, Universal Pictures. Produced by Robert Latham Brown, written by Don Mancini, directed by Jack Bender.

Chungking Express. 1994, Jet Tone Production Co. Ltd. Produced by Chan Yi-kan and Jeffrey Lau, written and directed by Wong Kar-wai.

City of Hope. 1991, The Samuel Goldwyn Company. Produced by Harold Welb and John Sloss, written and directed by John Sayles.

Cleopatra. 1963, 20th Century Fox. Produced by Walter Wanger, written by Joseph L. Mankiewicz et al., directed by Joseph L. Mankiewicz.

Crimes and Misdemeanors. 1989, Orion Pictures. Produced by Robert Greenhut, written and directed by Woody Allen.

Crimson Tide. 1995, Hollywood Pictures. Produced by Don Simpson and Jerry Bruckheimer, written by Michael Schiffer, directed by Tony Scott.

Dallas Buyers Club. 2013, Focus Features. Produced by Robbie Brenner and Rachel Winter, written by Craig Borten and Melisa Wallack, directed by Jean-Marc Vallee.

Dances with Wolves. 1990, Orion Pictures. Produced by Jim Wilson and Kevin Costner, written by Michael Blake, directed by Kevin Costner.

Dawn of the Planet of the Apes. 2014, 20th Century Fox. Produced by Peter Chernin et al., written by Rick Jaffa et al., directed by Matt Reeves.

Days of Heaven. 1978, Paramount Pictures. Produced by Bert Schneider and Harold Schneider, written and directed by Terrence Malick.

Death Proof. 2007, Dimension Films. Produced by Quentin Tarantino et al., written and directed by Quentin Tarantino.

Demonlover. 2002, SND Films. Produced by Xavier Giannoli, written and directed by Olivier Assayas.

Die Hard. 1988, 20th Century Fox. Produced by Lawrence Gordon and Joel Silver, written by Jeb Stuart and Steven E. de Souza, directed by John McTiernan.

Le Dîner de Cons. 1998, Gaumont. Produced by Alain Poiré, written and directed by Francis Veber.

Donnie Darko. 2001, Newmarket Films. Produced by Sean McKittrick et al., written and directed by Richard Kelly.

Don't Look Up. 2021, Netflix. Produced by Adam McKay and Kevin Messick, written and directed by Adam McKay.

Dune. 1984, Universal Studios. Produced by Raffaella De Laurentiis, written and directed by David Lynch.

8½. 1963, Cineriz. Produced by Angelo Rizzoli, written by Federico Fellini et al., directed by Federico Fellini.

Eraserhead. 1977, American Film Institute. Produced, written, and directed by David Lynch.

Eternals. 2021, Walt Disney Studios. Produced by Kevin Feige and Nate Moore, written by Chloé Zhao, Patrick Burleigh, Kaz Firpo, et al., directed by Chloé Zhao.

Eternal Sunshine of the Spotless Mind. 2004, Focus Features. Produced by Steve Golin and Anthony Bregman, written by Charlie Kaufman, directed by Michel Gondry.

Far from Heaven. 2002, Focus Features. Produced by Jody Allen and Christine Vachon, written and directed by Todd Haynes.

Fargo. 1996, Polygram Filmed Entertainment. Produced, written, and directed by Joel Coen and Ethan Coen.

The Fast and the Furious. 2001, Universal Pictures. Produced by Neal H. Moritz, written by Gary Scott Thompson, Erik Bergquist, and David Ayer, directed by Rob Cohen.

Fatal Attraction. 1987, Paramount Pictures. Produced by Stanley R. Jaffe and Sherry Lansing, written by James Dearden, directed by Adrian Lyne.

A Few Good Men. 1992, Columbia Pictures. Produced by Rob Reiner et al., written by Aaron Sorkin, directed by Rob Reiner.

Fifty Shades of Grey. 2015, Universal Pictures. Produced by Dana Brunetti et al., written by Kelly Marcel, directed by Sam Taylor-Johnson.

Fight Club. 1999, 20th Century Fox. Produced by Art Linson et al., written by Jim Uhls, directed by David Fincher.

Four Weddings and a Funeral. 1994, Polygram Filmed Entertainment. Produced by Duncan Kenworthy, written by Richard Curtis, directed by Mike Newell.

Freaks. 1932, Metro-Goldwyn-Mayer. Produced by Tod Browning et al., written by Willis Goldbeck and Leon Gordon, directed by Tod Browning.

Freaky Friday. 1976, Walt Disney Productions. Produced by Ron Miller, written by Mary Rodgers, directed by Gary Nelson.

Freaky Friday. 2003, Walt Disney Pictures. Produced by Andrew Gunn, written by Heather Hach and Leslie Dixon, directed by Mark Waters.

From Dusk Till Dawn. 1996, Miramax Films. Produced by Gianni Nunnari and Meir Teper, written by Quentin Tarantino, directed by Robert Rodriguez.

Frozen. 2013, Walt Disney Studios. Produced by Peter Del Vecho, written by Jennifer Lee, directed by Chris Buck and Jennifer Lee.

Fruitvale Station. 2013, The Weinstein Company. Produced by Nina Yang Bongiovi and Forest Whitaker, written and directed by Ryan Coogler.

Futureworld. 1976, American International Pictures. Produced by Paul N. Lazarus III and James T. Aubrey, written by Mayo Simon and George Schenck, directed by Richard T. Heffron.

Get Out. 2017, Universal Pictures. Produced by Jordan Peele et al., written and directed by Jordan Peele.

Ghostbusters: Afterlife. 2021, Columbia Pictures. Produced by Ivan Reitman, written by Gil Kenan and Jason Reitman, directed by Jason Reitman.

Ghostbusters: Frozen Empire. 2024, Columbia Pictures. Produced by Ivan Reitman, Jason Reitman, and Jason Blumenfeld, written by Gil Kenan and Jason Reitman, directed by Gil Kenan.

Glass. 2019, Universal Pictures. Produced by M. Night Shyamalan, Jason Blum, Marc Bienstock, et al., written and directed by M. Night Shyamalan.

Glass Onion: A Knives Out Mystery. 2022, Netflix. Produced by Rian Johnson and Ram Bergman, written and directed by Rian Johnson.

The Grand Budapest Hotel. 2014, Fox Searchlight Pictures. Produced by Wes Anderson et al., written and directed by Wes Anderson.

Hellraiser. 1987, Entertainment Film Distributors. Produced by Christopher Figg, written and directed by Clive Barker.

Hidden Figures. 2017, 20th Century Fox. Produced by Donna Gigliotti, Peter Chernin, Theodore Melfi, et al., written by Allison Schroeder and Theodore Melfi, directed by Theodore Melfi.

High Anxiety. 1977, 20th Century Fox. Produced by Mel Brooks, written by Mel Brooks et al., directed by Mel Brooks.

The Holdovers. 2023, Miramax. Produced by Mark Johnson, Bill Block, and David Hemingson, written by David Hemingson, directed by Alexander Payne.

The House That Jack Built. 2018, Zentropa. Produced by Louise Vesth, written and directed by Lars von Trier.

How to Lose a Guy in 10 Days. 2003, Paramount Pictures. Produced by Lynda Obst et al., written by Kristen Buckley et al., directed by Donald Petrie.

The Hurt Locker. 2008, Summit Entertainment. Produced by Kathryn Bigelow et al., written by Mark Boal, directed by Kathryn Bigelow.

I'm Thinking of Ending Things. 2020, Netflix. Produced by Charlie Kaufman, Anthony Bregman, Robert Salerno, et al., written and directed by Charlie Kaufman.

Inception. 2010, Warner Bros. Pictures. Produced by Emma Thomas and Christopher Nolan, written and directed by Christopher Nolan.

Inland Empire. 2006, Studio Canal. Produced by Mary Sweeney and David Lynch, written and directed by David Lynch.

Inside Out. 2015, Walt Disney Studios. Produced by Jonas Rivera, written by Pete Docter, Meg LeFauve, and Josh Cooley, directed by Pete Docter.

Insurgent. 2015, Lions Gate. Produced by Douglas Wick, Lucy Fisher, and Pouya Shabazian, written by Brian Duffield, Akiva Goldsman, and Mark Bomback, directed by Robert Schwentke.

In the Blue Box. 2010, StudioCanal. Produced by Frederic Leconte, interviews and editing by Yannis Polinacci. Featured on the 2017 Australian Blu-ray release of *Mulholland Drive*, 2001.

The Irishman. 2019, Netflix. Produced by Martin Scorsese et al., written by Steven Zaillian, directed by Martin Scorsese.

I Spit on Your Grave. 1978, Cinemagic Pictures. Produced by Joseph Zbeda, written and directed by Meir Zarchi.

Jaws. 1975, Universal Pictures. Produced by Richard D. Zanuck and David Brown, written by Peter Benchley and Carl Gottlieb, directed by Steven Spielberg.

The Jazz Singer. 1927, Warner Bros. Pictures. Produced by Darryl F. Zanuck, written by Alfred A. Cohn, directed by Alan Crosland.

Kill Bill: Volume 1. 2003, Miramax Films. Produced by Lawrence Bender, written and directed by Quentin Tarantino.

Kill Bill: Volume 2. 2004, Miramax Films. Produced by Lawrence Bender, written and directed by Quentin Tarantino.

Kingdom of the Planet of the Apes. 2024, 20th Century Studios. Produced by Wes Ball, Rick Jaffa, Amanda Silver, et al., written by Josh Friedman, directed by Wes Ball.

Knight of Cups. 2015, Broad Green Pictures. Produced by Nicolas Gonda et al., written and directed by Terrence Malick.

Knives Out. 2019, Lionsgate. Produced by Rian Johnson and Ram Bergman, written and directed by Rian Johnson.

Knocked Up. 2007, Universal Pictures. Produced by Judd Apatow et al., written and directed by Judd Apatow.

L.A. Confidential. 1997, Warner Bros. Pictures. Produced by Arnon Milchan et al., written by Brian Helgeland and Curtis Hanson, directed by Curtis Hanson.

Lady Chatterley. 2006, Ad Vitam Distribution. Produced by Gilles Sandoz, written by Roger Bohbot and Pascale Ferran, directed by Pascale Ferran.

The Last Laugh. 1924, UFA. Produced by Erich Pommer, written by Carl Mayer, directed by F. W. Murnau. 2004 DVD release, Eureka.

The Last Samurai. 2003, Warner Bros. Pictures. Produced by Tom Cruise et al., written by John Logan et al., directed by Edward Zwick.

Lethal Weapon. 1987, Warner Bros. Pictures. Produced by Richard Donner and Joel Silver, written by Shane Black, directed by Richard Donner.

Lightyear. 2022, Walt Disney Studios. Produced by Galyn Susman, written by Jason Headley and Angus MacLane, directed by Angus MacLane.

The Little Mermaid. 1989, Walt Disney Studios. Produced by Howard Ashman and John Musker, written and directed by John Musker and Ron Clements.

The Little Mermaid. 2023, Walt Disney Studios. Produced by Rob Marshall, Marc Platt, Lin-Manuel Miranda, et al., written by David Magee, directed by Rob Marshall.

The Lobster. 2015, Film4. Produced by Yorgos Lanthimos, Ceci Dempsey, Ed Guiney, et al., written by Yorgos Lanthimos and Efthimis Filippou, directed by Yorgos Lanthimos.

The Lone Ranger. 2013, Walt Disney Pictures. Produced by Jerry Bruckheimer and Gore Verbinski, written by Justin Haythe et al., directed by Gore Verbinski.

The Lord of the Rings: The Fellowship of the Ring. 2001, New Line Cinema. Produced by Peter Jackson, Fran Walsh, Tim Sanders, et al., written by Peter Jackson, Fran Walsh, and Philippa Boyens, directed by Peter Jackson.

The Lord of the Rings: The Two Towers. 2002, New Line Cinema. Produced by Peter Jackson, Fran Walsh, Tim Sanders, et al., written by Peter Jackson, Fran Walsh, Philippa Boyens, et al., directed by Peter Jackson.

The Lord of the Rings: The Return of the King. 2003, New Line Cinema. Produced by Peter Jackson, Fran Walsh, Tim Sanders, et al., written by Peter Jackson, Fran Walsh, and Philippa Boyens, directed by Peter Jackson.

Lost Highway. 1997, October Films. Produced by Mary Sweeney et al., written by David Lynch and Barry Gifford, directed by David Lynch.

The Machinist. 2004, Paramount Classics. Produced by Carlos Fernandez, written by Scott Kosar, directed by Brad Anderson.

Mad Max. 1979, Roadshow Film Distributors. Produced by Byron Kennedy, written by James McCausland and George Miller, directed by George Miller.

Malcolm X. 1992, Warner Bros. Pictures. Produced by Marvin Worth and Spike Lee, written by Arnold Perl and Spike Lee, directed by Spike Lee.

Mama Mia! 2008, Universal Pictures. Produced by Judy Craymer and Gary Goetzman, written by Catherine Johnson, directed by Phyllida Lloyd.

The Marvels. 2023, Walt Disney Studios. Produced by Kevin Feige, written by Nia DaCosta, Megan McDonnell, and Elissa Karasik, directed by Nia DaCosta.

Masquerade. 1965, United Artists. Produced by Michael Relph, written by William Goldman and Michael Relph, directed by Basil Dearden.

The Matrix. 1999, Warner Bros. Pictures. Produced by Joel Silver, written and directed by the Wachowskis.

Memento. 2000, Summit Entertainment. Produced by Suzanne Todd and Jennifer Todd, written and directed by Christopher Nolan.

Mission: Impossible. 1996, Paramount Pictures. Produced by Tom Cruise and Paula Wagner, written by David Koepp and Robert Towne, directed by Brian De Palma.

Moana. 2016, Walt Disney Studios. Produced by Osnat Shurer, written by Jared Bush, directed by John Musker and Ron Clements.

Modern Times. 1936, United Artists. Produced, written, and directed by Charlie Chaplin.

Monsters University. 2013, Walt Disney Studios. Produced Kori Rae, written by Dan Gerson, Robert L. Baird, and Dan Scanlon, directed by Dan Scanlon.

Moonlight. 2016, A24. Produced by Adele Romanski, Dede Gardner, and Jeremy Kleiner, written and directed by Barry Jenkins.

mother! 2017, Paramount Pictures. Produced by Scott Franklin and Ari Handel, written and directed by Darren Aronofsky.

Mulholland Drive. 2001, Universal Pictures. Produced by Mary Sweeney et al., written and directed by David Lynch.

Murder on the Orient Express. 1974 Paramount Pictures. Produced by John Brabourne and Richard Goodwin, written by Paul Dehn, directed by Sidney Lumet.

Murder on the Orient Express. 2017, 20th Century Fox. Produced by Ridley Scott et al., written by Michael Green, directed by Kenneth Branagh.

My Big Fat Greek Wedding. 2002, IFC Films. Produced by Gary Goetzman et al., written by Nia Vardalos, directed by Joel Zwick.

The Neon Demon. 2016, Amazon Studios. Produced by Lene Børglum and Nicolas Winding Refn, written by Nicolas Winding Refn, Mary Laws, and Polly Stenham, directed by Nicolas Winding Refn.

A Nightmare on Elm Street. 1984, New Line Cinema. Produced by Robert Shaye, written and directed by Wes Craven.

Nomadland. 2020, Searchlight Pictures. Produced by Chloé Zhao, Frances McDormand, Peter Spears, et al., written and directed by Chloé Zhao.

No Time to Die. 2021, EON Productions. Produced by Michael G. Wilson and Barbara Broccoli, written by Neal Purvis, Robert Wade, Cary Joji Fukunaga, and Phoebe Waller-Bridge, directed by Cary Joji Fukunaga.

Not Quite Hollywood: The Wild, Untold Story of Ozploitation! 2008, Madman Films. Produced by Michael Lynch and Craig Griffin, written and directed by Mark Hartley.

O Brother, Where Art Thou? 2000, Universal Pictures. Produced by Ethan Coen, written by Ethan Coen and Joel Coen, directed by Joel Coen.

Onward. 2020, Walt Disney Studios. Produced by Kori Rae, written by Dan Scanlon, Jason Headley, and Keith Bunin, directed by Dan Scanlon.

Oppenheimer. 2023, Warner Bros. Pictures. Produced by Emma Thomas, Charles Roven, and Christopher Nolan, written and directed by Christopher Nolan.

Parasite. 2019, CJ Entertainment. Produced by Bong Joon-ho, Kwak Sin-ae, Moon Yang-kwon, et al., written by Bong Joon-ho and Han Jin-won, directed by Bong Joon-ho.

Phantom Thread. 2017, Universal Pictures. Produced by JoAnne Sellar et al., written and directed by Paul Thomas Anderson.

Planet of the Apes. 1968, 20th Century Fox. Produced by Arthur P. Jacobs, written by Michael Wilson and Rod Serling, directed by Franklin J, Schaffner.

Planet of the Apes. 2001, 20th Century Fox. Produced by Richard D. Zanuck, written by William Broyles Jr. et al., directed by Tim Burton.

Planet Terror. 2007, Dimension Films. Produced by Robert Rodriguez et al., written and directed by Robert Rodriguez.

Porky's. 1981, 20th Century Fox. Produced by Don Carmody and Bob Clark, written and directed by Bob Clark.

The Prestige. 2006, Warner Bros. Pictures. Produced by Emma Thomas et al., written by Jonathan Nolan and Christopher Nolan, directed by Christopher Nolan.

Primer. 2004, IFC Films. Produced, written, and directed by Shane Carruth.

Pulp Fiction. 1994, Miramax Films. Produced by Lawrence Bender, written and directed by Quentin Tarantino.

Raging Bull. 1980, United Artists. Produced by Irwin Winkler and Robert Chartoff, written by Paul Schrader and Mardik Martin, directed by Martin Scorsese.

Raiders of the Lost Ark. 1981, Paramount Pictures. Produced by Frank Marshall, written by Lawrence Kasdan, directed by Steven Spielberg.

Ready Player One. 2018, Warner Bros. Pictures. Produced by Steven Spielberg et al., written by Zak Penn and Ernest Cline, directed by Steven Spielberg.

The Revenant. 2015, 20th Century Fox. Produced by Alejandro G. Iñárritu, Arnon Milchan, Mary Parent, et al., written by Alejandro G. Iñárritu and Mark L. Smith, directed by Alejandro G. Iñárritu.

Rise of the Planet of the Apes. 2011, 20th Century Fox. Produced by Peter Chernin et al., written by Rick Jaffa and Amanda Silver, directed by Rupert Wyatt.

Risky Business. 1983, Warner Bros. Pictures. Produced by Jon Avnet and Steve Tisch, written and directed by Paul Brickman.

Rocketman. 2019, Paramount Pictures. Produced by David Furnish et al., written by Lee Hall, directed by Dexter Fletcher.

Rocky. 1976, United Artists. Produced by Irwin Winkler and Robert Chartoff, written by Sylvester Stallone, directed by John G. Avildsen.

Rocky IV. 1985, United Artists / Metro-Goldwyn-Mayer. Produced by Robert Chartoff and Irwin Winkler, written and directed by Sylvester Stallone.

Romance. 1999, Rezo Films. Produced by Jean-Francois Lepetit, written and directed by Catherine Breillat.

Roxane. 2019, Quad Films. Produced by Foucauld Barre and Nicolas Duval Adassovsky, written by Michaël Souhaité, directed by Melanie Auffret.

Saltburn. 2023, Amazon MGM Studios. Produced by Emerald Fennell, Josey McNamara, and Margot Robbie, written and directed by Emerald Fennell.

San Andreas. 2015, Warner Bros. Pictures. Produced by Beau Flynn, written by Carlton Cuse, directed by Brad Peyton.

Saw. 2004, Lions Gate Films. Produced by Gregg Hoffman, Oren Koules, and Mark Burg, written by Leigh Whannell, directed by James Wan.

Schindler's List. 1993, Universal Pictures. Produced by Steven Spielberg et al., written by Steven Zaillian, directed by Steven Spielberg.

Scream. 1996, Dimension Films. Produced by Cathy Konrad and Cary Woods, written by Kevin Williamson, directed by Wes Craven.

Serene Velocity. 1970, Ernie Gehr. Produced, written, and directed by Ernie Gehr.

Shutter Island. 2010, Paramount Pictures. Produced by Mike Medavoy et al., written by Laeta Kalogridis, directed by Martin Scorsese.

Silence of the Lambs. 1991, Orion Pictures. Produced by Kenneth Utt et al., written by Ted Tally, directed by Jonathan Demme.

The Sixth Sense. 1999, Hollywood Pictures. Produced by Frank Marshall et al., written and directed by M. Night Shyamalan.

The Social Network. 2010, Sony Pictures. Produced by Scott Rudin et al., written by Aaron Sorkin, directed by David Fincher.

Some Like It Hot. 1959, United Artists. Produced by Billy Wilder, written by Billy Wilder and I. A. L. Diamond, directed by Billy Wilder.

The Sound of Music. 1965, 20th Century Fox. Produced by Robert Wise, written by Ernest Lehman, directed by Robert Wise.

Spaceballs. 1987, Metro-Goldwyn-Mayer. Produced by Mel Brooks, written by Mel Brooks et al., directed by Mel Brooks.

Spider-Man: Across the Spider-Verse. 2023, Sony Pictures Releasing. Produced by Amy Pascal, Phil Lord, Christopher Miller, et al., written by Phil Lord, Christopher Miller, and Dave Callaham, directed by Joaquim Dos Santos, Kemp Powers, and Justin K. Thompson.

Spider-Man: Beyond the Spider-Verse. 2027, Sony Pictures Releasing. Produced by Amy Pascal, Phil Lord, Christopher Miller, et al., written by Phil Lord, Christopher Miller, and Dave Callaham, directed by Joaquim Dos Santos, Kemp Powers, and Justin K. Thompson.

Split. 2017, Universal Pictures. Produced by Jason Blum et al., written and directed by M. Night Shyamalan.

Star Trek: The Motion Picture. 1979, Paramount Pictures. Produced by Gene Roddenberry, written by Alan Dean Foster and Harold Livingston, directed by Robert Wise.

Star Wars. 1977, 20th Century Fox. Produced by Gary Kurtz, written and directed by George Lucas.

Star Wars: Episode VII—The Force Awakens. 2015, Walt Disney Studios. Produced by Kathleen Kennedy et al., written by Michael Arndt et al., directed by J. J. Abrams.

Stealing Beauty. 1996, Fox Searchlight Pictures. Produced by Jeremy Thomas, written by Susan Minot, directed by Bernardo Bertolucci.

Sunset Boulevard. 1950, Paramount Pictures. Produced by Charles Brackett, written by Charles Brackett et al., directed by Billy Wilder.

Taxi Driver. 1976, Columbia Pictures. Produced by Julia Phillips and Michael Phillips, written by Paul Schrader, directed by Martin Scorsese.

Tenet. 2020, Warner Bros. Pictures. Produced by Emma Thomas and Christopher Nolan, written and directed by Christopher Nolan.

Thank You for Smoking. 2005, Fox Searchlight Pictures. Produced by David O. Sacks, written and directed by Jason Reitman.

Thelma and Louise. 1991, Metro-Goldwyn-Mayer. Produced by Ridley Scott and Mimi Polk Gitlin, written by Callie Khouri, directed by Ridley Scott.

The Thing. 1982, Universal Pictures. Produced by David Foster and Lawrence Turman, written by Bill Lancaster, directed by John Carpenter.

This Is the End. 2013, Columbia Pictures. Produced by Seth Rogen, Evan Goldberg, and James Weaver, written and directed by Seth Rogen and Evan Goldberg.

Thor: Ragnarok. 2017, Walt Disney Studios. Produced by Kevin Feige, written by Eric Pearson, Craig Kyle, and Christopher L. Yost, directed by Taika Waititi.

Thor: Love and Thunder. 2022, Walt Disney Studios. Produced by Kevin Feige and Brad Winderbaum, written by Taika Waititi and Jennifer Kaytin Robinson, directed by Taika Waititi.

Thoroughly Modern Millie. 1967, Universal Pictures. Produced by Ross Hunter, written by Richard Morris, directed by George Roy Hill.

Titane. 2021, Diaphana Distribution. Produced by Jean-Christophe Reymond, written and directed by Julia Ducournau.

Titanic. 1997, Paramount Pictures. Produced by James Cameron and Jon Landau, written and directed by James Cameron.

To All the Boys I've Loved Before. 2018, Netflix. Produced by Jordan Levin, Matthew Kaplan, and Dougie Cash, written by Sophie Alvarez, directed by Susan Johnson.

Top Gun. 1986, Paramount Pictures. Produced by Don Simpson and Jerry Bruckheimer, written by Jim Cash and Jack Epps Jr., directed by Tony Scott.

Toto le Heros. 1991, Canal Plus. Produced by Dany Geys and Luciano Gloor, written by Jaco Van Dormael et al., directed by Jaco Van Dormael.

Toy Story 3. 2010, Walt Disney Studios. Produced by Darla K. Anderson, written by Michael Arndt, directed by Lee Unkrich.

Toy Story 4. 2019, Walt Disney Studios. Produced by Mark Nielsen and Jonas Rivera, written by Andrew Stanton and Stephany Folsom, directed by Josh Cooley.

Transformers. 2007, DreamWorks Pictures and Paramount Pictures. Produced by Lorenzo di Bonaventura et al., written by Roberto Orci and Alex Kurtzman, directed by Michael Bay.

The Truman Show. 1998, Paramount Pictures. Produced by Scott Rudin et al., written by Andrew Niccol, directed by Peter Weir.

12 Years a Slave. 2013, Film4. Produced by Steve McQueen, Brad Pitt, Dede Gardner, et al., written by John Ridley, directed by Steve McQueen.

Twilight. 2008, Summit Entertainment. Produced by Greg Mooradian, Mark Morgan, and Wyck Godfrey, written by Melissa Rosenberg, directed by Catherine Hardwicke.

Twin Peaks: Fire Walk with Me. 1992, New Line Cinema. Produced by Gregg Fienberg, written by David Lynch and Robert Engels, directed by David Lynch.

2001: A Space Odyssey. 1968, Metro-Goldwyn-Mayer. Produced by Stanley Kubrick, written by Stanley Kubrick and Arthur C. Clarke, directed by Stanley Kubrick.

Unbreakable. 2000, Buena Vista Pictures. Produced by Barry Mendel et al., written and directed by M. Night Shyamalan.

Up. 2009, Walt Disney Studios. Produced by Jonas Rivera, written by Bob Peterson and Peter Docter, directed by Peter Docter.

The Usual Suspects. 1995, Gramercy Pictures. Produced by Bryan Singer and Michael McDonnell, written by Christopher McQuarrie, directed by Bryan Singer.

Valley of Love. 2015, Le Pacte. Produced by Cyril Colbeau-Justin et al., written and directed by Guillaume Nicloux.

Venredi Soir. 2002, Canal Plus. Produced by Bruno Pesery, written by Claire Denis and Emmanuele Bernheim, directed by Claire Denis.

War for the Planet of the Apes. 2017, 20th Century Fox. Produced by Peter Chernin et al., written by Mark Bomback and Matt Reeves, directed by Matt Reeves.

Werckmeister Harmonies. 2000, 13 Productions. Produced by Bela Tarr, written by Laszlo Krasznahorkai, directed by Bela Tarr, codirected by Agnes Hranitzky.

West Side Story. 1961, United Artists. Produced by Robert Wise, written by Ernest Lehman, directed by Jerome Robbins and Robert Wise.

Westworld. 1973, Metro-Goldwyn-Mayer. Produced by Paul N. Lazarus III, written and directed by Michael Crichton.

Wild at Heart. 1990, The Samuel Goldwyn Company. Produced by Steve Golin et al., written and directed by David Lynch.

The Wizard of Oz. 1939, Metro-Goldwyn-Mayer. Produced by Mervyn LeRoy, written by Noel Langley et al., directed by Victor Fleming.

The Wolf of Wall Street. 2013, Paramount Pictures. Produced by Martin Scorsese et al., written by Terence Winter, directed by Martin Scorsese.

Yesterday. 2019, Universal Pictures. Produced by Tim Bevan et al., written by Richard Curtis, directed by Danny Boyle.

Young Frankenstein. 1974, 20th Century Fox. Produced by Michael Gruskoff, written by Gene Wilder and Mel Brooks, directed by Mel Brooks.

You've Got Mail. 1998, Warner Bros. Pictures. Produced by Lauren Shuler Donner and Nora Ephron, written by Nora Ephron and Delia Ephron, directed by Nora Ephron.

You Were Never Really Here. 2017, Film4. Produced by Lynne Ramsay, Rosa Attab, Pascal Caucheteux, et al., written and directed by Lynne Ramsay.

Television Series

Breaking Bad. 2008–2013, Sony Pictures Television, US. Created by Vince Gilligan.

Coronation Street. 1960–, ITV Studios, UK. Created by Tony Warren.

CSI: Crime Scene Investigation. 2000–2015, CBS, US. Created by Anthony E. Zuiker.

Eastenders. 1985–, BBC Studios, UK. Created by Julia Smith and Tony Holland.

Extras. 2005–2007, British Broadcasting Corporation, UK. Created by Ricky Gervais and Stephen Merchant.

JAG. 1995–2004, NBC and CBS, US. Created by Donald P. Bellisario.

The Larry Sanders Show. 1992–1998, Sony Pictures Television, US. Created by Garry Shandling and Dennis Klein.

Law & Order. 1990–, NBC, US. Created by Dick Wolf.

NCIS: Naval Criminal Investigation Service. 2003–, CBS Studios, US. Created by Donald P. Bellisario and Don McGill.

The Office. 2005–2013, NBC Universal, US. Developed by Greg Daniels based on *The Office*, created by Ricky Gervais and Stephen Merchant.

Planet of the Apes. 1974, 20th Century Fox Television, US. Developed by Anthony Wilson.

Return to the Planet of the Apes. 1975–1976, 20th Century Fox Television, US. Developed by David H. DePatie and Friz Freleng.

The Sopranos. 1999–2007, HBO Entertainment, US. Created by David Chase.

Stranger Things. 2016–, Netflix, US. Created by Matt Duffer and Ross Duffer.

True Detective. 2014–, HBO Entertainment, US. Created by Nic Pizzolatto.

Twin Peaks. 1990–1991, American Broadcasting Company, US. Created by Mark Frost and David Lynch.

The Walking Dead. 2010–2022, AMC Studios, US. Created by Frank Darabont.

The West Wing. 1999–2006, Warner Bros. Television, US. Created by Aaron Sorkin.

BIBLIOGRAPHY

Adams, Douglas. *The Hitchhiker's Guide to the Galaxy.* Pan Books, 1979.

Alberge, Dalya. "Ennio Morricone: Good Film Scores Have Been Replaced by the Bad and the Ugly." *The Guardian*, June 3, 2015. https://www.theguardian.com/music/2015/jun/03/ennio-morricone-good-film-scores-replaced-by-bad-and-ugly.

Alcolea-Banegas, Jesus. "Visual Arguments in Film." *Argumentation* 23, no. 2 (2009): 259–275.

Alcorn, Chauncey. "'Fifty Shades' Trilogy Takes First Three Spots on the Top 10 Best-Selling Novels of the Decade List." *CNN*, December 19, 2019. https://edition.cnn.com/2019/12/19/business/50-shades/index.html#:~:text=The%20first%20%E2%80%9CFifty%20Shades%E2%80%9D%20book,selling%20book%20of%20the%202010s.

Alesi, Tamara. "TV Watchers around the World Spread Their Attention across Other Devices." *YouGov*, December 10, 2020. https://today.yougov.com/entertainment/articles/33396-multi-screening-global-poll.

Aristotle. *The "Art" of Rhetoric.* Translated by John Henry Freese. Heinemann, 1926.

———. *The Art of Rhetoric.* Translated by Hugh Lawson-Tancred. Penguin, 2004.

———. *Nicomachean Ethics.* Translated by C. D. C. Reeve. Hackett, 2014.

———. *Poetics.* Translated by Malcolm Heath. Penguin, 1996.

———. *The Poetics of Aristotle.* Translated by S. H. Butcher. Macmillan, 1907.

Arnold, Ann. "The Economics of Movie Making: Is There Any Money Left to Be Made in Film?" *ABC News*, February 27, 2017. http://www.abc.net.au/news/2017-02-25/economics-of-movie-making/8292352.

Aronofsky, Darren. "Master Class of Darren Aronofsky in OIFF." Odessa International Film Festival. YouTube, December 29, 2015. https://www.youtube.com/watch?v=B6LeXVCiOOM&t=3s.

Aronson, Linda. *Screenwriting Updated: New (and Conventional) Ways of Writing for the Screen*. Allen & Unwin, 2000.

Bakhtin, Mikhail. *The Dialogic Imagination: Four Essays*. Edited by Michael Holquist. Translated by Caryl Emerson and Michael Holquist. University of Texas Press, 1981.

Barnes, Brooks. "It Wasn't a Wreck, Not Really." *New York Times*, October 17, 2011. https://www.nytimes.com/2011/10/18/movies/john-lasseter-of-pixar-defends-cars-2.html.

Barthes, Roland. "The Death of the Author." *Aspen*, no. 5 and 6 (1967).

———. *S/Z: An Essay*. Farrar, Straus and Giroux, 1974.

Beaty, Bart. "Superhero Fan Service: Audience Strategies in the Contemporary Interlinked Hollywood Blockbuster." *Information Society* 32, no. 5 (2016): 318–325.

Behrens, Laurence. "The Argument in Film: Applying Rhetorical Theory to Film Criticism." *Journal of the University Film Association* 31, no. 3 (1979): 3–11.

Belloni, Matthew, and Stephen Galloway. "Director Roundtable: Mel Gibson, Denzel Washington and 4 More on Paralyzing Fears, Cast and Crew Complaints." *Hollywood Reporter*, December 8, 2016. https://www.hollywoodreporter.com/features/director-roundtable-mel-gibson-denzel-washington-4-more-paralyzing-fears-cast-crew-complain.

Bennett, Bruce. "Film as Argument." *Humanities* 28, no. 6 (2007). https://www.neh.gov/humanities/2007/novemberdecember/feature/film-argument.

Berg, Andrew Scott. *Goldwyn: A Biography*. Knopf, 1989.

Beugnet, Martine. "Cinema and Sensation: Contemporary French Film and Cinematic Corporeality." *Cinema and the Senses* 31, no. 2 (2008): 173–188.

———. *Cinema and Sensation: French Film and the Art of Transgression*. Southern Illinois University Press, 2007.

Boller, Paul F., Jr., and Ronald L. Davis. *Hollywood Anecdotes*. William Morrow, 1987.

Booth, Wayne. *The Rhetoric of Fiction*. University of Chicago Press, 1961.

Bordwell, David. "Common Sense + Film Theory = Common-Sense Film Theory?" *David Bordwell's Website on Cinema*, May 2011. http://www.davidbordwell.net/essays/commonsense.php.

Bordwell, David, Janet Staiger, and Kristin Thompson. *The Classical Hollywood Cinema*. Columbia University Press, 1985.

Bordwell, David, Kristin Thompson, and Jeff Smith. *Film Art: An Introduction*. 12th ed. McGraw-Hill, 2018.

Boulle, Pierre. *La Planète des Singes*. Rene Julliard, 1963.

Bourdieu, Pierre. *Outline of a Theory of Practice*. Cambridge University Press, 1972.

Brenes, Carmen. "Quoting and Misquoting Aristotle's 'Poetics' in Recent Screenwriting Bibliography." *Communication and Society* 27, no. 2 (2014): 55–78.

Brooks, Xan. "Room to Dream by David Lynch and Kristine McKenna—Review." *The Guardian*, June 24, 2018. https://www.theguardian.com/books/2018/jun/24/room-to-dream-david-lynch-biography-review.

Buckmaster, Luke. "Why *Mulholland Drive* Is the Greatest Film since 2000." *BBC*, August 23, 2016. http://www.bbc.com/culture/story/20160822-why-mulholland-drive-is-the-greatest-film-since-2000.

Burke, Seán. *The Death and Return of the Author: Criticism and Subjectivity in Barthes, Foucault and Derrida*. Edinburgh University Press, 2008.

Campbell, Joseph. *Hero of a Thousand Faces*. Commemorative ed. Princeton University Press, 2004.

Campora, Matthew. *Subjective Realist Cinema: From Expressionism to Inception*. Berghahn Books, 2014.

Carroll, Noël. "Philosophizing through the Moving Image: The Case of Serene Velocity." In *Thinking through Cinema: Film as Philosophy*, edited by Murray Smith and Thomas E. Wartenberg, 173–185. Blackwell, 2006.

———. "The Power of Movies." *Daedalus* 114, no. 4 (1985): 79–103.

Cavell, Stanley. *Pursuits of Happiness: The Hollywood Comedy of Remarriage*. Harvard University Press, 1981.

Cavna, Michael. "Pixar Tips: 'Brave' Artist Emma Coats Shares Her Storytelling Wit and Wisdom on Twitter (#FollowHer)." *Washington Post*, June 25, 2012. https://www.washingtonpost.com/blogs/comic-riffs/post/pixar-tips-brave-artist-emma-coats-shares-her-storytelling-wit-and-wisdom-on-twitter%20followher/2012/06/25/gJQADaxd2V_blog.html.

Coleridge, Samuel Taylor. *Biographia Literaria*. Edinburgh University Press, 2014.

Conan Doyle, Arthur. *The Complete Sherlock Holmes*. Doubleday, 1930.

Conor, Bridget. "Gurus and Oscar Winners: How-To Screenwriting Manuals in the New Cultural Economy." *Television & New Media* 15, no. 2 (2014): 121–138.

Cousineau, Phil. *The Painted Word: A Treasure Chest of Remarkable Words and Their Origins*. Cleis Press, 2012.

Cox, Damian, and Michael Levine. *Thinking through Film*. Wiley-Blackwell, 2012.

Crowe, Cameron. "Hot Shot in Top Gun." *Interview Magazine*, 1986. http://www.theuncool.com/journalism/tom-cruise-interview-magazine/.

Dancyger, Ken, and Jeff Rush. *Alternative Screenwriting*. 5th ed. Focal Press, 2013.

Deleuze, Gilles. *Desert Islands and Other Texts (1953–1974)*. Translated by Mike Taormina. Semiotext(e), 2003.

———. *Negotiations*. Translated by Martin Joughin. Columbia University Press, 1995.

Dyer, Richard. *Only Entertainment*. Routledge, 1992.

Eisenstein, Sergei. *Film Form: Essays in Film Theory*. Translated by Jay Leyda. Harvest Books, 1969.

Elsaesser, Thomas. "The Mind-Game Film." In *Puzzle Films: Complex Storytelling in Contemporary Cinema*, edited by Warren Buckland, 13–41. Blackwell, 2009.

Falzon, Christopher. *Philosophy Goes to the Movies*. Routledge, 2002.

Fear, David, Brandon Geist, Tim Grierson, Kory Grow, and Eric Hynes. "25 Best Modern Exploitation Movies." *Rolling Stone*, July 6, 2015. http://www.rollingstone.com/movies/lists/25-best-modern-exploitation-movies-20150706/crank-2006-20150701.

Field, Syd. *Screenplay: The Foundations of Screenwriting*. Rev. ed. Random House, 2005.

Fisher, Walter R. *Human Communication as Narration: Toward a Philosophy of Reason, Value and Action*. University of South Carolina Press, 1989.

Fox, Killian. "David Lynch: 'It's Important to Go Out and Feel the So-Called Reality.'" *The Guardian*, June 30, 2019. https://www.theguardian.com/film/2019/jun/30/david-lynch-interview-manchester-international-festival.

Giddens, Anthony. *New Rules of Sociological Method*. Basic Books, 1976.

Gleiberman, Owen. "Film Review: 'Mother!" *Variety*, September 5, 2017. https://variety.com/2017/film/reviews/mother-review-jennifer-lawrence-venice-film-festival-1202545924/.

Green, Melanie C., and Timothy C. Brock. "The Role of Transportation in the Persuasiveness of Public Narratives." *Journal of Personality and Social Psychology* 79, no. 5 (2000): 701–721.

Haase, Christine. *When Heimat Meets Hollywood: German Filmmakers and America, 1985–2005*. Boydell & Brewer, 2007.

Hager, Paul. "Refurbishing MacIntyre's Account of Practice." *Journal of Philosophy of Education* 45, no. 3 (2011): 545–561.

Harari, Yuval Noah. "How AI Will Shape Humanity's Future." YouTube, March 5, 2024. https://www.youtube.com/watch?v=2w37ty9gGU8.

———. *Sapiens: A Brief History of Humankind*. Harper, 2015.

Hitchcock, David. "Enthymematic Arguments." *Informal Logic* 7, no. 2 (1985): 83–97.

Homer. *The Odyssey*. Translated by Robert Fagles. Penguin, 1997.

Hooton, Christopher. "Darren Aronofsky Defends Mother! after F Rating: 'I Wanted to Howl, and This Was My Howl.'" *Independent*, September 22, 2017. https://www.independent.co.uk/arts-entertainment/films/news/mother-film-movie-darren-aronofsky-2017-jennifer-lawrence-f-rating-reviews-critical-response-a7961051.html.

Kauffman, Stanley. "Stanley Kauffman on Films: Sense and Sensibility." *New Republic,* October 29, 2001. https://newrepublic.com/article/92197/david-lynch-mulholland-drive.

Kaye, Don. "Human See, Human Do: A Complete History of 'Planet of the Apes.'" *Rolling Stone,* July 1, 2014. https://www.rollingstone.com/movies/movie-news/human-see-human-do-a-complete-history-of-planet-of-the-apes-107958/.

Keegan, Rebecca. "Jordan Peele on the 'Post-racial Lie' That Inspired Get Out." *Vanity Fair,* October 30, 2017. https://www.vanityfair.com/hollywood/2017/10/jordan-peele-get-out-screening.

Kerin, Roger A., P. Rajan Varadarajan, and Robert A. Peterson. "First-Mover Advantage: A Synthesis, Conceptual Framework, and Research Propositions." *Journal of Marketing* 56, no. 4 (1992): 33–52.

Kivy, Peter. *Once-Told Tales: An Essay in Literary Aesthetics.* John Wiley, 2011.

Kwapis, Ken. *What I Really Want to Do Is Direct: Lessons from a Life Behind the Camera.* St. Martin's Griffin, 2020.

Lacey, Nicola. "MacIntyre, Feminism and the Concept of Practice." In *After MacIntyre: Critical Perspectives on the Work of Alasdair MacIntyre,* edited by John Horton and Susan Mendus, 265–282. Blackwell, 1994.

Leigh, Danny. "Is Terrence Malick Ahead of His Time or Out of Date?" *The Guardian,* March 10, 2017. https://www.theguardian.com/film/2017/mar/09/is-terrence-malick-ahead-of-his-time-or-out-of-date.

———. "What Is David Lynch's Inland Empire About?" *The Guardian,* March 9, 2007. https://www.theguardian.com/film/filmblog/2007/mar/09/whatisdavidlynchsinlandem.

Leitch, Thomas. *Film Adaptation and Its Discontents: From "Gone with the Wind" to "The Passion of the Christ."* Johns Hopkins University Press, 2007.

Lewis, Robyn. "Nice Film—If You Can Get It." *The Guardian,* January 17, 2002. https://www.theguardian.com/culture/2002/jan/17/artsfeatures.davidlynch.

Liveley, Genevieve. *Narratology.* Oxford University Press, 2019.

Livingston, Paisley. *Cinema, Philosophy, Bergman: On Cinema as Philosophy.* Oxford University Press, 2009.

———. "Theses on Cinema as Philosophy." In *Thinking through Cinema: Film as Philosophy,* edited by Murray Smith and Thomas E. Wartenberg, 11–18. Blackwell, 2006.

Lovell, Alan, and Gianluca Sergi. *Cinema Entertainment: Essays on Audiences, Films and Film Makers.* Open University Press, 2009.

Lynch, David. *Catching the Big Fish: Meditation, Consciousness and Creativity.* Tarcherperigee, 2006.

Lynch, David, and Kristine McKenna. *Room to Dream.* Random House, 2018.

Macdonald, Ian W. *Screenwriting Poetics and the Screen Idea*. Palgrave Macmillan, 2013.

MacDowell, James. *Happy Endings in Hollywood Cinema: Cliché, Convention and the Final Couple*. Edinburgh University Press, 2014.

MacIntyre, Alasdair. *After Virtue: A Study in Moral Theory*. 2nd ed. University of Notre Dame Press, 1981.

Mackendrick, Alexander. *On Film-Making*. Faber & Faber, 2004.

Main, Douglas. "Even in the Middle Ages, People Didn't Think the Earth Was Flat." *Newsweek*, January 28, 2016. https://www.newsweek.com/even-middle-ages-people-didnt-think-earth-was-flat-420775.

Mamet, David. *On Directing Film*. Penguin, 1992.

———. "They Think It's All Over." *Guardian*, May 16, 2003. https://www.theguardian.com/film/2003/may/16/artsfeatures.davidmamet.

Maras, Steven. *Screenwriting: History, Theory and Practice*. Wallflower Press, 2009.

Mateer, John. "Directing for Cinematic Virtual Reality: How the Traditional Film Director's Craft Applies to Immersive Environments and Notions of Presence." *Journal of Media Practice* 18, no. 1 (2017): 14–25.

McCarthy, Todd. "Brave: Film Review." *Hollywood Reporter*, June 10, 2012. https://www.hollywoodreporter.com/movies/movie-reviews/brave-film-review-335633/.

McGowan, Todd. "Accumulation and Enjoyment on *Mulholland Drive*." *Comparitist* 39 (October 2015): 101–115.

———. "Lost on *Mulholland Drive*: Navigating David Lynch's Panegyric to Hollywood." *Cinema Journal* 43, no. 2 (2004): 67–89.

McKee, Robert. *Story: Substance, Structure, Style, and the Principles of Screenwriting*. HarperCollins, 1998.

Mellor, Louisa. "Robert Zemeckis Interview: The Walk, Modern Filmmaking." *Den of Geek*, October 5, 2015. http://www.denofgeek.com/movies/robert-zemeckis/37195/robert-zemeckis-interview-the-walk-modern-filmmaking.

Metz, Christian. *The Imaginary Signifier: Psychoanalysis and the Cinema*. Translated by Celia Britton, Annwyl Williams, Ben Brewster, and Alfred Guzzetti. Indiana University Press, 1982.

Meyer, Stephenie. *Twilight*. Little, Brown, 2005.

Miller, David. "Virtues, Practices and Justice." In *After MacIntyre: Critical Perspectives on the Work of Alasdair MacIntyre*, edited by John Horton and Susan Mendus, 245–264. Blackwell, 1994.

Mittell, Jason. *Complex TV: The Poetics of Contemporary Television Storytelling*. New York University Press, 2015.

———. "Haunted by Seriality: The Formal Uncanny of *Mulholland Drive*." *Cinephile* 9, no. 1 (2013): 27–33.

Morrison, Blake. "Life after James." *The Guardian*, February 6, 2003. https://www.theguardian.com/uk/2003/feb/06/bulger.ukcrime.

Mueller, Eric. "What Is the Bechdel Test and How Has It Changed Representation in Film?" *Reference*, November 27, 2023. https://www.reference.com/history-geography/bechdel-test-history.

Mulhall, Stephen. *On Film: Thinking in Action*. Routledge, 2002.

Mulvey, Laura. "Visual Pleasure and Narrative Cinema." *Screen* 16, no. 3 (1975): 6–18.

Nolan, Christopher. "Christopher Nolan: You're Not Meant to Understand Everything in 'Tenet.'" YouTube, February 4, 2024. https://www.youtube.com/watch?v=3C-AzyS2lWQ.

Novelly, Thomas. "'Top Gun' Boosted Recruiting and Brought the Tailhook Scandal. So What Happens after the Blockbuster Sequel?" *Military.com*, August 11, 2022. https://www.military.com/daily-news/2022/08/11/top-gun-boosted-recruiting-and-brought-tailhook-scandal-so-what-happens-after-blockbuster-sequel.html.

Oxford English Dictionary. Oxford University Press, 1989.

Panek, Elliot. "The Poet and the Detective: Defining the Psychological Puzzle Film." 30th Anniversary Special Double Issue on Complex Narratives. *Film Criticism* 31, no. 1/2 (2006): 62–88.

Parker, Alan. *Will Write and Direct for Food*. Southbank, 2007.

Patten, Dominic. "'Walking Dead' Lawsuit Settled for $200m between Frank Darabont, CAA & AMC." *Deadline*, July 16, 2021. https://deadline.com/2021/07/walking-dead-lawsuit-settled-frank-darabont-caa-amc-1234794718.

Peele, Jordan. *Get Out*. "Deleted Scene Alternate Ending Director's Commentary." Blu-ray ed. Universal Pictures, 2017.

Perez, Rodrigo. "'Star Wars: The Force Awakens,' the Legacy-quel, and the Rising Danger of Fan Service." *Indiewire*, December 21, 2015. https://www.indiewire.com/2015/12/star-wars-the-force-awakens-the-legacy-quel-and-the-rising-danger-of-fan-service-95872/.

Phillips, Melanie Anne, and Chris Huntley. *Dramatica Dictionary*. Screenplay Systems, 2001.

———. *Dramatica: A New Theory of Story*. 4th ed. Screenplay Systems, 2001.

Plantinga, Carl R. *Rhetoric and Representation in Nonfiction Film*. Cambridge University Press, 1997.

Plunkett, John. "Breaking Bad Creator Vince Gilligan: How Long Can Anyone Stay at the Top?" *The Guardian*, August 19, 2013. https://www.theguardian.com/media/2013/aug/18/breaking-bad-vince-gilligan-walter-white.

Propp, Vladimir. *Morphology of the Folk Tale*. 2nd ed. Translated by Laurence Scott. University of Texas Press, 1968.

Pulver, Andrew. "Spy Who Loved Me Director Lewis Gilbert Dies Aged 97." *The Guardian*, February 28, 2018. https://www.theguardian.com/film/2018/feb/27/spy-who-loved-me-alfie-lewis-gilbert-dies-michael-caine-james-bond.

Queenan, Joe. "Dumb and Dumber." *The Guardian*, September 4, 2007. https://www.theguardian.com/film/2007/sep/04/features.juddapatowfilm.

Reddit. "Is Carrie from Four Weddings and a Funeral the Most Unlikable Female Love Interest Ever to Be Seen in a Beloved Romcom?" *Reddit*, 2024. https://www.reddit.com/r/movies/comments/mi4bje/is_carrie_from_four_weddings_and_a_funeral_the/?rdt=47479.

Roche, David. "The Death of the Subject in David Lynch's *Lost Highway* and *Mulholland Drive*." *Electronic Journal of Studies on the English-Speaking World* 2, no. 2 (2004). https://journals.openedition.org/erea/432.

Rose, Lacey, and Lesley Goldberg. "Executive Quiz: What's the difference between a 'Miniseries,' 'Limited' or 'Event' Series?" *Hollywood Reporter*, February 28, 2014. https://www.hollywoodreporter.com/news/heroes-24-whats-difference-between-683563.

Rosenblum, Ralph, and Robert Karen. *When the Shooting Stops . . . the Cutting Begins*. Da Capo Press, 1996.

Russell, Keith. "The Glimpse and Fan Service: New Media, New Aesthetics." *International Journal of the Humanities* 6, no. 5 (2008): 105–110.

Screen Australia. "Australian Screen Stories Are Important to Australians." 2011. https://www.screenaustralia.gov.au/getmedia/c1d643d6-ee81-4b3b-a194-9faefa5325f4/Australian-Screen-Stories-Research.pdf?ext=.pdf.

Seger, Linda. *Making a Good Script Great*. 2nd ed. Samuel French, 1994.

Shanley, Patrick. "Darren Aronofsky Responds to 'Mother!'s 'F' Cinemascore." *Hollywood Reporter*, September 21, 2017. https://www.hollywoodreporter.com/heat-vision/darren-aronofsky-responds-mothers-f-cinemascore-1042005.

Sheets, Hilarie M. "David Lynch, Who Began as a Visual Artist, Gets a Museum Show." *New York Times*, August 28, 2014. https://www.nytimes.com/2014/08/31/arts/design/museum-show-for-david-lynch-who-began-as-a-visual-artist.html.

Shoard, Catherine. "Francis Ford Coppola: Scorsese Was Being Kind—Marvel Movies Are Despicable." *The Guardian*, October 21, 2019. https://www.theguardian.com/film/2019/oct/21/francis-ford-coppola-scorsese-was-being-kind-marvel-movies-are-despicable.

———. "Martin Scorsese Says Marvel Movies Are 'Not Cinema.'" *The Guardian*, October 4, 2019. https://www.theguardian.com/film/2019/oct/04/martin-scorsese-says-marvel-movies-are-not-cinema.

Sinek, Simon. *Start with Why: How Great Leaders Inspire Everyone to Take Action*. Penguin, 2011.

Sinnerbrink, Robert. *Cinematic Ethics: Exploring Ethical Experience through Film*. Routledge, 2016.

———. "Emotional Engagement and Moral Evaluation." In *Social Aesthetics and Moral Judgment: Pleasure, Reflection and Accountability*, edited by Jennifer A. McMahon, 196–212. Routledge, 2018.

———. *New Philosophies of Film*. Continuum, 2011.

Smith, Daniel. "Why Do We Tell Stories? Hunter-Gatherers Shed Light on the Evolutionary Roots of Fiction." *The Conversation*, December 6, 2017. https://theconversation.com/why-do-we-tell-stories-hunter-gatherers-shed-light-on-the-evolutionary-roots-of-fiction-88586.

Smith, Murray. "Film Art, Argument and Ambiguity." Special Issue: Thinking through Cinema: Film as Philosophy. *Journal of Aesthetics and Art Criticism* 64, no. 1 (2006): 33–42.

Snyder, Blake. *Save the Cat: The Last Book on Screenwriting You'll Ever Need*. Michael Wiese, 2005.

Stefansky, Emma. "How TV's Demons, Aliens and Dragons Are Getting More Cinematic." *Vanity Fair*, June 13, 2018. https://www.vanityfair.com/hollywood/2018/06/emmys-visual-effects-game-of-thrones-stranger-things.

Stevens, George, Jr. *Conversations with the Great Moviemakers of Hollywood's Golden Age at the American Film Institute*. Vintage Books, 2006.

Suggitt, Connie. "Five Record-Breaking Book Facts for National Bookshop Day." *Guinness World Records*, October 4, 2018. https://www.guinnessworldrecords.com/news/2018/10/5-page-turning-book-facts.

Tabachnikova, Olga. *Russian Irrationalism from Pushkin to Brodsky: Seven Essays in Literature and Thought*. Bloomsbury, 2016.

Thomas, William. "Star Trek: The Motion Picture Review." *Empire*, January 1, 2000. https://www.empireonline.com/movies/reviews/star-trek-motion-picture-review/.

Thompson, Kristin. *Storytelling in Film and Television*. Harvard University Press, 2003.

Todorov, Tzvetan. *Grammaire du Décaméron*. De Gruyter Mouton, 1969.

Tolkien, J. R. R. "On Fairy-Stories." In *The Monsters and the Critics and Other Essays*, edited by Christopher Tolkien, 109–161. HarperCollins, 1983.

Travers, Peter. "Mulholland Drive." *Rolling Stone*, October 19, 2001. https://www.rollingstone.com/movies/movie-reviews/mulholland-drive-94077/.

Truffaut, François. *Hitchcock*. Rev. ed. Simon & Schuster, 1985.

Tuttle, Brad. "Movie Theaters Make 85% Profit at Concession Stands." *Time*, December 7, 2009. http://business.time.com/2009/12/07/movie-theaters-make-85-profit-at-concession-stands/.

Twain, Mark. *The Adventures of Huckleberry Finn*. Charles L. Webster, 1885.

Vogler, Christopher. *The Writer's Journey: Mythic Structure for Writers*. Boxtree Limited, 1998.

Wartenberg, Thomas E. "Beyond Mere Illustration: How Films Can Be Philosophy." In *Thinking through Cinema: Film as Philosophy*, edited by Murray Smith and Thomas E. Wartenberg, 19–32. Blackwell, 2006.

———. "Film as Argument." *Film Studies* 8, no. 1 (2006): 126–137.

Watts, Naomi. "Interview with Naomi Watts." *Mulholland Drive*, Australian Blu-ray, 2017.

Weiss, Joanna. "In 'Fifty Shades of Grey,' It's Not the Sex; It's the Stuff." *Boston Globe*, February 12, 2015. https://www.bostonglobe.com/opinion/2015/02/12/fifty-shades-grey-not-sex-stuff/YV9Wgu1n2IbndLoeHMkyRK/story.html.

Wetstein, Aleen. "One Girl Chorus: If Goldwyn Has a Message He'll Keep It on a Telegram." *Pittsburgh Press*, July 27, 1940.

Williams, Eric R. *The Screenwriters Taxonomy: A Roadmap to Creative Storytelling*. Routledge, 2017.

Wolff, Janet. *The Social Production of Art*. Macmillan, 1981.

Yeo, Colin. "Will the Superhero Films Ever End? The Business of Blockbuster Movie Franchises." *The Conversation*, June 15, 2017. http://theconversation.com/will-the-superhero-films-ever-end-the-business-of-blockbuster-movie-franchises-78834.

Yorke, John. *Into the Woods: A Five-Act Journey into Story*. Harry N. Abrams, 2015.

INDEX

ABOUT THE AUTHOR

DARREN PAUL FISHER is an international multi-award-winning screenwriter, director, producer, and academic, and Head of Film, Screen and Creative Media at Bond University, Australia. He works across both the large and small screens, and holds a PhD in narrative feature filmmaking.

We are also grateful to those individuals who participated in our Build a Book Program. They are:

Anonymous (5), Robert Abrams, Debra Allbery, Maggie Anderson, Jean Ball, Sally Ball, Adria Bernardi, Richard Blanchard, Laurel Blossom, Lee Briccetti, Anne Babson Carter, Jennifer Christman, Aaron Coleman, Peter Coyote, Elinor Cramer, Michael Anna de Armas, Brian Komei Dempster, Patrick Donnelly, Lynn Emanuel, Joan Frank, Rigoberto Gonzalez, Elizabeth T. Gray Jr., David and Joan Grubin, Naomi Guttman and Jonathan Mead, Beth Harrison, Jeffrey Harrison, KT Herr, Carlie Hoffman, Elizabeth Jackson, Linda Susan Jackson, Marilyn Johnson, Deborah Jonas-Walsh, Maeve Kinkead, David Lee and Jamila Trindle, Rodney Terich Leonard, Jen Levitt, Howard Levy, Owen Lewis and Susan Ennis, Ralph and Mary Ann Lowen, Maja Lukic, Ricardo Alberto Maldonado, Cleopatra Mathis, Victoria McCoy, Lupe Mendez, Mary Jane Nealon, Nicole Nevadunsky, Kimberly Nunes, Cathy McArthur Palermo, Veronica Patterson, Eileen Pollack, Martha Rhodes, Soraya Shalforoosh, Sarah Stone, Yerra Sugarman, Marjorie and Lew Tesser, Reed Turchi, Maria Walsh, and Calvin Wei